# YOUNG STUDENTS ENCYCLOPEDIA

Specially prepared with the Staff of
MY WEEKLY READER

**1**
**Aardvark**
**Ancient Civilizations**

Xerox Education Publications

Middletown, Connecticut

Copyright © 1977 by Xerox Corporation,
1974, 1972 by Funk & Wagnalls, Inc.
and Xerox Corporation
Library of Congress Catalog Card Number:
76-43151. Printed in U.S.A.

XEROX® is a trademark of XEROX CORPORATION.

4 5 / 81 80 79

# EDITORIAL STAFF

**for Xerox Education Publications**

The original YOUNG STUDENTS ENCYCLOPEDIA was prepared by Funk & Wagnalls in cooperation with Xerox Education Publications, the publishers of My Weekly Reader.

PUBLISHER
John E. Schmid

EDITORIAL DIRECTOR
George H. Wolfson

MANAGING EDITOR
Mary Lou Kennedy

EDITOR
Richard Harkins

ASSISTANT EDITOR
Jeanine Basinger

DESIGNER
David L. Brady

PRODUCTION MANAGER
William F. Miller

Geography and U.S. History:
John Maynard, Editor, Current Events

Literature and World History:
George Thiffault, Staff Writer, Issues Today

Physics, Chemistry, Earth Sciences, Astronomy, and Mathematics:
Walter Scott Houston, Staff Writer, Science Unit Books

Anthropology, Biology, and Medicine:
Erwin Steinkamp, Staff Writer, Current Science

Sports and Games:
James W. Crayton, Editor, My Weekly Reader 4

**for Funk & Wagnalls**

PROJECT DIRECTOR
Leonard Dal Negro

EDITORIAL DIRECTOR
Harold J. Blum

EDITOR IN CHIEF
Jean F. Blashfield

EXECUTIVE EDITOR
Patricia Maloney Markun

SENIOR EDITORS
Kathleen McLane
Frank L. Meltzer
Phyllis Price
Priscilla Rosenfeld

EDITORS
Lucille Allred
Sylvia Cave
Kendra Crossen
Jennifer Daly
Harry Foster
Judith Siegel Kremen
Maryann Macdonald
David Pitts, Captions

EDITORIAL ASSISTANTS
Allison Hall
Carol Harding Kelleher
Harold O. Wang

ART DIRECTOR
Mike Roy

ART DEPARTMENT
Sally J. Tassler
Larry Workman

PICTURE EDITORS
Kristi Brown, Chief
Charlotte M. Mitchell

INDEXER
Marilyn Duffin Rowland

FORMAT DESIGN
Albert Storz

PRODUCTION EXECUTIVE
Edward Haas

**for Revised Edition**

This revised edition of YOUNG STUDENTS ENCYCLOPEDIA was prepared for Xerox Education Publications by Laurence Urdang Inc.

For XEROX EDUCATION PUBLICATIONS:
EDITORIAL DIRECTOR
George H. Wolfson

For LAURENCE URDANG INC.:

EDITOR IN CHIEF
Laurence Urdang

MANAGING EDITOR
Robert B. Costello

SENIOR EDITORS
Walter C. Kidney
George C. Kohn

EDITORS
John Daintith
Stella Stiegeler
Elizabeth Martin
Valerie Pitt
Alan Isaacs

ART DIRECTOR
Penelope J. Guilmette

PICTURE EDITOR
Eleanor Eccleston

INDEXER
Hope Gilbert

# Foreword

The wide acceptance of *Young Students Encyclopedia* since its first publication has led the publishers to undertake a new edition. The world changes as time passes. New nations appear. Populations grow and shift. In the United States another presidential election takes place. The body of scientific knowledge expands. The human mind, embodied in Viking, reaches Mars.

This new edition of *Young Students Encyclopedia* reflects these and other changes in the world. Dozens of new and rewritten articles have been written and many others brought up to date. New illustrations have been added where they were needed. Maps and population figures have been revised.

To make the information concerning measurements as useful as possible, metric equivalents have been indicated, along with the traditional measurements, throughout. Detailed information about the metric system can be found in Volume 12, page 1484, under MEASUREMENT and in Volume 13, page 1510, under METRIC SYSTEM.

The purpose of all these changes and additions has been to make *Young Students Encyclopedia* an even more interesting and helpful learning tool than it has been in the past. We think we have succeeded.

—The Publishers.

# Introduction

Mankind's recorded history and ideas are the cornerstone for the future. As man's world shrinks and as his past becomes more distant, it becomes important to preserve that past and build on those ideas. Education tries to serve that purpose, increasingly aware that the time to begin is at the elementary school level.

To this end, we have now published the YOUNG STUDENTS ENCYCLOPEDIA to provide a basic introduction to man's ideas, language and world. The encyclopedia was designed for young people, for use as an early reference and activities source at home or at school. The articles provide fundamental information relating to man's development. They are reinforced by full-color photographs, maps, diagrams, and activities that build on the curiosity and creativity of children.

The YOUNG STUDENTS ENCYCLOPEDIA was developed specifically for children. Three fundamental concerns determined its content: coverage of those ideas most often included in school curriculums, variation in reading abilities, and encouragement of active reader participation.

### COVERAGE

Approximately a hundred categories were chosen for particular emphasis, from ancient history to physics to personal relationships. They represent the prime concepts underlying current elementary school programs of study as well as children's outside interests. These categories serve as a basic introduction and "umbrella" for the more than 2,400 articles that highlight and explore further various aspects of the major categories.

The major subjects are generally recognizable in the text by their length and the special form of cross reference through which the reader is guided to supplementary and related articles. The form of cross reference starts with *"For further information on:"* and then outlines the main areas of interest in the category.

## READING LEVEL

Reading level was of paramount concern in developing the articles but is purposely not uniform throughout. A reader's ability to deal effectively with a given topic usually depends on the prior experiences he brings to the topic. As a result, those topics which are familiar to most children or deal with concrete ideas can be comprehended by students at lower reading levels. Unfamiliar or complicated topics are, by their nature, useful only at higher reading and comprehension levels. The entire encyclopedia thus becomes usable for a wider age group of readers. A concerted effort has been made to provide interesting and readable articles for a wide range of readers. Educators recognize, however, that *a young student's ability to understand information generally extends well beyond his ability to read.* Parents and teachers are, therefore, urged to provide assistance when needed.

## LEARNING BY DOING

"Learning by doing" is a basic premise upon which many sound educational programs and activities have been developed. The YOUNG STUDENTS ENCYCLOPEDIA employs that basic premise by inviting the young student to participate at every opportunity.

Blue type is used throughout the encyclopedia to show a suggested activity. Any illustration needed to help with the activity has the same blue background. The activities vary greatly. They were selected to help the reader understand more clearly the ideas presented or to stretch his own view of the ideas.

In addition to providing suggested activities, articles often call attention to curious information or ask questions, leading the young student to reach his own conclusions on what he has read.

## FORMAT

Size and style of print, column format, illustrations, and an index are important parts in the planning of any encyclopedia, but they were considered particularly vital to the YOUNG STUDENTS ENCYCLOPEDIA. The most readable type has been used throughout in order to provide information in its clearest form. Important elements are highlighted through type, color, and organization.

Full-color pictures, maps, charts, and tables have been carefully selected and arranged to contribute to a reader's more complete understanding of a given idea. Photographs, rather than drawings, were chosen to illustrate the bulk of the material. Today's young readers, with their prior experience of visual media, demand photographic accuracy and realism.

Important information can be overlooked by a young student in an article that is long or involved. Therefore, a complete index to all concepts is found in the last volume, providing a guide to the location of related material. The student should always be encouraged to "look it up in the index" before starting to explore a new subject.

In addition to the foregoing, the YOUNG STUDENTS ENCYCLOPEDIA includes the following important elements:

- More than 2,400 articles arranged in alphabetical order, letter by letter, except when a comma appears in the title. For example, **CAT, WILD** appears before **CATACOMBS**, but **HORSEPOWER** appears before **HORSE RACING**. For the most part, article titles are in singular rather than plural form.
- An interlacing chain of cross references that guide the young student to related information. At the ends of articles, they appear as ALSO READ: followed by one or more article titles. In alphabetical order where a subject might be expected to appear but instead has been incorporated into another article, a slightly different form of cross reference has been used; for example, **ACCIDENT PREVENTION** see SAFETY, or **ADENOIDS** see BREATHING.
- An index providing three major types of information that expand its usefulness: (1) a simple guide to pronunciation for all words unfamiliar to the average reader, (2) birth and death dates for all people mentioned in the encyclopedia, and (3) the scientific names for many plants and animals. Complete directions for the best use of the index appear at its start in the last volume.
- Tables of information with each U.S. President, U.S. state, Canadian province, and nation that highlight some of the basic data about each.
- Glossaries of terms commonly used in relation to the subject of an article. For examples, see **BOXING, CATTLE,** or **MUSIC.**
- Maps created specially for the YOUNG STUDENTS ENCYCLOPEDIA that represent geographical and historical information in easy-to-use fashion.
- Special "nuggets" of information, which appear in yellow boxes in the outside column. These provide contrasts, records, special examples, and so on.
- Instructions on how to play various games, in the belief that a good reference tool can be helpful for play as well as study. The article **CHILDREN'S GAMES** lists the games that appear in regular alphabetical order.

The YOUNG STUDENTS ENCYCLOPEDIA was developed around children's interests and abilities, to provide them with a basic information and activities source for their pleasure and enlightenment. To this end, it is hoped that young readers, their parents, and their teachers will find the regular use of this new encyclopedia an exciting and rewarding foundation for the future.

*John F. Fanning*

John F. Fanning *B.S., M.Ed., Ed.D.*
Chief Consultant

# Consultants

Chief Consultant
John F. Fanning, Ed.D.
Deputy Superintendent of Schools, Lower Merion County, Pa.

Science Consultant
Alex Costea, Ph.D.
Teacher, Arlington County Public Schools, Arlington, Va.

Social Studies Consultant on Content of Selected Articles
Peter H. Martorella, Ph.D.
Associate Professor of Curriculum and Instruction, Social Studies Education, Temple University, Philadelphia, Pa. (and Reading, Pa.)

Language Arts Consultant
Marciene S. Mattleman, Ed.D.
Associate Professor of English Education, Temple University, Philadelphia, Pa.

Mathematics Consultant
George I. McCune, M.Ed.
Assistant Superintendent of Schools, Concord, Mass.

Human Growth and Development, Fine Arts Consultant
Carol A. Millsom, Ph.D.
Professor of Human Growth and Development, New York University, N.Y.C., N.Y.

Geographical Consultants:

Latin American Consultant
Betty Didcoct, B.A., M.A.
American Assoc. of American Geographers.

Far East Consultant
Hattie Kawahara Colton, Ph.D.
Specialist in Far Eastern Studies.

Middle East Consultant
Harry N. Howard, Ph.D.
Adjunct Professor, American University.

Africa Consultant
Ann Madison Reid, M.A., M.Sc.
Specialist in African Studies.

Southeast Asia Consultant
Ralph T. Jans, Ph.D.
Specialist in Asian Studies.

Europe Consultant
William C. Kinsey, M.A.
Retired Foreign Service Officer, Dept. of State.

South Asia Consultant
Robert Rossow, B.S. in F.S.
Retired Foreign Service Officer, Dept. of State.

# Contributors

**SIGRID ABBOTT, B.A.**
Europe
  Reporter, DAILY OKLAHOMAN and OKLAHOMA CITY TIMES.

**JOY ANDERSON, B.S.**
Asia, Central America, South America
  Author of several children's books, one for WEEKLY READER CHILDREN'S BOOK CLUB.

**JOYCELYN ARUNDEL, B.A.**
Zoology
  Naturalist and author of several books on animals for young people.

**JEAN F. BLASHFIELD, B.A.**
Mammals
  Editor-in-Chief, YOUNG STUDENTS ENCYCLOPEDIA.

**MARY JO BORRESON, B.A.**
Education, Language Arts, Speech, Written Language
  Editor of publications, Montgomery County Schools, Rockville, Md.

**FRANCES CAVANAH, B.A.**
The Presidents
  Author of many children's books; formerly editor of CHILD LIFE.

**ANNE CHANEY, B.A.**
Graphic Arts, Sculpture (with Earl Palmatier)
  Art Resource Teacher, Prince George's County Public Schools, Md.

**HARRIET DOUTY DWINELL, B.A.**
International Relations
  Free-lance writer; contributing editor, WASHINGTONIAN.

**ELEANOR MALONEY FEATHERSTONE, B.A.**
Reference Tools
  Former Children's Librarian, Fairfax County, Va.

**G. HOWARD GILLELAN, B.A.**
Reptiles and Amphibians, Sports, Trees
  Washington and Archery editor for OUTDOOR LIFE; conservationist.

**RAY E. HIEBERT, Ph.D.**
American History, Civil War, Communications
  Head of Dept. of Journalism and Professor at University of Maryland.

**RICHARD HOOVER, B.S.**
Light, Physics
  Physicist specializing in space optics and X-ray astronomy.

**MARION BOND JORDON, B.A.**
Citizenship, Negro
  Teacher of black history; NAACP field director; YWCA national board.

**MARTIN KEEN, B.S.**
Biology, Geology, Medicine, Physiology
  Author of 27 books for children; writer for several encyclopedias.

**ELIZABETH SEARLE LAMB, B.M., B.A.**
Choral Music, Music, Musical Instruments
  Concert harpist; composer; writer for children; prize-winning poet.

**PATRICIA MALONEY MARKUN, B.A.**
Art History
  Executive Editor, YOUNG STUDENTS ENCYCLOPEDIA; author of several books.

**H. STEPHEN MORSE, B.A.**
Mathematics, Philosophy
  Mathematics teacher at Sidwell Friends School, Washington, D.C.

**PHYLLIS NAYLOR, B.A.**
Child Care, Personal Relationships
  Author of 17 books for children.

**HARRY EDWARD NEAL**
Business, Economics, Ecology
  Author of 28 books for young people.

**EARL PALMATIER, B.S., M.Ed.**
Graphic Arts, Sculpture (with Anne Chaney)
  Editorial Board, ART EDUCATION JOURNAL; Art supervisor, Prince George's County, Md.

**DAN PATTERSON, B.A., M.A.**
American Indians, Polar Regions, Topography
  Free-lance writer; editor of CLASSROOM MAGAZINE.

**BRITTMARIE JANSON DE PEDRESCHI**
Languages
  Translator of radio broadcasts in Central America; linguist.

**LEANNE G. REES, B.A.**
Government, U.S. Government
  Free-lance writer; former newspaper columnist; wife of California Congressman.

**CORINNE MADDEN ROSS, A.A.**
Ancient Civilizations, Literature, Myths and Legends
  Free-lance writer-editor, children's book and story field.

**BARBARA BATTLE RYAN, B.A., B.S. in F.S.**
Clothing and Fashion, Hobbies
  Free-lance writer and copy-editor; former jr. high teacher.

**JAMES SCHEFTER, B.A.**
Astronomy, Oceanography, Space
  Free-lance science writer; airplane pilot; author of book on space.

**RALPH SLATER, B.A.**
Aviation, Military and Weaponry
  Overseas National Airlines public relations; author of books on aviation.

**SHIRLEY THOMSON, B.A., M.A.**
Cities, Exploration, North America
  Author of children's books; former asst. secretary of UNESCO for Canada.

**JOHN TOTTLE, B.S.**
States of the U.S.
  Author of several books for young people; former editor of classroom weekly.

Other Contributors:

WILL BARKER, B.S.

VANA EARLE

ELOISE ENGLE, B.A.

LUCY FRISBEE, B.A.

ROBERT WEST HOWARD, B.S.

HELEN LILLIE, M.A.

CHARLES SCOTT MARWICK, M.A.

GLORIA MOSESSON, B.A., M.S.

R. G. VAN PEURSEM, B.A.

JAMES P. SWEENEY, Ph.D.

# Acknowledgments

All photographs supplied by Armando Curcio Editore, SpA, except for the following:

Abby Aldrich Rockefeller Folk Art Collection—page 110 bottom.

John T. Allen—page 36 top.

Bell Aerospace Division of Textron—page 57 bottom.

E. Bennett/Photo Researchers—page 92.

The Bettmann Archive, Inc.—pages 37 bottom, 51 top, 80 bottom, 81 upper left, 89 upper right, 93 bottom, 101, 103 bottom, 119 top.

Jean F. Blashfield—pages 36 lower left, 86 bottom.

The Boeing Company—pages 65 lower left, 69.

British Aircraft Corporation—page 68 top.

V. Bucher/Photo Researchers—page 70 top.

Bureau of Indian Affairs—pages 83 top, 90 top, 94 bottom.

Children's Television Workshop—page 27 top.

Colonial Williamsburg, Williamsburg, Virginia—page 109 upper right, 109 lower right.

Department of Transportation, Official Photograph—page 72 top.

Editorial Photocolor Archives—page 95.

Environmental Protection Agency—page 71 top.

EPA/Photo Researchers—page 11.

Federal Aviation Agency, Official Photograph—page 76 top.

The Goodyear Tire & Rubber Company—page 75 bottom.

Grumman Aerospace Corporation—page 99 top.

Grumman Aerospace Corporation/U.S. Department of Transportation—page 58 top.

International Harvester Company—pages 48 top, 51 center, 51 bottom, 52.

Henry J. Kaufman & Associates, Inc. for Quality Motels, Inc.—page 35 bottom.

Library of Congress—pages 15, 30 center, 93 top, 100 bottom, 105 upper left.

Jan Lukas/Editorial Photocolor Archives—page 112 top left.

T. McHugh/Photo Researchers—page 96.

Merck Sharp & Dohme—page 95 bottom.

NASA—pages 37 top, 89 bottom.

National Wildlife Magazine (Oct.-Nov. 1970 issue); by George H. Harrison—page 16.

North American Aviation, Inc.—page 61 bottom.

Overseas National Airway, Inc.—page 62 top, 62 bottom.

The Phillips Collection, Washington—page 18 center.

Robert Rapelye from Editorial Photocolor Archives—page 28.

J-L Ray—C.E.P.A.—pages 28 top, 32 bottom.

State of Alabama Bureau of Publicity and Information—pages 78 bottom, 79 top, 80 top.

Herb Taylor from Editorial Photocolor Archives—page 115.

United Press International Photo—page 94 top.

United States Air Force, Official Photograph—page 60 center, 60 bottom, 61 top.

United States Capitol Historical Society—page 119 bottom.

United States Navy, Official Photograph—page 55 bottom, 56 top, 56 bottom.

University of Illinois at Chicago—page 30 bottom.

Wayne Corporation—page 105 upper right.

Cathleen L. Yordi—page 45 upper right.

State flags courtesy of Hammond, Inc.

Canadian armorial bearings of provinces and territories from the Dominion Bureau of Statistics, courtesy of Information Canada

Maps from the Pictograph Corporation

We gratefully acknowledge the co-operation given by Juliana F. DeWitt, Picture Editor of *Funk & Wagnalls New Encyclopedia.*

▲ *Kikuyu dancers in bright costumes perform a tribal war dance. (See* AFRICA.*)*

# Aa

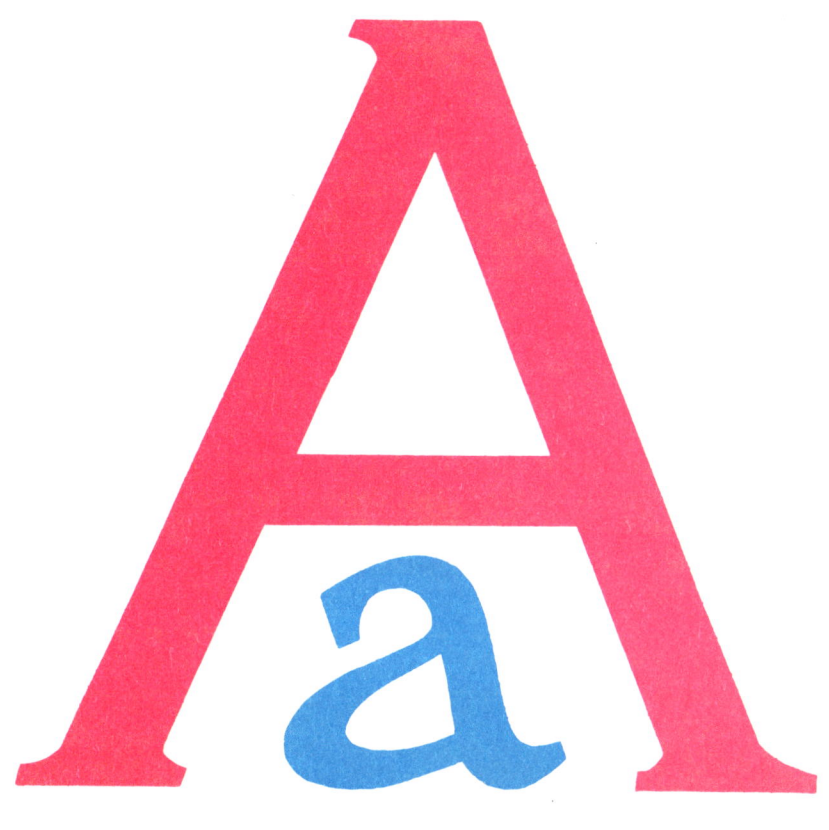

**AARDVARK** An aardvark is a strange animal of Africa. It is so unusual that scientists place it in an order of mammals by itself—order Tubulidentata, which means "tube-toothed." Its teeth have no roots or strong enamel. But the aardvark does not really need strong teeth because it eats termites and ants that don't need to be chewed.

The aardvark is about five to six feet long, including its thick tail. Very few bristly hairs adorn its pinkish-gray skin, although some
[5-6 ft.=1.5-1.8m]
aardvarks have been seen with long, full coats of hair. An aardvark's narrow head is topped by large donkey-like ears. Its ears can pick up the faint sounds termites make in their nests. The animal uses its strong front claws to tear open the large, concrete-hard "castles" termites build. The insects do, of course, attack the aardvark, but even their sharp pincers cannot go through its tough skin. The animal just goes on slurping in more food with its sticky tongue. Then it retires to an underground burrow to

▲ *An aardvark is an animal of Africa. It eats termites and lives in a burrow.*

◀ *A drawing of a western abacus. This one has three rows of beads. But some abacuses have more rows. You can tell that no adding is being done here, since no beads are touching the center strip. A real abacus does not have the numbers written on the beads as this one does. Each abacus in the six drawings shows a different number—(a) 3; (b) 7; (c) ?; (d) 73; (e) 98; and (f) ?. What do abacus (c) and abacus (f) show?*

sleep away the day. If an enemy, such as a lion, threatens the aardvark while away from its burrow, the aardvark may turn, lie on its back, and fight. Blows by its strong tail or slashes from its powerful claws usually stop an attacker.

The animal's name means "earth pig," and was given the animal by Dutch settlers in South Africa. Aardvarks live south of the Sahara Desert, where there are termites.

ALSO READ: MAMMAL.

**ABACUS** An abacus is a device that helps a person count and do arithmetic problems. As you can see in the diagram, an abacus uses beads to keep track of the numbers. The beads slide along rods. Each rod has seven beads—five on the left and two on the right of the center strip. The beads should be pushed away from the center strip before starting a problem, because that is where the numbers are counted.

The more rows of beads on an abacus, the larger the numbers you can count. Each row stands for a different *power of ten*. Powers of ten are 1, 10, 100, 1,000, and so on, adding as many zeroes as you like.

The five beads on the left in every row each stand for *one* of the unit of that row. The two beads on the right are each *five* of the unit. Numbers are formed by bringing the beads from their starting position to the center strip. To count a number on an abacus, you push enough beads into the center to equal your number. To subtract a number, you push the right number of beads away from the center.

You can make an abacus. You will need a picture frame, string, beads, and thumbtacks. Many abacuses have 13 rows of beads. But you can make a "little" one, with only five rows, and still count up to 166,665. To make a five-row abacus, first cut five pieces of string the same length—long enough to cross the picture frame plus three inches for tying knots. Tie a knot one-fourth of the way down each piece of string. Make the knots fat, so no beads can pass them. The knots will be the center strip in your abacus. Now carefully put five evenly spaced thumbtacks on each side of the picture frame. Slide five beads onto one string at the end that is farther from the knot. Put two beads onto the short end. Tie the ends of the string to the first thumbtack on either side of the frame, with the group of five beads at the left. Then load the other four strings with beads and tie them to the other four pairs of tacks.

Hold your abacus flat, with the groups of five beads toward your left, and you are ready to try a simple problem. First, count 3 on your abacus. Push three beads on the bottom row to the right until

[3 in.=7.6 cm]

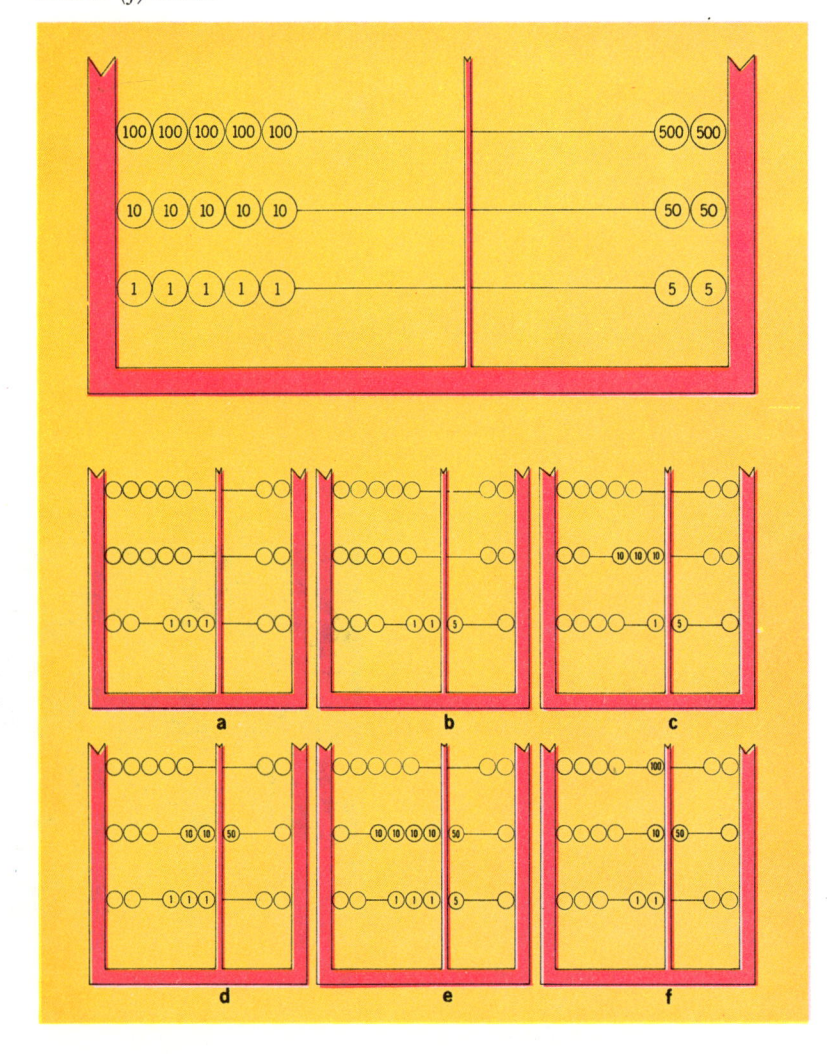

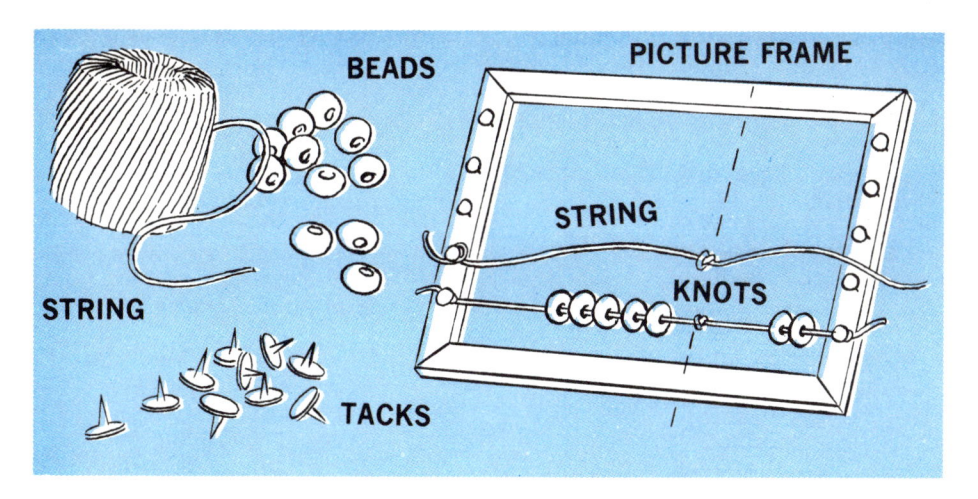

they touch the center strip (the knot). Now add 5. Do this by pushing one right-hand bead on the bottom row to the left until it touches the center strip, too. You have just completed an addition problem. What is the total? Now try subtracting 6 from the total. What answer do you get? (Remember, to subtract, you push the right number of beads *away* from the center strip.) Next, add 210 to the number on your abacus. You can read this number in three parts—two hundreds (200), one ten (10), and no ones (0). If you work carefully, the total that your abacus shows will be 212. You can solve very difficult problems with the help of your abacus. And with practice you can use your abacus to solve problems more quickly than you can with pencil and paper.

People in the United States and in other western countries do not use abacuses very often. But almost every businessman in Asia uses one. So do Asian schoolchildren and their teachers. Different countries use different abacuses. But the only difference is the number of beads on each row.

ALSO READ: ARITHMETIC, CALCULATOR, COMPUTER.

**ABBREVIATION** To abbreviate means to make shorter. Words and phrases are often shortened to save time and space in speaking and writing. Abbreviations, acronyms, and contractions are some ways of shortening language.

Abbreviations are letters that stand for common, well-known words and phrases. The letters often have periods after them to show that other letters have been left out. There are no basic rules for forming abbreviations. Perhaps somebody just decided to shorten a word or phrase in a certain way. It soon became accepted and understood. Sometimes just the beginning of the word is used, such as *doz.* for "dozen" or *St.* for "Street." Other abbreviations use the first and last letters, such as *Rd.* for "Road" or *Dr.* for "Doctor." And still others use just the first letter. *FBI* stands for "Federal Bureau of Investigation."

Some abbreviations do not look like the words they stand for. Such abbreviations usually come from ancient Latin or Greek words or from modern foreign languages. *A.M.* means "before noon." It is an abbreviation of the Latin *ante meridiem*. The shortened form for *pound* is *lb.*, from the Latin word *libra*, which was a unit of weight. *R.S.V.P.* means "Please answer." It stands for the French words, *Répondez, s'il vous plaît*.

Abbreviated words can be confusing. Several words may share the same abbreviation. The letters *St.* can mean either "Street" or "Saint." And *Fr.* may mean "Father," "France," or "French." It is

## SOME COMMON ABBREVIATIONS

**abbr.** abbreviation
**ABC** American Broadcasting Company
**A.D.** *anno Domini*, "in the year of our Lord"
**adj.** adjective
**adv.** adverb, advertisement
**Ala., AL** Alabama
**Alas., AK** Alaska
**A.M., a.m.** *ante meridiem*, "before noon"
**anon.** anonymous, "author unknown"
**Apr.** April
**Ariz., AZ** Arizona
**Ark., AR** Arkansas
**assn.** association
**asst.** assistant
**atty.** attorney
**Aug.** August
**Ave.** Avenue
**b.** born
**BBC** British Broadcasting Corporation
**B.C.** before Christ; British Columbia
**bldg.** building
**Blvd.** Boulevard
**bros.** brothers
**C** Celsius; centigrade
**Calif., CA** California
**CBC** Canadian Broadcasting Corporation
**CBS** Columbia Broadcasting System
**cc** cubic centimeter
**Co.** Company; County
**c/o** in care of
**C.O.D.** cash on delivery
**Colo., CO** Colorado
**conj.** conjunction
**Conn., CT** Connecticut
**cont.** continued
**Corp.** Corporation
**CST** Central Standard Time
**d.** died
**D.A.** district attorney
**D.C., DC** District of Columbia
**D.D.S.** Doctor of Dental Surgery
**Dec.** December
**Del., DE** Delaware
**Dem.** Democrat
**Dr.** Doctor; Drive
**DST** Daylight Saving Time
**E.** east
**e.g.** *exempli gratia*, "for example"
**Eng.** English; England
**EST** Eastern Standard Time
**etc.** *et cetera*, "and so forth"
**f.** female
**F** Fahrenheit
**Feb.** February

**Fla., FL** Florida
**Fr.** Father; French; France
**Fri.** Friday
**ft.** foot; feet
**Ft.** Fort
**Ga., GA** Georgia
**Gov.** Governor
**H.I., HI** Hawaii
**Hon.** Honorable
**HRM** His (Her) Royal Majesty
**I.** Island
**Ia., IA** Iowa
**Id., ID** Idaho
**i.e.** *id est*, "that is", "in other words"
**ill., illus.** illustration
**Ill., IL** Illinois
**in.** inch; inches
**Inc.** incorporated
**Ind., IN** Indiana
**IOU** I owe you
**IQ** intelligence quotient
**Jan.** January
**Jr.** Junior
**Kans., KS** Kansas
**km.** kilometer
**Ky., KY** Kentucky
**La., LA** Louisiana
**m.** male
**Mar.** March
**Mass., MA** Massachusetts
**Md., MD** Maryland
**Me., ME** Maine
**Mich., MI** Michigan
**Minn., MN** Minnesota
**Miss., MS** Mississippi
**Mo., MO** Missouri
**Mon.** Monday
**Mont., MT** Montana
**mpg** miles per gallon
**mph** miles per hour
**Mr.** Mister
**Mrs.** Mistress (used for a married woman)
**Ms.** written form of address for any woman
**MST** Mountain Standard Time
**Mt.** Mount; Mountain
**n.** noun
**N.** north
**NBC** National Broadcasting Company
**N.C., NC** North Carolina
**N.Dak., ND** North Dakota
**Nebr., NB** Nebraska
**Nev., NV** Nevada
**N.H., NH** New Hampshire
**N.J., NJ** New Jersey
**N.Mex., NM** New Mexico
**no.** number
**Nov.** November
**N.Y., NY** New York
**O., OH** Ohio
**Oct.** October
**Okla., OK** Oklahoma

**Ore., OR** Oregon
**p.** page
**Pa., Penn., PA** Pennsylvania
**pat.** patent
**PBS** Public Broadcasting Service
**pl.** plural
**Pl.** Place
**P.M., p.m.** *post meridiem*, "after noon"; *post mortem*, "after death"
**P.O.** post office
**pp.** pages
**prep.** preposition
**pron.** pronoun
**P.S.** *post scriptum*, "postscript"; Public School
**PST** Pacific Standard Time
**R.** River
**Rd.** Road
**Rep.** Republican
**R.I., RI** Rhode Island
**rpm** revolutions per minute
**R.R.** railroad
**R.S.V.P.** *Répondez, s'il vous plaît*, "please reply"
**S.** south
**Sat.** Saturday
**S.C., SC** South Carolina
**S.Dak., SD** South Dakota
**Sept.** September
**sing.** singular
**sq.** square
**Sr.** Senior
**St.** Saint; Street
**Sun.** Sunday
**Tenn., TN** Tennessee
**Terr.** Terrace; Territory
**Tex., TX** Texas
**Thur., Thurs.** Thursday
**Tues.** Tuesday
**U., UT** Utah
**UHF** ultra-high frequency
**UN** United Nations
**U.S.** United States
**U.S.A.** United States of America
**U.S.S.R.** Union of Soviet Socialist Republics
**v.** verb
**Va., VA** Virginia
**VHF** very high frequency
**VI** Virgin Islands
**Vt., VT** Vermont
**W.** west
**Wash., WA** Washington
**Wed.** Wednesday
**Wis., WI** Wisconsin
**W.Va., WV** West Virginia
**Wyo., WY** Wyoming
**YMCA** Young Men's Christian Association
**YWCA** Young Women's Christian Association

up to the reader to decide what an abbreviation means by looking at the rest of the sentence.

An *acronym* is an abbreviation that is actually a word, because it can be easily pronounced. *NATO* is an acronym for *North Atlantic Treaty Organization*. Another well-known acronym is *NASA*, which stands for *National Aeronautics and Space Administration*.

A *contraction* is a shortened phrase that, when written, has an apostrophe to show that letters are missing. Contractions, such as "isn't" and "won't," are used more often in speaking than in writing.

You probably know more abbreviations than you think you do. Find out. Print one letter of the alphabet on each of 26 small pieces of paper. Mix them up in a bag and draw five pieces of paper. How many different abbreviations can you make from the five letters you drew? Have a contest with a friend and see who can make the most abbreviations.

In the short list of common abbreviations printed here, the regular shortened form of a state's name is followed by the official two-letter U.S. Post Office abbreviation. For example, Minn. and MN are shown for Minnesota.

ALSO READ: WRITTEN LANGUAGE.

**ABOLITION** Slaves first arrived in the United States during the 1600s. Even then, there were people who thought that slavery was wrong. These people were part of the *anti-slavery* movement. By the 1800s, even more people were outraged about slavery. These people refused to obey laws that helped slave owners. They hid runaway slaves. They gave speeches and wrote books and newspaper articles against slavery. They decided that slavery had to be *abolished* (ended) as quickly as possible. These people were called *abolitionists*.

One of the most famous abolitionists was William Lloyd Garrison. From 1831 to the end of the Civil War in 1865, he published an anti-slavery newspaper called *The Liberator*. Another important abolitionist was Frederick Douglass, a black journalist. His newspaper, *The North Star*, urged blacks and whites to help slaves escape from the South. Charles Lenox Remond, a black abolitionist speaker, traveled through the country, speaking wherever people would listen.

Harriet Beecher Stowe wrote *Uncle Tom's Cabin* in 1852. This novel told a dramatic tale of how slaves were forced to live. It told about beatings and about how slave families were separated, when the mother or father was sold to another slave owner. The book made many people examine their own attitudes toward slavery.

Some people did not like the abolitionists. People threw stones and rotten eggs at William Lloyd Garrison when he made speeches against slavery. An angry mob in Boston once grabbed Garrison while he was speaking. They tied a rope around his neck and dragged him through the streets. Another abolitionist editor, Elijah P. Lovejoy, was murdered by a mob.

Some people thought that speaking and writing against slavery was not enough. John Brown tried to

◀ *Charles Lenox Remond, a respected black speaker for abolition.*

convince the slaves to start a revolution. In 1859, he and some followers captured the U.S. arsenal, a place where guns and ammunition were kept, at Harpers Ferry, Virginia (now in West Virginia). He hoped the raid would be a signal to all slaves to fight for their freedom. But many of his followers were killed by soldiers. Brown was captured and hanged for treason.

People who were afraid of abolitionists lived all over the U.S. They thought abolitionists caused trouble and did not try to find a workable solution to the problem. Some southerners tried to silence the abolitionists, even in Congress. But those who spoke out boldly against slavery finally won their battle. On January 1, 1863, President Abraham Lincoln made his Emancipation Proclamation, freeing the slaves in the Confederate States. The Thirteenth Amendment was added to the U.S. Constitution in 1865, and slaves were freed in all of the United States.

ALSO READ: BROWN, JOHN; CIVIL WAR; DOUGLASS, FREDERICK; EMANCIPATION PROCLAMATION; SLAVERY; STOWE, HARRIET BEECHER; UNDERGROUND RAILROAD.

**ABOMINABLE SNOWMAN** The abominable snowman is a creature some people believe lives high in the Himalaya Mountains of Asia. The Sherpas, a tribe of people in Tibet, call the snowman the *yeti*. Their tribal stories tell of a large, hairy, long-armed beast. It walks standing up, and has a man-like face. They tell stories about the yeti leaving the snowy regions and coming down to villages from time to time. No one has yet proved the yeti exists.

Many people have seen large, strange footprints in the snow of the Himalayas. Some people believe these are the yeti's prints. Others think they are footprints of a running bear. A bear's hind feet may land partly on the prints made by its front feet, when it runs. These two sets of prints may, together, look like a large print of a man. Other large prints are probably formed when snow melts around a group of several small animal footprints. Explorers of the Himalayas have seen huge footprints of some mysterious animal, since the 1890s. The Sherpas have pieces of hair and dried scalp, which they claim are from the yeti. But scientists know these pieces are from bears, yaks, mountain antelopes, and other animals.

Sir Edmund Hillary, an explorer, led an expedition to the Himalayas in 1960, to search for the creature. No abominable snowman was found, dead or alive. Maybe some day it will be.

ALSO READ: HILLARY, SIR EDMUND; HIMALAYA MOUNTAINS.

**ABORIGINE** The first people to live in any region are called *aborigines*. The term comes from the Latin words, *ab origine*, which mean "from the beginning."

The name "aborigine" is most often given to the earliest known people of Australia. These people were living in Australia when Europeans began to explore that continent in the 1700s. Scientists call these aborigines *Australoids*, tribes who moved to Australia from Southeast Asia 12,000 years ago.

Between 150,000 and 300,000 aborigines lived in Australia when Europeans settled there in 1788. The number of natives has gone down since then. Many were killed by diseases brought by white men. Most aborigines now live among white people, often working on cattle and sheep ranches. Others have kept their old tribal ways of life, living on reservations in the Northern Territory, Queensland, and Western Australia. Very few of them are farmers. Most are fishermen and hunters. Their hunt-

▼ *This huge footprint may have been left by America's Abominable Snowman. This mysterious creature, called Bigfoot, is said to roam the woods of the northwestern United States.*

ing weapons are the *boomerang*, the *waddy* (a war club), and the *womera* (a throwing stick with a three-pronged spear in front). They sometimes carry decorated shields.

Most aborigines have small skulls, low foreheads, and heavy brows. Their faces are short and broad, with small chins and wide noses. Their skin color can be reddish-brown to dark brown. Not many aborigines are tall. The Australian aborigines speak about 200 different languages, none of them like languages spoken elsewhere.

ALSO READ: AUSTRALIA, BOOMERANG, MAN.

**ABSORPTION** Liquid spilled on a table top can be soaked up by a sponge, a napkin, or a paper towel. This soaking up is absorption. Many things can be soaked up, or absorbed, by other substances or objects. Gas, liquid, light, heat, and even sound can be absorbed.

Let a glass of *cold* water stand in sunlight. You will see small air bubbles form on the sides of the glass. The bubbles rise through the water to the surface. These bubbles are air that was absorbed in the water. The air was forced out as the water warmed up because warm water cannot hold so much air as cold water can.

Absorption is an important process for living things. Fish breathe the air that is absorbed in water. In man and other animals, digested food is absorbed by the blood through the vessels of the small intestine and then carried to all parts of the body where it is used for energy. Plants absorb water from the soil. The water keeps them alive and healthy, and enables them to stand up straight. What happens if you put a partly wilted flower in a glass of water?

Light and heat can also be absorbed. Dark objects are better heat and light absorbers than light-colored ones. You can prove this with a simple experiment that was first done a long time ago. On a cold, sunny day, put two thermometers on the ground. Be sure they show the same temperature. Put a black cloth over one and a white one over the other. Which thermometer shows the highest temperature after half an hour?

ALSO READ: COLOR, DIGESTION, GAS, HEAT AND COLD, LIGHT, LIQUID, PLANT, SOUND.

**ABSTRACT ART** You probably know that "subtract" means "take away." *Abstract* means "to take what is important away from what is not." Abstract art shows what is important in a scene and leaves out unimportant details.

Look at the picture of the bison, horses, and deer on the next page. It was painted on the wall of a cave near Lascaux, France, thousands of years ago. It is a simple painting. The cave man left out details. He arranged the animals to fit the picture, not as they really looked prowling around outside his cave. The picture is *not* "realistic," just like life. It is *abstract art*.

In the 1880s in France, some artists began to make painting less realistic. Why? For one thing, the camera had been invented. A photograph could be made to get an

▲*An Australian aborigine. At one time all the people of Australia were aborigines. But now only one in a hundred Australians is one of these people.*

# ABSTRACT ART

▲ *An ancient painting in a cave at Lascaux, France.*

▼ *Arrival of the Circus by Paul Klee.*

▼ *Jackson Pollock's The Wooden Horse.*

exact likeness of something or someone. So the French painters began new ways of painting. "Looking like something" became less important. Two French painters, Paul Cézanne and Georges Seurat, found that people could see the shapes of nature more easily if the shapes were painted simply, without all the details used in realistic art. Cézanne tried to see in nature the simple shapes of the block, the ball, and the cone.

Some years later another artist, Pablo Picasso, began to paint abstractly, too. Only he went much further. To him, abstraction was whatever had to be done to nature to make it fit a picture. He would change nature to what he thought a picture should be. As artists began doing abstract sculpture, they ignored the exact form of a real-life object. The feel and texture and shape of a sculpture were more important to these artists than showing exact form.

Look at Paul Klee's painting of a circus arriving in town. See the circus parade with a dog leading it? The painter uses no perspective in this picture, so things that might be farther away don't look smaller. Instead, the picture is in layers. Nearly everyone in the painting is wearing a funny hat. Why? Many things are happening at the same time, as in a real circus. Look for details, such as the boy holding a balloon over his head. Banners often mean fun and excitement. How many do you see here? See how Klee has "framed" his picture with dark paint in a smudgy way. Is the picture a dream of long ago?

How would your community look if a circus were arriving? Make a picture of it on a big piece of paper. Show things in an abstract way, not a realistic one.

Do you see the horse in the Jackson Pollock painting, *The Wooden Horse*? What does the rest of the picture look like to you? Could those tangled lines be paths the horse followed? Could the yellow splotches be places the horse rested? Do the red lines show a really fast ride? Think what fun it would be to take off along those trails. You may want to paint a picture story of an exciting horseback ride. Or a bicycle ride that was an adventure.

Of course, you may see Pollock's painting in a very different way. That is the fun of abstract art. You can see it in a new way every time you look at it. Some people feel that abstract art is more exciting than a realistic painting or sculpture which looks exactly like the real scene or object every time you see it.

ALSO READ: CÉZANNE, PAUL; MODERN ART; PICASSO, PABLO; SCULPTURE.

**ABU SIMBEL** Abu Simbel is the site of two ancient temples on the Nile River in Egypt. The temples were carved into a sandstone cliff about 1250 B.C. by order of Ramses II, an Egyptian pharaoh.

The Great Temple reached almost 200 feet into the side of the cliff. The entrance was guarded by four statues of Ramses II. Each statue was 67 feet high. Ramses II wished to honor the sun god. The pharaoh had the temple built so that the sun's early-morning rays shone through the halls and touched the carved figure of the sun god deep inside. The smaller temple had six figures, each 33 feet high, at its entrance. Four were of Ramses II and two were of his queen, Nefertari.

Egypt planned a great dam on the Nile River in the 1960s. But the plan called for the valley of the temples to be flooded. Egypt asked the United Nations to help save the temples before the dam was built. More than 50 nations gave over 17 million dollars for the project. The temples were cut into huge blocks, some weighing 30 tons. The blocks were moved to high, safe ground and put together again. Egypt finished the Aswan High Dam in 1968, and a lake now covers the old site.

ALSO READ: EGYPT, ANCIENT; NILE RIVER.

**ACADEMY AWARD** The Academy of Motion Picture Arts and Sciences was founded in May, 1927. The Academy is made up of several thousand people in every area of movie making. Its main purpose is to help the movie industry improve the art and science of film making.

▲ *The giant statues of the Temple of Abu Simbel on the Nile River, where they used to be. When the Aswan High Dam was built, they were moved to higher ground above the water.*

[200 ft.=61 m]
[67 ft.=21 m]

[33 ft.=10.2 m]

[30 tons=27.2 metric tons]

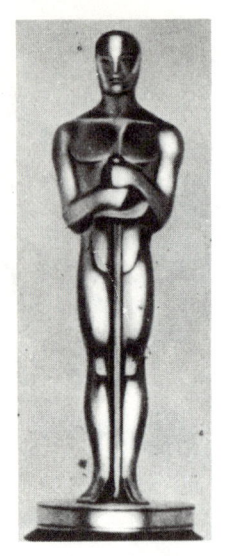

▲ *Oscar, the little statue given as an Academy Award for good work in American movies.*

In 1931, the Academy Award statue was accidentally nicknamed "Oscar" by Academy librarian Margaret Herrick. When she first saw the statue, she said, "Why, it looks like my Uncle Oscar!" A newspaperman heard her remark and printed it in his newspaper.

▲ *An accordion is like an organ. The player squeezes the bellows in and out while playing a melody on the keys.*

ACANTHUS

The Academy also honors outstanding film achievements with its Academy Awards. The members of the Academy vote by secret ballot on who should win.

Once each year in Hollywood, California, small gold statues are awarded for the best performances by actors and actresses in leading and supporting roles and for best direction, music, costume design, photography, writing, sound recording, and other areas of production. An award is also given for the best movie of the year. Each award is a 13½-inch-high statue of a man, nicknamed "Oscar." This statue weighs 8½ pounds, and is made of bronze covered with a layer of gold.

The first movie to win an Oscar was *Wings* in 1928. In recent years, *The Godfather* (1972) and *The Godfather, Part II* (1974) received the Best Picture award. *One Flew Over the Cuckoo's Nest* swept all five major awards for 1975, including Best Picture, Best Actor (Jack Nicholson), Best Actress (Louise Fletcher), Best Director, and Best Screenplay. This was the first film to win all since 1934.

ALSO READ: ACTORS AND ACTING, MOTION PICTURES.

**ACANTHUS** see GREEK ART.

**ACCELERATION** see MOTION.

**ACCIDENT PREVENTION** see SAFETY.

**ACCORDION** An accordion is a musical instrument that works like a reed-organ. The accordion hangs from the player's shoulders by straps.

The first accordion-like instrument was made by Friedrich Buschmann in Germany in 1822. An Austrian, Cyrillys Damian, soon made some improvements. He named his instrument "akkordion." About the same time, Charles Wheatstone of England invented the concertina, which is like the accordion.

The accordion is mainly a bellows. The player stretches the bellows to let in air. He then closes, or squeezes, the bellows, and the air is forced out through metal parts called *tongues* or *reeds*. These tongues are of different sizes, so they produce different musical notes. Attached to the bellows on the right side is a keyboard, like a part of a piano. The accordionist plays the melody on the keyboard. On the left are buttons which he presses to produce bass notes and chords.

Accordions are popular in many parts of the world. In Europe, accordionists play music for folk dancing and singing at festivals. Pioneers traveling west across the United States in covered wagons often played accordions to keep their spirits high.

ALSO READ: MUSICAL INSTRUMENTS, ORGAN.

**ACCOUNTING AND BOOKKEEPING** A businessman must keep records of the money he takes in and the money he spends. The work of keeping such records is called *bookkeeping*. The work of deciding how the records should be set up is called *accounting*. An *accountant* also finds out, by studying the records, whether or not a business is doing well. The accountant must know many things about the business.

Suppose a man owns a small clothing store. He keeps records that show that he spent money for newspaper advertising, and for suits, coats, shirts, shoes, and neckties to sell to his customers. He had to pay a young man to help him in the store. He also paid rent and had other expenses.

At the end of the year, he must take an *inventory*. That is, he counts how many pieces of clothing he has on hand. Then he must find out exactly how many he sold, how much money he took in, and how

ACIDS AND BASES

much money he spent in running the business. If he took in more than he spent, he made a *profit* for the year. If he spent more than he took in, he suffered a *loss*. He depends on his store accounting records to get all this information.

The owner of a small clothing store can keep records without much trouble. But a giant oil company, an insurance company, or a big bank has many difficult accounting problems. The company must know how much money is to be paid by its *debtors* (people who owe the company money) and how much it owes other companies (*creditors*) for supplies. It must know how much the company's buildings and machines are worth, and how much the company has lost in *depreciation,* or wear and tear, of its equipment. All of this information must be kept in the company's accounts. Big companies employ many accountants.

After a company's accountants finish their yearly count, their work must be *audited.* Experts from outside the company double-check the records to be sure the accounts are correct.

**How Bookkeeping Works**

Try keeping records of your own money. Suppose your weekly allowance is 75 cents. Your grandmother gives you two dollars as a gift. A candy bar costs you 12 cents, and a balsa-wood glider costs 50 cents. You want to go to the movies on Saturday, and you also want to save some money.

Make a chart with three columns on a lined sheet of paper. Mark the first column "Received," the second column "Spent," and the third column "Balance" (meaning the money you have left). What numbers go in what columns? How much money will you be able to save if the movies cost you one dollar?

This is a simple way to do *bookkeeping.* It is a record of money received, or *income,* and money paid out, or *expenses.* Your mother or father may keep records like this of food and other home expenses.

Today, many bookkeeping and accounting records are made by electronic machines. But men and women still have to provide the information the machines need to do the jobs.

ALSO READ: CALCULATOR, ECONOMICS, MONEY.

**ACHILLES** see TROJAN WAR.

**ACIDS AND BASES** Have you ever tasted a green apple? It has a sour taste. The juice of a lemon is very sour. Vinegar is sour, too. What makes these things taste sour? It is *hydrogen ions.* An ion is an atom with too many or too few electrons. An *acid* is a substance that forms hydrogen ions when added to water. You cannot see the ions, but if the acid is strong, it makes many hydrogen ions, which taste sour. Never taste (or touch) a very strong acid.

▲*Two hydrangea flowers. Chemicals in the soil act on a substance in the flowers called* pigment *to produce the different colors. Alkaline (basic) soil produces pink hydrangeas. Acid in the soil produces blue hydrangeas.* ▼

# ACIDS AND BASES

Oxygen and hydrogen are both gases, and oxygen forms part of Earth's air. The letter H stands for hydrogen, and O stands for oxygen. Water is two parts hydrogen and one part oxygen. It is written $H_2O$.

Acids usually have a sour taste. Some bases taste bitter. A *base* is a substance that forms *hydroxide ions* when added to water. A hydroxide ion is made up of one part oxygen and one part hydrogen. This incomplete molecule is written with the symbol OH.

### The "In-Between" Substances

But not all substances are acids or bases. If equal amounts of an acid and a base are mixed, the mixture is "in-between," neither an acid or a base. It is called a *neutral* liquid. The liquid is neutral because it contains the same number of H ions and OH ions. The H and OH ions have joined and formed water. A *salt* is also formed, but you can see it only when the water evaporates. There are many kinds of acids and many kinds of bases. The type of salt formed depends on the acid and base mixed together. One type of salt is the kind that we use to season our food.

Some substances change color when they are put into an acid or base. One of these is a dye called *litmus*. Litmus is red in an acid and blue in a base.

You can make your own dye to show acids and bases. Chop up a few of the outer leaves of a red cabbage. Put them in a pan with enough water to cover them. Boil the water until it turns purple, probably about 20 minutes. Remove the cabbage leaves by straining the liquid into a container.

When the liquid has cooled, put part of it into a jar and add a little lemon juice. The color changes from purple to red. Next, put some of the dye into another jar. Add a little baking soda. This time, the liquid changes to greenish blue. Why?

You are now ready to test some of the liquids around your home to see if they are acid or base. For example, put a drop of liquid soap into some of the basic purple liquid. Does it change color? Now put some soap with the red, or acid, indicator. Does it change color this time? What is soap, a base or an acid? What happens when a substance you test is neutral?

### Acids and Bases Are Useful

A small amount of acid gives flavor to our food. The tart taste of an apple or orange is caused by the acid in the fruit. We add vinegar, another mild acid, to pickles, lettuce, and other foods to give them a slightly sour taste.

The ions in acids carry electricity. Sulfuric acid is very strong (contains many ions), so it is used in the battery of a car. Hydrochloric acid, another common acid, is found in human stomachs. In very small amounts, it helps humans digest food.

Bases are useful, too. Windows sparkle when washed with water containing ammonia, a common base. Another is sodium hydroxide, used in making soap. Car tires are made with the help of bases. And the pages of a book as well as some of the clothes you wear are made with the help of bases.

Bees, wasps, and jellyfish all have stingers. If one of these animals stings you, the "bite" hurts. The sting is really a small amount of acid injected into your skin through the hollow, needle-like stinger. The acid is what makes the sting hurt. You can take away the pain of the sting if you add a base to the acid. If you are stung by a bee or some other animal, try putting a paste of baking soda and ammonia on the bite. This is a good way to take the hurt out of a sting.

ALSO READ: ATOM, CHEMISTRY, ELECTRICITY, ELEMENT, FIRST AID, POISON.

**ACNE** see SKIN.

---

Strong acids will dissolve most metals, but they do not affect gold. One way of testing whether something is gold or an imitation is to test it with acid. This is the origin of the phrase "to give something the acid test." Gold is dissolved in the laboratory by a mixture of hydrochloric and nitric acids: this is called *aqua regia* (Latin for "royal water").

# ACROBATICS

**ACROBATICS** The word "acrobat" comes from two Greek words that mean "one who walks on tiptoes" and "one who climbs high." Thousands of years ago, Egyptians and Greeks admired performers who could move quickly and keep their balance at heights or in dangerous places. Acrobatics were sport and exercise for these people. At the same time, in China, acrobats often entertained large groups of people.

You have probably climbed something, a tree with low branches, or a Jungle Gym on a playground. But just being able to climb or swing does not make you an acrobat. An acrobat must have strong muscles and good control of them (called *coordination*). He or she must be in top physical condition, and must spend many years training to be an acrobat.

## Circus Acrobats

The most dangerous and spectacular forms of acrobatics are seen in circuses. *Aerialists*, or high-trapeze artists, have been thrilling audiences for many years. Perhaps you've heard an old song called "The Daring Young Man on the Flying Trapeze." A *trapeze* is a small swinging bar suspended by two ropes. Most trapeze performers use trapezes that are very high above the ground. Performers climb up to their high equipment on a rope ladder. Some performers are so strong they can go up a rope hand-over-hand, without using their legs.

Both men and women trapeze artists can do some almost unbelievable tricks. They usually work in teams. An act may begin with the artists standing on two high platforms. One flyer begins to swing from his trapeze. A partner swings from the opposite platform. The first flyer changes his position on the swinging bar, so that he hangs by his knees. His partner—with perfect timing—lets go of his trapeze, dives through the air, and catches the first person's hands in midair. A third flyer may join in, to do a triple somersault through the air between the other two performers. All of the act is done with split-second timing, and to the sound of gasps from the audience below.

Acrobats called *tightrope walkers* do more than walk across a rope (actually a heavy wire cable). When they do walk on the rope, they wear special shoes with soft soles. But they also do handstands and somersaults. Some ride bikes and even motorcycles on the narrow cable. One performer invented an unusual handstand. Instead of balancing himself on one hand, he balanced on one finger!

Another kind of acrobatics is performed by *high-wire* artists. One of the most famous high-wire groups is the Wallenda family. Perhaps their most spectacular act was the "human pyramid," performed without a net beneath them. Four members of the family balanced on a wire, with a long rod placed across their shoulders. Two others stood on that rod, with another rod on their shoulders. On the very tiptop stood a lone girl, far above the crowd. Three members of the family have been killed in falls, and another was seriously injured. Even so, the Wallendas who are left have not given up acrobatics. The Wallendas train younger members of the family, and they continue to thrill and entertain audiences.

## Acrobatic Safety

Circus acrobats are always trying to develop new acts, such as balancing on a moving ladder, like the five acrobats pictured. Acrobats attract big crowds when they advertise a new stunt that nobody has seen before. Their urge to do new things sometimes leads them to try dangerous tricks. Many trapeze artists have been killed in falls. Most cir-

▲ *These acrobats need great skill. They are doing expert stunts on a moving ladder.*

▲ *A circus girl spends many years training her muscles before she can hang by her toes.*

Karl Wallenda, head of the famous family of acrobats, walked across Tallulah Gorge in Georgia in July, 1970, on a high wire 750 feet above the gorge. He walked an 821-foot-long wire in 20 minutes, stopping twice to stand on his head.

[750 ft.=228.7 m; 821 ft.=250.5 m]

ACROPOLIS

cuses now have large rope nets stretched under the acrobats because of the danger of their falling. If a performer loses his balance or his grip, he falls into the net. To finish his act, a trapeze expert may purposely drop into the net. He bounces on it, then drops gracefully to the ground.

ALSO READ: CIRCUS, GYMNASTICS.

▲ The "Porch of the Maidens" on the Erechtheum, another famous temple on the Acropolis.

▲ These old ruins were once temples. They stand on the Acropolis at Athens. The one in front is the Parthenon, most famous of them all. It was built in honor of the goddess Athena.

[500 ft.=152.5 m]

When Lord Elgin was the British ambassador to Greece in the early 1800s, he sent ancient marble sculptures to London to prevent their destruction in war. Now called the "Elgin marbles," they are in the British Museum.

**ACROPOLIS** In the city of Athens, Greece, stands a hill 500 feet high. This hill is the Acropolis. The word "acropolis" means "upper city." The ancient Greeks used hills as forts, because fighting uphill was hard for enemies. Handsome buildings called *temples* were built on these hills to honor the gods and goddesses of the Greeks. Many cities in ancient Greece had an acropolis, but the most famous one is in Athens. See how the buildings in the photograph seem to be standing guard over Athens.

Over 400 years before Christ, several magnificent marble temples were built on the Athens Acropolis in honor of the goddess Athena. The great gatehouse of the Acropolis, called the *Propylaea*, was the Athenians' favorite building.

The most famous temple is the *Parthenon*, designed by Phidias, one of the most noted architects of all time. Most people think that the Parthenon is one of the most beautiful buildings ever built. Inside it stood a 40-foot-tall gilded statue of Athena, which was lost long ago.

Another temple, the *Erechtheum*, is known for its "Porch of the Maidens." The six "maidens" are *caryatides*, statues of women that hold up the roof of the porch.

Many parts of the Acropolis temples were destroyed by time and war. But some of them have now been rebuilt.

ALSO READ: ATHENS; GODS AND GODDESSES; GREECE, ANCIENT; GREEK ART.
[40 ft.=12.4 m]

**ACTION** see PEACE CORPS.

**ACTORS AND ACTING** Everyone is an actor sometimes. Playing "make-believe" is acting. So is dressing up in your parents' old clothes. Trying to get out of doing something unpleasant by saying you are sick is acting, too.

An actor pretends to be someone else. He *impersonates* a *character* (person) in a story or play in front of a group of people called an *audience*. To impersonate means to study the character, or *role*, that an actor will play, and then act in such a way that an audience believes he is that character.

No one knows when man first started acting, but it is a very ancient art. It probably began with hunting and victory dances, such as the dances of the American Indians.

Many religious rites or events were acted out. The story was most important in these ceremonies.

**The Ups and Downs of Acting**
The Greeks were writing plays and performing them in outdoor theaters by the fourth century B.C. The ancient Romans later copied the Greeks. Actors became very important. Many of them did not have to pay taxes or fight wars. *Pantomime*, which is acting without speaking, became popular. Pantomime actors use their bodies and faces to tell a story.

Little by little, foolish and silly plays produced in Rome made acting less serious. Many actors quit. The Romans then trained slaves to act. So people began to think of acting as a bad thing.

Acting was still not popular during the Middle Ages in Europe. Actors—and plays—almost disappeared. Jugglers, acrobats, and singers took their place, and traveled all over Europe.

Plays began to be performed again during the late Middle Ages. Many of them were Bible stories performed in churches. James Burbage built the first theater in England, in 1576. Many companies of actors were formed during the reign of Elizabeth I. William Shakespeare was a famous playwright and actor of that time. Many people, even the ladies and gentlemen of the royal court, came to the theaters.

The Puritans closed down the theaters in England in 1642, because they thought plays were sinful. But theaters reopened when King Charles II came to the throne in 1660. Plays were popular again by the end of the seventeenth century. Women began to act on the English stage for the first time. Boys had played women's parts in Shakespeare's time. Nell Gwynn was one of the most famous actresses of the seventeenth century. Plays have remained popular ever since then. Today, actors and actresses have many opportunities for careers on the stage, in television, and in movies.

**Acting in the Theater**
Some of the greatest actors in theater history are Richard Burbage (James's son), David Garrick, Henry Irving, Sarah Bernhardt, Sir Laurence Olivier, Eleanora Duse, Katharine Cornell, and the Barrymore family. Many of these people, as well as other world-famous actors, have performed in New York City. This city is the center of professional theater in the United States. Touring companies, college and high school acting groups, summer theaters, community theaters, and children's theaters are located all over the U.S.

An actor uses his education, his talent, and his imagination to create a role for the stage. He must use both his voice and his body when he acts. To be a successful actor, he must study and practice. He must observe other people and understand their emotions. He must learn the *motivations* (reasons) for people's behavior, so that his acting is believable.

▲ *An actor in pantomime must play many different parts. By his movements, this actor makes people think he is a merchant, a thief, an innkeeper, and a storyteller.*

## ACTORS AND ACTING

### Acting in the Movies
Many movie actors and actresses are more famous than kings and presidents, because millions of people all over the world watch movies. Hollywood, California, the capital of the movie industry, created the star system. A *star* is an actor or actress who is considered to be an outstanding performer, and who has leading roles in movies. Charlie Chaplin was a famous pantomimist in silent films. Shirley Temple was one of the best-loved child actresses. Paul Newman and Elizabeth Taylor have both reached the top of their profession.

Working in movies is different from working in the theater. An actor performs in a whole play in front of people. In a movie, he works in bits and pieces in front of a camera. He may perform the last scenes first, and weeks later do the first scene. He must sometimes travel to distant places, or "go on location," to film some sections of a movie.

### Acting in Television and Radio
Acting for television is somewhat different from stage acting. The television screen is small and intimate (close). Actors must make smaller movements and gestures, because the audience is very close to the television screen. Actors must work under very hot lights and use microphones. They must stand where there are chalk marks on the floor. Actors do not have so much freedom on television as on stage.

Radio actors and comedians were important in the 1930s and 1940s. Jack Benny, Fred Allen, and Orson Welles are three people made famous by radio. *Soap operas*, stories that continue from day to day, were very popular. After television arrived, radio lost some of its popularity. Not many plays are produced on radio now. Today, radio has mainly news, music, and sports.

### Acting Styles
There are two basic styles of acting. To be a good actor, it is probably best to combine the two styles. The first style uses *external techniques* alone. An actor uses gestures, movements, and vocal and facial expressions to create a believable character. A skillful actor can make his audience feel emotions through his movements and voice, even when he does not feel all the emotion himself. This kind of acting can sometimes seem faked when done by a poor actor.

▲ *Some children are famous actors. Shirley Temple was a popular child star of the thirties. She starred in this movie with Gary Cooper.*

▶ *Did you ever wish you were someone else? Actors often play people we would like to be. Here, Clark Gable is playing a cowboy. He has just roped a horse.*

# ACTORS AND ACTING

*◀Big Bird is an actor on television's Sesame Street. He helps children learn the alphabet, numbers, and other useful things.*

The second type of acting uses *internal techniques*. The most famous internal method is called the *Stanislavski method*, named after the Russian actor and director Konstantin Stanislavski, or "method" acting. People who believe method acting is better say that an actor can make his part believable only when he really feels the emotions of his character. If an actor is playing an unhappy person, he tries to feel sad himself. An unskilled actor may get careless using this method. He may not speak clearly, or he may not respond properly to another actor's words. Skilled actors try to use a combination of both techniques.

You and a half dozen friends might like to do some acting. One game that is fun is "paper bag theater." Divide the group into two teams. Each group puts into a paper bag five or six things, such as a comb, a handkerchief, a doll, a seashell, and so on. Each group trades its bag with the other. From its bagful of surprises, each group makes up a play using all the items in the bag and then, after about an hour, presents their play to the other group. You'll be amazed at the plays and the acting started by a few things in a paper bag.

## Becoming an Actor

To become a good actor, a person must train his body, voice, and mind to express what a character is really like. One way a person can get training as an actor is to perform in plays produced in his school, college, or town. But if he wants to become a professional actor, he usually goes to a special school. Many colleges and universities have classes in acting and drama. Students can even earn bachelor's and master's degrees in drama at some universities. There are also many acting schools in large cities, such as the Actor's Studio in New York City. While an actor studies his craft, he usually continues to *audition* (try out) for plays or movies, hoping some day he will get an important leading role.

## Rewards of Acting

Professional actors and actresses today are given many honors, besides the pleasure of being known and admired all over the world. Some actors even become knights, in Great Britain. The most famous actors earn large sums of money. One of the best-known awards is the Academy Award. *Oscar*, a statue, is presented every year by

*▲Many animals "act" with human actors. Chimpanzees, like this one, are easy to train because they love to show off.*

*A director helps the actors do the best job possible. Here, he tells some young actors how to play a scene.*

*Could you act under hot lights and with many people crowding in around you? Movie actors often have to do that.*

the Academy of Motion Picture Arts and Sciences, to actors and actresses who give best performances in movies. The best television actors win *Emmy* awards presented by the Academy of Television Arts and Sciences. Stage actors are given awards, too. Most famous is the Antoinette Perry Award, called the *Tony*.

An actor's greatest reward is probably the response of the audience. When an actor makes an audience weep or laugh, the applause of the audience at the end of a performance is what makes all of his hard work worthwhile.

ALSO READ: ACADEMY AWARD; DRAMA; MOTION PICTURES; PANTOMIME; SHAKESPEARE, WILLIAM; THEATER.

**ADAMS, JOHN** (1735-1826) A man named Henry Adams came to Massachusetts in 1636. He, his sons, his grandsons, and his great-grandsons were farmers. But two of his great-great-grandsons, Samuel and John Adams, became political leaders. Both of them signed the Declaration of Independence. Samuel Adams was an important leader of the American Revolution. John Adams, his cousin, was the second President of the United States.

John Adams first studied at Harvard College to become a minister. But he decided to study law instead. He became known throughout Massachusetts as an honest, courageous, and able lawyer. He was a leader in the American colonies' fight for independence from Great Britain. In 1774, he went to the First Continental Congress. He signed the Declaration of Independence at the Second Congress, in 1776. He worked hard to convince the colonies to accept the Declaration. Adams went to France and the Netherlands during the American Revolution, to urge those countries to support the colonists. John Adams, Benjamin Franklin, and John Jay worked on the peace treaty with England, in 1783. Adams served as George Washington's Vice President after the Revolution.

Adams himself became President in 1797. The United States was almost at war again. The people of France had revolted against royalty eight years earlier. Kings of other European countries supported the French royalty. So France, controlled by the people, fought a series of wars with several European countries.

Many Americans, led by Thomas Jefferson, wanted to help France. Other Americans, led by Alexander Hamilton, wanted to join the supporters of royalty. President Adams realized that the U.S. was not strong enough to fight a war. He

---

**SECOND PRESIDENT  MARCH 4, 1797–MARCH 4, 1801**

**Born:** October 30, 1735, Braintree, Massachusetts (Now Quincy)
**Parents:** John and Susanna Boylston Adams
**Education:** Harvard College
**Religion:** Unitarian
**Occupation:** Lawyer
**Political Party:** Federalist
**Married:** 1764 to Abigail Smith (1744–1818)
**Children:** 3 sons, 2 daughters (1 died in infancy)
**Died:** July 4, 1826, Quincy, Massachusetts
**Buried:** First Unitarian Church, Quincy, Massachusetts

**JOHN ADAMS**

worked out a treaty with France that kept the U.S. out of the wars in Europe.

The treaty was probably a good idea for the country, but it made President Adams very unpopular, especially with his own political party, the Federalists. Thomas Jefferson was elected President in 1803. Adams lost the election because so many Federalists were angry at him.

John Adams was one of the most famous members of this noted American family. Another interesting family member was John's wife, Abigail, probably the best-informed woman of her day. She is remembered for the intelligent, amusing letters she wrote to her husband during his stay in Europe. You can find out more about Abigail by reading her letters. The eldest son of John and Abigail, John Quincy Adams, was the sixth U.S. President.

ALSO READ: ADAMS, JOHN QUINCY; ADAMS, SAMUEL; CONTINENTAL CONGRESS; HAMILTON, ALEXANDER; JEFFERSON, THOMAS; PRESIDENCY.

**ADAMS, JOHN QUINCY (1767-1848)** The American Revolution began when John Quincy Adams was eight. He and his mother watched the Battle of Bunker Hill from a nearby field. Later, he went with his father, John Adams, on a government mission to France. They sailed safely through a line of enemy British ships, but they were shipwrecked in Spain. Riding mules, they took three months to reach Paris. When he was 14, John was an aide to the first U.S. diplomat to go to Russia. He later went with his father to the peace treaty conferences between the United States and Great Britain at the end of the American Revolution. John Quincy Adams was an experienced traveler and diplomat by the time he graduated from Harvard College in 1787.

Adams served as an ambassador for President George Washington, and then for his own father, who followed Washington as President. Then John Quincy, too, entered politics. He was elected to the Senate in 1803. But he angered his own political party, the Federalists, because he did not always vote the

▲ *This is how the U.S. Capitol looked when John Adams was President. The building was not finished, and the city of Washington, D.C., was hardly begun.*

Two famous presidents of the United States died on the same day—July 4, 1826, the fiftieth anniversary of the Declaration of Independence. They were Thomas Jefferson, who had written much of the Declaration, and John Adams, who had also signed it.

◄ *In 1825, during John Quincy Adams's first year of office, the Erie Canal was opened. The canal linked the Hudson River with Lake Erie.*

---

**SIXTH PRESIDENT    MARCH 4, 1825–MARCH 4, 1829**

**Born:** July 11, 1767, Braintree, Massachusetts (now Quincy)
**Parents:** John and Abigail Smith Adams
**Education:** University of Leyden, the Netherlands; Harvard College
**Religion:** Unitarian
**Occupation:** Lawyer
**Political Party:** Federalist, then National Republican
**Married:** 1797 to Louisa Catherine Johnson (1775–1852)
**Children:** 3 sons, 1 daughter (died in infancy)
**Died:** February 23, 1848, Washington, D.C.
**Buried:** First Unitarian Church, Quincy, Massachusetts

**JOHN QUINCY ADAMS**

*Samuel Adams, American patriot.*

*Jane Addams.*

*Hull House, where Jane Addams worked to give people a better life. It is now part of the University of Illinois at Chicago.*

way they wanted him to. After five years, they elected a new Senator. President Madison then asked Adams to become a diplomat again and sent him to Europe. President Monroe made Adams his Secretary of State in 1817. Adams bought Florida from Spain, and he helped write the Monroe Doctrine.

In the Presidential election of 1824, Adams was one of four candidates. Andrew Jackson received the most votes, but not enough to win. The House of Representatives had to decide who would be President, and they picked Adams. The men in Congress who had supported Jackson argued constantly with President Adams. He had good ideas, but they were not accepted, because he was not popular. In 1828, Andrew Jackson won the election.

Adams went back to Washington in 1831, this time as a congressman from Massachusetts. He served for 17 years. He believed that slavery was wrong and should be stopped. He spoke about it so often that slave owners called him the "Madman from Massachusetts." In 1848, he collapsed at his desk in the House of Representatives, and he died two days later.

ALSO READ: ADAMS, JOHN; JACKSON, ANDREW; PRESIDENCY.

**ADAMS, SAMUEL (1722-1803)** "A hot-headed radical!" "An arch traitor!" These were just two of many names the British called Samuel Adams of Boston in the years before the American Revolution. Sam went to Harvard College, like his younger cousin John Adams. Also, like John, Sam never stopped fighting for the independence of the American colonies from Great Britain.

Sam Adams constantly gave speeches to tell the colonists they had to be free from British rule. He urged the colonists to protest the Stamp Act and other examples of England's "taxation without representation." He helped organize groups of rebels, such as the Sons of Liberty. He led the Boston Tea Party. Sam and his friend Patrick Henry were both delegates to the Continental Congress. They urged the other delegates to demand immediate independence for the colonies. He voted for and signed the Declaration of Independence.

Adams served in the Continental Congress during the Revolution. Then he returned to Boston. He was governor of Massachusetts from 1794 to 1797. The British may have called Samuel Adams a traitor, but in American history he is remembered as an important leader of the American Revolution.

ALSO READ: ADAMS, JOHN; BOSTON TEA PARTY; CONTINENTAL CONGRESS; DECLARATION OF INDEPENDENCE; HENRY, PATRICK; PRESIDENCY.

**ADAPTATION** see EVOLUTION.

**ADDAMS, JANE (1860-1935)** "She belongs to all the people." "She was everybody's friend." Jane Addams earned this praise from a lifetime spent helping people. She worked for the poor, for immigrants and minority groups, for women and children.

Born in Cedarville, Illinois, Jane graduated from nearby Rockford College. She had been born with a badly curved back. She wanted to be a doctor, but her handicap kept her from finishing medical school.

Her family sent her to Europe to rest. In London she visited a *settlement house*—a gathering place and education center for poor people. She decided to start such a place for the poor of Chicago. Hull House was the result. Jane and her friend, Ellen Starr, worked hard at Hull House. Kindergarten was held in the morning, teenagers' classes in the afternoon, and classes for grownups in the evening.

Jane Addams called social work the profession of helping people in need—in need of food, clothing, housing, education, work, or play. She helped women win the right to vote. All her life she battled for peace. Her work for world peace won her the Nobel Peace Prize when she was 71.

ALSO READ: SOCIAL WORK.

**ADDICTION** Using some drugs for a long time can make a person need to keep on taking them. This need is called *addiction*. The drug user, or *addict*, becomes addicted when he takes a habit-forming drug often, for a long time. His need for the drug is called a *habit*. His habit makes him take larger and larger amounts of the drug.

There are different kinds of addictive drugs and two kinds of addictions. Some drugs, such as sleeping pills and "pep pills," act on the body's central nervous system. The addict thinks he needs such drugs, especially during times of stress. This need of the mind is called *mental dependence*. Other drugs, called *narcotics*, set up such a need that the addict's body cannot do without them. This kind of need is called *physical dependence*. If the drugs are taken away from an addict with a physical dependence, he experiences *withdrawal* symptoms. One of these symptoms is intense pain. People who use *heroin* and then stop must suffer through withdrawal. Unlike most drugs, heroin has no known medical use. It is used only by drug addicts.

Many drugs that cause physical or mental dependence are dangerous and illegal. There are four main kinds of drugs. (1) *Pain killers*, such as opium, morphine, and codeine, are given to patients by doctors to stop severe pain. But if a person takes these drugs over a period of time, he develops physical dependence. (2) *Depressants* slow, or relax, the central nervous system. Sleeping pills *(sedatives)* are depressants. (3) Other drugs called *stimulants* pep up the central nervous system. These include *amphetamines*, which are called "speed." (4) *Hallucinogens* are the fourth main kind of drug. They are drugs that make a person see colors and objects and hear sounds that are not really there. Marijuana is an hallucinogen. LSD (lysergic acid diethylamide) and similar chemicals are the strongest and most dangerous hallucinogens. Drug users usually do not become physically addicted to hallucinogens, but the drugs often cause mental dependence, and may lead users to try narcotics.

Drug addiction and misuse have grown greatly in recent years. Treatment of addicts has become a big community problem. Addicts hurt themselves by using drugs; and they can hurt, or even kill, other people when they try to steal money to buy drugs.

Most ways of treating addicts start by *withdrawing* the drug. "Hard" drug addicts, those on heroin or morphine, usually stay in treatment centers, to stop them from getting new supplies of drugs and to have help available during the pain of withdrawal. Many scientists are trying to develop safe drugs that can be given as substitutes for hard drugs during the withdrawal period. It is very, very difficult to break an addiction, and not many addicts are successful. Those who get past the withdrawal period need the help of doctors for a long time thereafter.

The best way to prevent addiction is to keep people from getting drugs, except when a doctor *prescribes* (gives) them. Growing, manufacturing, and importing illegal drugs must be stopped. Mental health and drug-education programs give information on drugs. Hopefully, such information will help young people avoid drugs.

ALSO READ: MOOD MODIFIERS.

**ADDITION** see ARITHMETIC.

*Konrad Adenauer, post-war German Chancellor.*

The German people fondly called Konrad Adenauer *Der Alte,* "the old one." He was in his 70s before doing the work history remembers him for.

▼ *This happy teenage smile belongs to an adolescent in New Guinea.*

**ADENAUER, KONRAD (1876-1967)** Konrad Adenauer was the first Chancellor (chief minister of state) of West Germany. He was elected in 1949—at age 73—when Germany was still suffering from its defeat in World War II. Adenauer was a strong leader, who helped rebuild his war-torn country. Today, West Germany is one of the major industrial nations in the world.

Adenauer was born in Cologne, Germany. He became a lawyer and entered politics when he was 30 years old. He was elected mayor of Cologne in 1917. He remained active in politics until 1933, when Adolph Hitler's Nazi party took over Germany. The Nazis removed Adenauer from office because he spoke up against them. They imprisoned him twice during the war.

After World War II, Adenauer organized a new political party, the Christian Democratic Union. He also helped write a constitution for Germany before he was elected Chancellor. As Chancellor, he helped improve Germany's relations with the United States and other European nations. Adenauer signed a "Treaty of Cooperation" with France in 1963. This treaty helped end hundreds of years of hostility between Germany and France. Konrad Adenauer retired in 1963, knowing that Germany was again a strong nation respected by the rest of the world.

ALSO READ: GERMAN HISTORY; HITLER, ADOLF; WORLD WAR II.

**ADENOIDS** see BREATHING.

**ADJECTIVE** see PARTS OF SPEECH.

**ADOLESCENCE** Boys and girls usually look forward to becoming teenagers. These particular years of growing up are called *adolescence,* which is a time of many changes. The changes usually begin to take place in girls 10 to 13 and in boys 11 to 14. The changes of adolescence go on for several years.

**Physical Changes**
The adolescent's body changes in many ways. Girls are turning into women and boys into men. Hair begins to grow on various parts of the body. Girls' hips become rounder and their breasts larger. Boys' voices change, and their muscles develop. These changes are part of *puberty,* the stage of growing up when people become physically able to reproduce.

At first, it seems that girls are growing faster than boys of the same age. But boys soon catch up and then become taller and heavier than most of the girls. Some teenagers start growing very fast and then slow down. Others develop slowly at first and later speed up.

Because so many changes are taking place in the body, the adolescent often is very tired and needs extra sleep. Other times, he seems to have a great deal of energy. His body is sometimes changing so fast that he becomes very clumsy. He may be embarrassed because he develops pimples on his face.

But it helps the teenager to know that his or her friends are also going through these changes. In a few years they will look very much like the other young men and women who have grown up.

**Changes in Feelings**
Just as a small child gives up his wagon and blocks for two-wheelers and mystery books, adolescents' interests change, too. Boys lose interest in their bicycles and look forward to driving cars. Girls no longer want to spend time making doll clothes, but become interested in their own clothes instead. Both boys and girls become interested in each other. They spend a lot of time together and learn many things about getting along with the opposite sex, which will help them later when they want to marry.

An adolescent's feelings are confused because he is no longer a child but not quite a grown-up. Sometimes he cries very easily and other times he acts as though nothing can hurt him. Parents who are understanding can help make things easier for their adolescent. Teenagers still need the love and help of their parents, but of a different kind. They need support and encouragement, but they must also be free to make many decisions themselves, even though some will be mistakes.

Adolescence is a time of adventure. Teenagers begin thinking about what kind of work they want to do as adults. They also begin preparing for this work in school. They make plans about whether or not to go to college. Sometimes they take part-time jobs. They learn to do more and more things for themselves, so that they do not have to depend so much on their parents. They want to think out answers for themselves, and question the beliefs of others, searching for answers that seem honest to them. Many adolescents are very concerned with problems in their community and their nation, such as pollution and war and discrimination, and are well on their way to becoming responsible men and women.

ALSO READ: AGING, GROWTH, HUMAN BODY, REPRODUCTION.

**ADOPTION** Some children have no family because their parents are dead or are too sick or have too many problems to take care of them. Many men and women do not have children of their own, so they adopt children who have no families. To *adopt* means to become the legal parent of someone else's child. Often, if a person marries someone with children, he or she adopts those children. Sometimes a mother allows her new baby to be adopted because she knows that she cannot make a good home for him, and she wants him to be happy.

Adoption agencies have the job of making sure that the people who want to adopt children can give the children good, loving homes. These agencies try to keep brothers and sisters together.

A child cannot be adopted until an agency learns all about him and the people who want to adopt him. The child usually lives with his new family for a while. If the agency thinks that the child will be happy with his new family, a court makes the adoption legal. Then the child really becomes part of his new family. His last name is changed to theirs. And his natural parents—those to whom he was born—cannot take him from his adopted family.

Many agencies try hard to find good homes for children who need special love and understanding. Sometimes these are older children, or children who have physical or mental problems. Many people who adopt these children find special happiness in making the children part of their family.

ALSO READ: CHILD CARE.

**ADRIATIC SEA** Think of Italy as a boot sticking southward into the Mediterranean Sea. The Adriatic Sea lies along the back of the boot. The Adriatic is actually a gulf of the Mediterranean Sea. (See the map with the article on EUROPE.)

The Adriatic was named after the ancient town of Adria, once a major Roman port. Roman sailing ships, bulging with cargo, crisscrossed the Adriatic. Many vessels sailed through the Strait of Otranto into the open waters of the Mediterranean. Some Roman ships went all the way to Britain and the Far East. The place where Adria stood now lies 15 miles from the sea, because mud has piled up at the mouth of the Po River and pushed back the sea.

The Adriatic's Italian coastline is low-lying, and has few harbors. On the eastern side of the sea, the

[15 mi.=24.2 km]

▲ *The Adriatic Sea is between Italy and Yugoslavia. This sea has been a highway for travelers through many centuries.*

▼ *A poster of 1853 advertising buses. Before the days of radio and television, posters and handbills were very important forms of advertising.*

coasts of Yugoslavia and Albania have steep sides and good harbors. Many islands are near the Yugoslav shore. Wealthy Romans once built summer homes along this rugged coast. Today, vineyards cling to the slopes along the coast. Yugoslav fishermen sail from the harbors to cast nets into the Adriatic for sardines. Venice, the city of canals, lies at the top of the Adriatic.

ALSO READ: MEDITERRANEAN SEA, ROMAN EMPIRE, VENICE, YUGOSLAVIA.

**ADVERB** see PARTS OF SPEECH.

**ADVERTISING** Advertising is the business of trying to convince a *consumer* what to buy. A consumer is a buyer of products or a user of services. Business and industry provide more products and services than any one person can ever use.

One kind of product may be made by several different companies. So each company uses its own special name for a product. That special name is called the company's *brand name*. No other company can use that name. Coca-Cola and Kleenex are brand names.

**Ads Are Persuaders**

Advertising gives useful information about which products to buy. But modern advertising does more than give news about products and services. Today's advertisements, or ads, try to get consumers to buy certain brands. Writers of advertising are so skillful they can sometimes persuade a consumer to wear a certain kind of clothing, eat a special kind of cereal, or go to a movie. Consumers might never even want a product if they did not see or hear advertisements for it.

For example, you probably do not need the newest cereal in the supermarket. Your mother probably has many cereal brands on her shelves. She may not have space on a shelf for another. But if you see ads about a new cereal that is sugar-coated and has a toy submarine in the box, you may want it.

Advertising must get attention. It must be exciting, entertaining, or provide some pleasure to be effective. The ad writer's secret is that he offers a good idea as well as a product. The idea is what the ad is really selling. One example is an ad that says eating a certain cereal will make a boy do well in sports. A cereal brand may sell better if consumers think it offers strength and energy.

Suppose you are running a lemonade stand in your neighborhood. How would you advertise it?

First, you could decorate your stand with different colors of crepe paper. When you paint your sign, you can make it large and bright, so that people notice you.

The words in advertising are called *copy*. Your copy should say something about the lemonade to make people want to buy it. Think of good things about lemonade on a hot summer day. What words will you use?

If someone else has a lemonade stand on your block, he may take business away from you. If this happens, you can offer something he does not have, to win back business. You can make your lemonade with fresh lemons, perhaps, instead of a frozen mix. Many *advertisers* offer other things along with the ones they are trying to sell, such as prizes or trading stamps. Perhaps you could find something to offer with your lemonade.

### The Media

A communications *medium* is a means of carrying information to an audience. The plural form of medium is *media*. Some examples of media are television, films, newspapers, magazines, and radio. Advertising uses nearly all media.

Many ads can be found in the *print* media, such as newspapers, magazines, catalogues, telephone directories, posters, and billboards. Newspapers and magazines depend on advertising to pay the cost of printing them. Payments that newspapers and magazines get from advertisers give publishers enough money to sell their newspapers or magazines for much less than it costs to print and mail them. Successful magazines can almost afford to give their issues away, because of the amount of money they get from the advertising they carry. For example, *Time* magazine sells its outside back cover, printed in color, for $62,250. You can buy a copy for a dollar. Some special magazines *are* given away.

Ads go wherever people can see them. *Outdoor advertising* is mounted above the windows and doors of buses and subways. Taxicabs carry ads on boards attached to their roofs, in some cities. Ads are sometimes painted on sides of buildings. Big ads made of electric lights flash on and off at night in the downtown parts of cities.

*Direct mail* advertising uses letters and colorful brochures mailed to people's homes. The letters or brochures may ask people to subscribe to magazines, give money to charity, order books through the mail, or attend a special sale. Direct mail is a very successful way of advertising.

Ads that reach the most people are on television and radio. Many different kinds of ads are shown during a few hours of television broadcasting. Probably more people see one ad on TV at one time than will ever drive past one billboard on a highway. A company may have to pay several thousand dollars to buy even a few seconds of television time, to advertise a product. Not all companies can afford to advertise on TV.

### When Did Advertising Begin?

The first ads probably came from the town criers in ancient Greece. They called out what could be bought in the local marketplaces. Newsboys still hawk (advertise by shouting) papers in big cities as they walk down the street. The earliest billboards were in ancient Egypt. The Egyptians carved announcements on tall stones called *stelae*. Ads were first printed in 1480. William Caxton, one of the first English printers, nailed printed papers on church doors to advertise a religious book he was selling.

Many different newspapers and magazines appeared in Europe and America in the late nineteenth century. England took the lead in advertising in the print media. But, by the 1860s, American manufacturers took the lead.

▲*Piccadilly Circus in London glitters with advertising. "Spectaculars" sparkle in neon lights. On one wall a clock draws your eyes to an ad for beer. There are window ads, too. Even the double-deck buses carry ads.*

▼*Wouldn't it be fun to stay at a motel where there is a happy family like this? Attractive people are used as models in ads. They make it easier to sell the product.*

▲ *Years ago big wooden Indians stood outside cigar stores to advertise tobacco. The Indians were carved and painted, and often held cigars in their hands. Can you think of any stores that advertise with special signs?*

The red-and-white striped barber pole outside a barber shop was a form of advertising long ago. It was red, wrapped with a white bandage as a symbol of bloodletting, which was thought to cure illness. Before modern medicine, barbers were the local doctors and surgeons.

▼ *Would you like to visit some beautiful islands where European civilization started? The Aegean Sea is peppered with islands. An ancient Greek temple and a modern village stand side by side on this one.*

Advertising agencies grew into big businesses with the coming of radio and television in the twentieth century. J. Walter Thompson, one of the world's largest agencies, billed its clients, in a recent year, $900,100,000 for purchases of advertising. An agency provides advertising to the media for anyone with a product or service to sell. In advertising, a customer is called a *client*. A client can be one person or a huge company. A client has an *account* with an ad agency. An account includes the entire job of producing the client's ads and getting them into the media. An agency and a client agree on the media that will carry the ads. A team then goes to work. Most ads—even television ads—need an illustrator, a copy writer, a designer, and often a photographer. Recorded tapes need to be made for radio and television ads. Many exciting careers are available for young people in advertising agencies.

ALSO READ: PATENTS AND COPYRIGHTS, PROPAGANDA, PUBLIC RELATIONS.

**AEGEAN SEA** Lying between Greece and Turkey is the Aegean Sea. It is an arm of the Mediterranean Sea. Crete, the largest island belonging to Greece, lies at its south end. About 400 other islands are also in the Aegean. (See the map with the article on EUROPE.)

This sea was important in Greek history and legend. Great cities were built around its natural ports. When men first discovered how to make bronze long ago, they carried this valuable alloy to other parts of the world on ships that crossed the Aegean. Adventurers searching for fortunes fought many battles in its waters. According to legend, the king of Crete kept a monster in the sea to scare away his enemies.

The Aegean Sea covers more than 69,000 square miles. It is about 200 miles wide at its widest point, and 400 miles long. Greece owns most of the Aegean islands. Many of them are "dead" volcanoes. Fishermen now live on many islands and fish in the nearby waters. Farmers grow grapes on the sunny slopes to make wine and raisins. Some islands have large quarries of beautiful white marble. That marble was used over 2,000 years ago to make temples and palaces, some of which are still standing.

ALSO READ: ANCIENT CIVILIZATIONS; GREECE, ANCIENT; MEDITERRANEAN SEA.

[69,000 sq.mi.=178,710 km²; 200 mi.=322 km; 400 mi.=644 km]

**AEROSOL** A fluffy white cloud in the blue sky overhead is one kind of aerosol. The unpleasant smog that stings your eyes and makes breathing difficult is an aerosol, too. An aerosol is a scattering of very tiny droplets of liquid or bits of a solid, in a gas such as air.

Clouds are droplets of water

▼ *Press down the top and the valve opens. Then the pressure of the gas forces the liquid up the tube, through the plunger, and out the top of an aerosol can.*

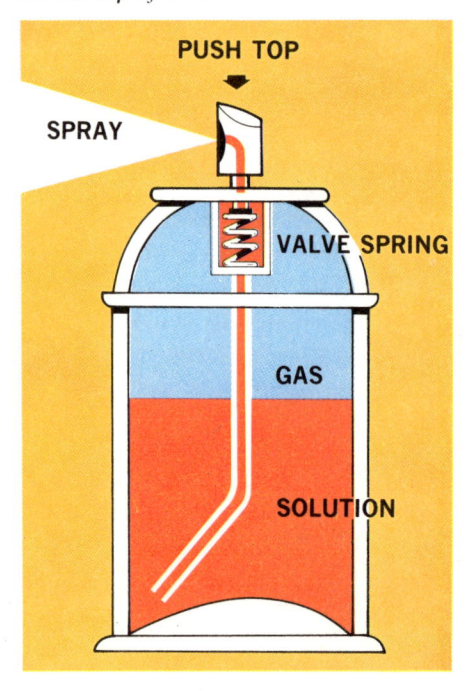

hanging in air. *Fog* is a cloud at ground level. Solid bits of carbon or ash in air form an aerosol called *smoke.* If smoke is mixed with fog, *smog* is the result. Clouds and smog are examples of natural aerosols.

Aerosols can also be man-made. Whipping cream, deodorants, and insect sprays are some things that come in *aerosol cans.* A harmless gas, called a *propellant,* is put in the can under such high pressure that it turns to a liquid. A useful product, such as deodorant, is mixed with the propellant. When a button on the can is pushed, the propellant sprays out, carrying the deodorant with it. The propellant turns to a gas and disappears. It is easy to store and use many products in aerosol cans. Can you think of other useful products in aerosols?

ALSO READ: AIR POLLUTION, GAS.

**AEROSPACE** The beginning of the Space Age added a new word to our vocabularies—*aerospace.* Scientists saw that the Earth's atmosphere and outer space together can be seen as one vast realm that includes everything from the surface of the Earth outward. This realm is *aerospace.*

The word also means the science of all flight within the realm of aerospace. This includes *aeronautics,* the science of navigating through air, and *astronautics,* the science of navigating through space. Craft that move through the air are *aircraft.* Craft that move through space are *spacecraft.* Scientists are now working on *aerospace craft,* which will fly like airplanes in the atmosphere and like rocket-driven spacecraft in space. One of the goals of aerospace science is to study the planets at close range. So the science of astronomy is also part of aerospace.

Man's desire to explore space led to the aerospace industry. Hundreds of thousands of new jobs were created. Engineers and technicians learned how to make large parts small — even smaller than the parts in tiny transistor radios — so they could be used in space travel. Experts found how to go beyond Earth's gravity, and how to keep man alive in space. Some of the things they learned are already part of everyday life. Television programs from other continents, improved telephone calls across the ocean, more accurate maps, and better weather forecasts are just some of the results. Even the photograph you see here of our planet Earth would not have been possible before aerospace research.

ALSO READ: APOLLO, ASTRONOMY, AVIATION, SPACE, SPACE RESEARCH, SPACE TRAVEL.

▲*The science of aerospace has given us a new view of our own world. This picture of planet Earth was taken by a satellite from 23,000 miles away.*
[23,000 mi.=37,030 km]

**AESOP (about 620-562 B.C.)** A marvelous storyteller named Aesop lived long ago in Greece. Very little is known about him except that he was a young slave on the island of Samos. Legend says that he was an ugly man, perhaps deformed. But he had a brilliant mind, and he enjoyed telling stories in which animals acted like human beings. Each tale taught people a lesson. These tales are called *fables.*

One legend tells that Aesop was freed from slavery. He was sent to divide money among the people of Delphi, a Greek city. But he found that they were dishonest, and he refused to give them the money. The angry people of Delphi threw Aesop over a cliff to his death.

In those days, stories were shared mostly by word of mouth. Aesop's stories were not written down until at least 200 years after he died. Since then, they have been translated from Greek into almost every language in the world.

Many people have laughed at Aesop's fable of the race between the slow, patient tortoise and the swift, bragging hare. Perhaps you know the stories about the goose that laid the golden egg, the grass-

▼*Aesop, Greek storyteller.*

▼*One of Aesop's fables tells of the race between the tortoise and the hare. The hare was sure he would win, so he played along the way. The tortoise kept plodding along, and he won.*

hopper and the ant, or the lion and the mouse. These are four of *Aesop's Fables,* some of the most familiar and best-loved stories of all time.

ALSO READ: FABLE.

**AFARS AND ISSAS** The French Territory of the Afars and Issas is a small, sun-baked area on the northeast African coast, at the entrance to the Red Sea. This bleak, dry desert territory was once called *French Somaliland.* The name was changed, in 1967, to Afars and Issas, for the territory's two largest native tribes. The Issa tribe is one of the tribes of people who are called *Somalis.* The other Somali tribe is the Ishaak. Somalis also live in nearby Somalia. (See the map with the article on AFRICA.)

main a French territory. The people voted "Yes." But most of the Issa people wanted independence and union with Somalia. France granted independence to the territory at the end of 1976.

ALSO READ: AFRICA, ETHIOPIA, SOMALIA.

**AFGHANISTAN** The land-locked mountain republic of Afghanistan is at the crossroads of Asia, surrounded by the nations of Iran, Russia, Pakistan, and China. Afghanistan's location has made it important throughout history. Main trade routes run through it, connecting Asia with the Western World. (See the map with the article on ASIA.)

Afghanistan is about the size of

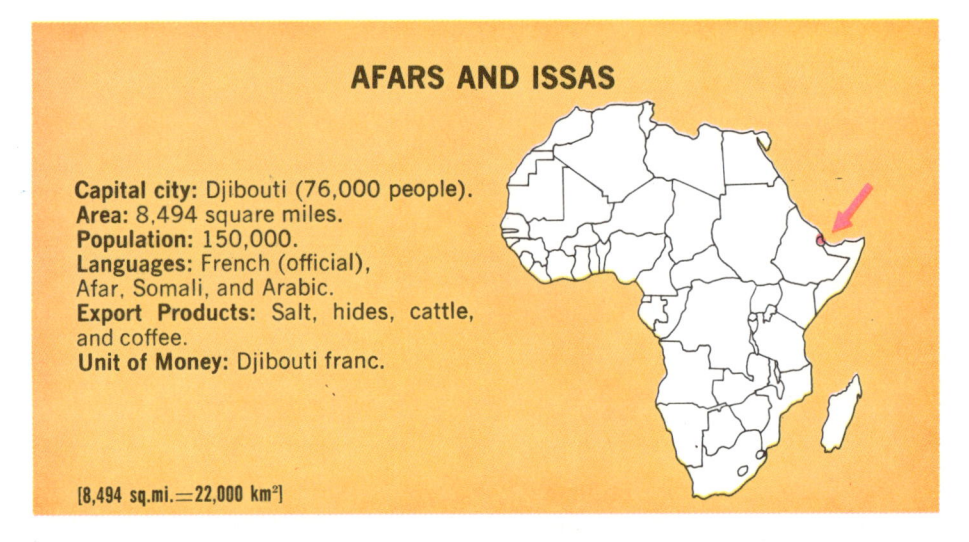

### AFARS AND ISSAS

**Capital city:** Djibouti (76,000 people).
**Area:** 8,494 square miles.
**Population:** 150,000.
**Languages:** French (official), Afar, Somali, and Arabic.
**Export Products:** Salt, hides, cattle, and coffee.
**Unit of Money:** Djibouti franc.

[8,494 sq.mi.=22,000 km²]

▼ *The busy Rimbaud city square in Djibouti, the capital and port of Afars and Issas in Africa. The tall tower is the Djibouti Mosque.*

Djibouti, the capital, is the important center of the Territory of the Afars and Issas. Half of neighboring Ethiopia's exports are carried by the Franco-Ethiopian Railway to the port of Djibouti. Ocean vessels dock at the city's harbor. An international airport is also located in the city. Most people living outside Djibouti are nomadic herders of goats and other livestock.

France gained the territory of Somaliland through treaties made with Somali rulers between 1883 and 1887. In 1967, France allowed the people in the territory to decide whether they wanted to re-

Texas. None of Afghanistan touches a sea. The high Hindu Kush Mountains separate Afghanistan into two sections. Nomads roam the rough mountain country, herding livestock. The Karakul lamb is one of the animals the nomads raise. The curly black Karakul fur is exported, to be made into Persian lamb coats. The low, dry land south of the mountains is a farm region where farmers use river water from the highlands to irrigate crops.

Afghanistan's ancient capital, Kabul, lies on the banks of Kabul River. Kabul has wide modern streets through which automobiles

## AFGHANISTAN

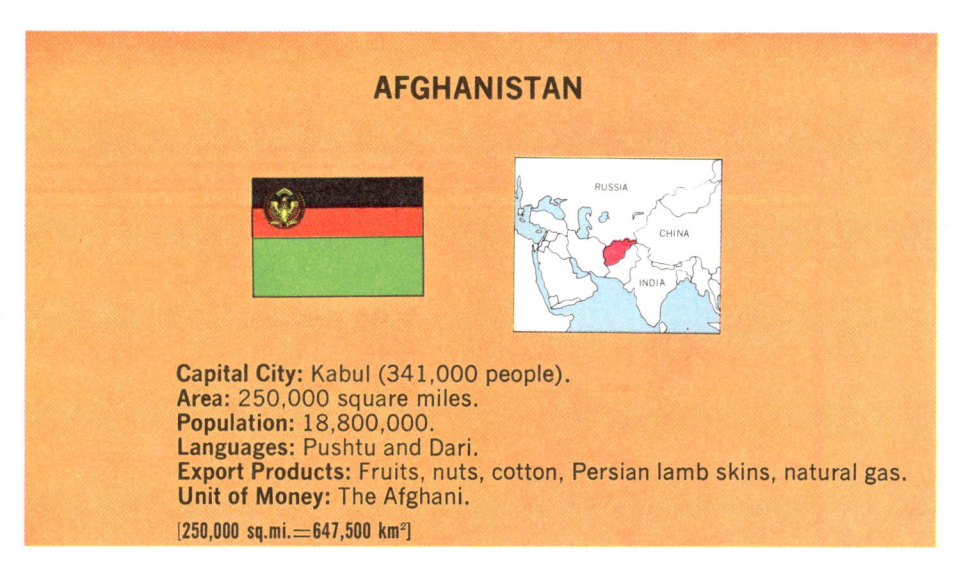

**Capital City:** Kabul (341,000 people).
**Area:** 250,000 square miles.
**Population:** 18,800,000.
**Languages:** Pushtu and Dari.
**Export Products:** Fruits, nuts, cotton, Persian lamb skins, natural gas.
**Unit of Money:** The Afghani.

[250,000 sq.mi.=647,500 km²]

▼ *Two men meet for a chat on a mountain road in Afghanistan.*

travel. But the old part of Kabul has unpaved, narrow streets surrounded by high walls of mud-brick houses. Merchants sell fruits, nuts, spices, furs, and jewels in outdoor bazaars (marketplaces).

Transportation beyond the cities is poor in Afghanistan. There are no railroads and few paved roads. People cross the mountains only on foot or on animals. Camel caravans carry goods along rocky roads and through steep mountain passes, such as the famous Khyber Pass. Alexander the Great conquered Afghanistan about 330 B.C., and led his armies through the Khyber Pass to India.

The Afghan people did not know the ways of the outside world for hundreds of years. Most Afghans live far from cities in small, walled villages. Very few nomads or villagers can read or write. Most Afghans still strictly obey the old laws of Islam. Many women wear face veils, as their ancestors did, and long dresses down to their feet. Men wear turbans and flowing robes.

Mohammed Daud is head of state, ruling the country with a Central Committee. Afghanistan is building schools, which the children who can reach them must attend until age 13. Many people are moving from villages into the growing cities. The Afghans remain loyal to their ancient traditions, but they are also working to become educated citizens of the twentieth-century modern world.

ALSO READ: ALEXANDER THE GREAT, ASIA.

**AFRICA** Africa is a giant continent, more than three times bigger than the United States. Africa is divided in two by the equator, so the continent is partly in the Northern Hemisphere and partly in the Southern Hemisphere. A narrow bridge of land in the northeast connects Africa to the Sinai Peninsula of Asia. The rest of the continent is surrounded by water. The Mediterranean Sea separates Africa from Europe to the north. The Atlantic Ocean is to the west, and the Red Sea, the Gulf of Aden, and the Indian Ocean are to the east. Several islands—including one of the world's largest, Madagascar—lie off the African mainland.

### The Land

People sometimes imagine that most of Africa is a steaming jungle of twisted vines and tangled bushes. Jungles are actually found only in a small part of central Africa. The rest of the continent is mainly desert and grassland. Tropical forests and woodlands occupy about one-fifth of the total area of Africa. The various land regions are distributed over a great *plateau* (a high, fairly

## AFRICA

**Total Population:**
375,000,000.

**Total Area:**
11,500,000 sq. miles.

**Highest Point:**
Mount Kilimanjaro in Tanzania (19,565 ft.).

**Lowest Point:**
Qattara Depression in northern Egypt (440 ft. below sea level).

**Longest River:**
Nile River (4,160 miles long).

**Largest Lake:**
Lake Victoria (26,828 sq. miles).

**Largest City:**
Cairo (5,517,000 people).

[11,500,000 sq.mi.=29,785,000 km²]
[19,565 ft.=6,065 m]
[440 ft.=136 m]
[4,160 mi.=6,698 km]
[26,828 sq.mi.=69,485 km²]

## AFRICAN NATIONS

| COUNTRY | YEAR OF INDEPENDENCE | AREA IN SQ. MILES | AREA IN SQ. KILOMETERS | CAPITAL | POPULATION |
|---|---|---|---|---|---|
| AFARS AND ISSAS | FRENCH TERRITORY | 8,494 | 22,000 | Djibouti | 150,000 |
| ALGERIA | 1962 | 919,353 | 2,381,124 | Algiers | 16,280,000 |
| ANGOLA | 1975 | 481,352 | 1,246,702 | Luanda | 6,000,000 |
| BENIN (DAHOMEY) | 1960 | 43,483 | 112,621 | Porto Novo | 3,030,000 |
| BOTSWANA | 1966 | 222,000 | 674,980 | Gaborone | 675,000 |
| BURUNDI | 1962 | 10,747 | 27,835 | Bujumbura | 3,680,000 |
| CAMEROON | 1960 | 183,377 | 474,946 | Yaoundé | 6,400,000 |
| CAPE VERDE | 1975 | 1,557 | 4,023 | Praia | 300,000 |
| CENTRAL AFRICAN REP. | 1960 | 238,224 | 617,000 | Bangui | 2,610,000 |
| CHAD | 1960 | 495,754 | 1,284,003 | Ndjamena | 4,035,000 |
| COMORO | 1975 | 863 | 2,235 | Moroni | 300,000 |
| CONGO | 1960 | 132,047 | 342,002 | Brazzaville | 1,060,000 |
| EGYPT | 1922 | 386,101 | 1,000,000 | Cairo | 37,240,000 |
| EQUATORIAL GUINEA | 1968 | 10,830 | 28,050 | Malabo | 315,000 |
| ETHIOPIA | About 1000 B.C. | 457,267 | 1,184,321 | Addis Ababa | 28,000,000 |
| GABON | 1960 | 103,089 | 267,000 | Libreville | 530,000 |
| GAMBIA | 1970 | 4,003 | 10,368 | Banjul | 515,000 |
| GHANA | 1957 | 91,843 | 237,873 | Accra | 9,855,000 |
| GUINEA | 1958 | 94,926 | 245,868 | Conakry | 4,410,000 |
| GUINEA-BISSAU | 1974 | 13,948 | 36,125 | Madina do Boe | 520,000 |
| IVORY COAST | 1960 | 124,503 | 322,463 | Abidjan | 4,900,000 |
| KENYA | 1963 | 224,960 | 592,646 | Nairobi | 13,360,000 |
| LESOTHO | 1951 | 11,716 | 30,344 | Maseru | 1,050,000 |
| LIBERIA | 1847 | 43,000 | 111,370 | Monrovia | 1,715,000 |
| LIBYA | 1951 | 679,360 | 1,704,903 | Tripoli + Benghazi | 2,455,000 |
| MALAGASY (MADAGASCAR) | 1960 | 227,700 | 589,743 | Tananarive | 7,700,000 |
| MALAWI | 1964 | 45,747 | 118,485 | Lilongwe | 5,015,000 |
| MALI | 1960 | 464,873 | 1,204,021 | Bamako | 5,560,000 |
| MAURITANIA | 1960 | 419,230 | 1,085,806 | Nouakchott | 1,320,000 |
| MAURITIUS | 1968 | 791 | 2,049 | Port Louis | 875,000 |
| MOROCCO | 1956 | 171,305 | 443,680 | Rabat-Salé | 17,435,000 |
| MOZAMBIQUE | 1975 | 302,328 | 783,030 | Lourenço Marques | 9,250,000 |
| NAMIBIA | IN DISPUTE—SOUTH AFRICA AND U.N. BOTH CLAIM IT. | 318,099 | 823,876 | Windhoek | 700,000 |
| NIGER | 1960 | 458,993 | 1,188,762 | Niamey | 4,480,000 |
| NIGERIA | 1960 | 356,669 | 923,773 | Lagos | 61,270,000 |
| REUNION | FRENCH OVERSEAS DEPARTMENT | 969 | 2,510 | St. Denis | 500,000 |
| RHODESIA | 1965 | 150,333 | 389,353 | Salisbury | 6,250,000 |
| RWANDA | 1962 | 10,169 | 26,338 | Kigali | 4,230,000 |
| SÃO TOMÉ and PRÍNCIPE | 1975 | 372 | 964 | São Tomé | 85,000 |
| SENEGAL | 1960 | 76,124 | 197,161 | Dakar | 4,425,000 |
| SEYCHELLES | 1976 | 107 | 277 | Victoria | 60,000 |
| SIERRA LEONE | 1961 | 27,925 | 72,326 | Freetown | 2,750,000 |
| SOMALIA | 1960 | 246,202 | 647,663 | Mogadishu | 3,170,000 |
| SOUTH AFRICA | 1931 | 472,359 | 1,223,410 | Cape Town | 25,520,000 |
| SUDAN | 1956 | 967,500 | 2,595,825 | Khartoum | 17,750,000 |
| SWAZILAND | 1968 | 6,704 | 17,363 | Mbabane | 500,000 |
| TANZANIA | 1964 (UNITED) | 362,820 | 939,704 | Dar es Salaam | 15,145,000 |
| TOGO | 1960 | 22,008 | 57,001 | Lomé | 2,220,000 |
| TUNISIA | 1956 | 48,332 | 125,180 | Tunis | 5,770,000 |
| UGANDA | 1962 | 93,981 | 243,411 | Kampala | 11,535,000 |
| UPPER VOLTA | 1960 | 105,839 | 274,123 | Ouagadougou | 6,045,000 |
| WESTERN SAHARA | In dispute | 102,703 | 266,001 | El Aaiún | 91,000 |
| ZAIRE | 1960 | 905,381 | 2,344,937 | Kinshasa | 24,885,000 |
| ZAMBIA | 1964 | 288,130 | 746,257 | Lusaka | 4,845,000 |

AFRICA
PLAINS
HIGHLANDS
MOUNTAINS
DESERTS
FRANCE
ITALY
SPAIN
Algiers
Tunis
TUNISIA
Rabat
MOROCCO
Atlas Mts.
Mediterranean Sea
Tripoli
Benghazi
Cairo
30° Canary Islands
ALGERIA
Libyan Desert
Qattara Depression (below Sea level)
El Aaiún
WESTERN SAHARA (in dispute)
Claims by Morocco, Mauritania, Algeria
S A H A R A
D E S E R T
Ahaggar Mts.
LIBYA
EGYPT
Tropic of Cancer
Nile R.
20°
MAURITANIA
Nouakchott
Tibesti Mts.
Red Sea
Cape Verde Is.
Praia
Senegal R.
MALI
Niger R.
NIGER
CHAD
Khartoum
SUDAN
Blue Nile R.
Dakar
SENEGAL
Banjul
GAMBIA
Bamako
UPPER VOLTA
Niamey
Madina do Boe
GUINEA-BISSAU
Ouagadougou
Lake Chad
Ndjamena
Lake Tana
Djibouti
AFARS & ISSAS
GUINEA
NIGERIA
Conakry
Freetown
SIERRA LEONE
Monrovia
LIBERIA
IVORY COAST
Abidjan
GHANA
Accra
TOGO
BENIN
Porto-Novo
Lagos
Lomé
Benue R.
CENTRAL AFRICAN REP.
Bangui
White Nile R.
Addis Ababa
ETHIOPIA
SOMALIA
Mogadishu
Malabo
EQUATORIAL GUINEA
Yaounde
CAMEROON
UGANDA
Kampala
KENYA
Libreville
GABON
Gulf of Guinea
EQUATOR
São Tome
SÃO TOME & PRINCIPE
10°
0°
CONGO (BRAZZAVILLE)
Congo R.
RWANDA
Kigali
Bujumbura
BURUNDI
Lake Victoria
Nairobi
19,565 ft.
Mt. Kilimanjaro
Seychelles Is.
Victoria
Brazzaville
Kinshasa
ZAIRE
Pemba
Zanzibar
TANZANIA
Dar es Salaam
Lake Tanganyika
CABINDA
Luanda
ATLANTIC OCEAN
ANGOLA (Port.)
Moroni
Comoro Is.
L. Nyasa
Lusaka
ZAMBIA
Zomba
MALAWI
Zambezi R.
Salisbury
RHODESIA
Tananarive
NAMIBIA
BOTSWANA
MOZAMBIQUE
Windhoek
Tropic of Capricorn
Gaborone
Limpopo R.
KALAHARI DESERT
MALAGASY
Mbabane
Lourenço Marques
SWAZILAND
Orange R.
Maseru
LESOTHO
SOUTH AFRICA
TRANSKEI
40°
50°
Cape Town
Cape of Good Hope
INDIAN OCEAN
30°

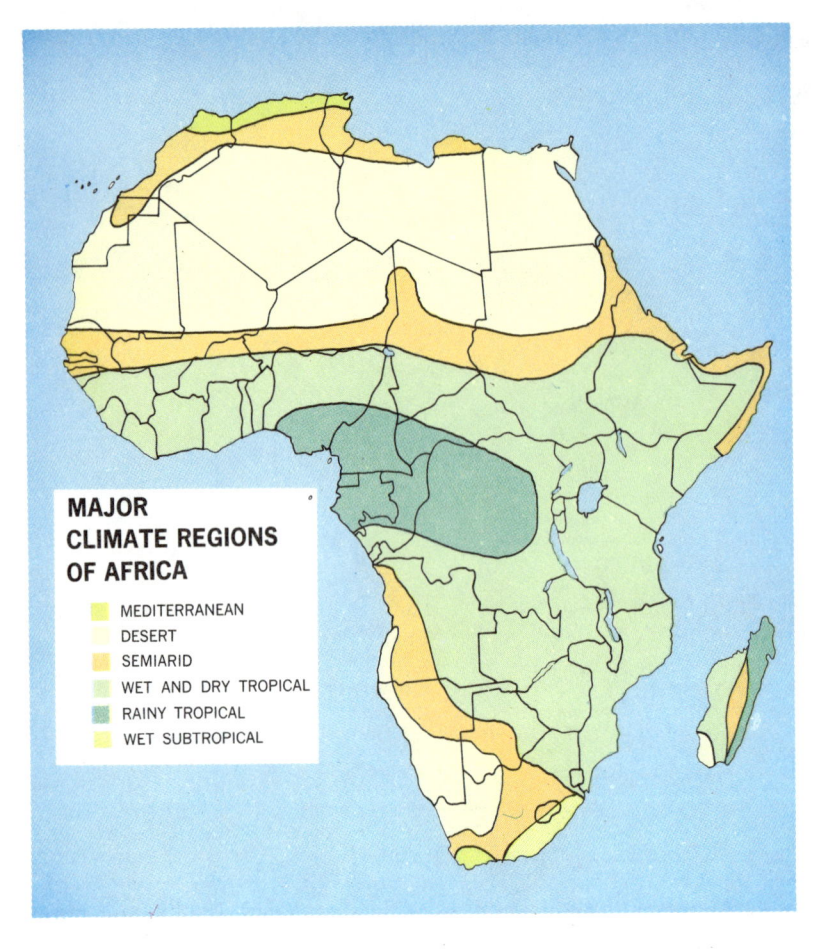

# AFRICA

**MAJOR CLIMATE REGIONS OF AFRICA**
- MEDITERRANEAN
- DESERT
- SEMIARID
- WET AND DRY TROPICAL
- RAINY TROPICAL
- WET SUBTROPICAL

▼ *Mount Kilimanjaro is the highest mountain in Africa. It stands in the East African country of Tanzania near the border with Kenya and has two volcanic peaks.*

level land mass). The plateau rises sharply from the low coastal plains and stretches across most of the continent.

The largest desert in the world—the Sahara—is the main feature of the northern plateau. Two smaller deserts, the Kalahari and the Namib, are in the southern plateau. The deserts are mostly dry and barren, although the Sahara has a few green spots, called oases, where date palms and cereals grow. The rain forests of central Africa, near the equator, are just the opposite. These moist tropical lands are thick with fruit trees, oil palms, and hardwood trees such as ebony and mahogany. The trees often grow so high and thick that sunlight can barely reach the ground.

Between the desert regions and the rain forests are *savannas*—lonely stretches of grassland with scattered trees and shrubs. These lands make up almost half the area of Africa. The dry savannas near the deserts have short, stubby grass. But the savannas close to the rain forests have coarse "elephant grass," which can grow tall enough to hide a person, or even a large animal.

Much of Africa lies in the tropics, but highland regions throughout the continent have a cool and comfortable climate. The Atlas Mountains in the northwest are Africa's longest range. The smaller Drakensberg mountain chain lies along the southeastern tip. Mount Kilimanjaro and Mount Kenya are in the east-central highlands. These mountains are close to the equator, but they are capped with snow all year. Also in the eastern ranges are Africa's largest lakes, including Lake Tanganyika, the longest freshwater lake in the world. The waters of the eastern lakes help feed three great rivers—the Nile, the Congo, and the Zambezi. Another important river, the Niger, drains the waters of west-central Africa. Steep waterfalls and rapids often occur at the places where these mighty rivers plunge from the high plateaus to the low coastal lands. The spectacular Victoria Falls, on the Zambezi River in southeastern Africa, drop about 355 feet [110 m].

**Animal Life**

Some of the world's most famous animals come from Africa. Giraffes, elephants, zebras, antelopes, and rhinoceroses feed on the plentiful grasses and shrubs of the savannas. Fierce meat-eaters such as lions, leopards and cheetahs also dwell in the grassy plains. Ostriches, the largest of all birds, are found in the sandy savanna lands near the Sahara. Many of these large animals are protected in special parks, because so many have been killed by hunters.

Crocodiles and hippopotamuses are common in warm rivers and swamps. The tropical rain forests are the home of gorillas, chimpanzees, monkeys, colorful birds, and a great variety of insects and snakes.

*Zebras roam the grassy plains of a national park in Kenya. Many of Africa's wild animals are protected in the national parks.*

The rock python is a giant African snake that squeezes its prey to death and swallows it whole. An especially dreaded insect of the tropical lands is the blood-sucking tsetse fly. It carries the germs that cause sleeping sickness and other diseases.

## People

Africa has an enormous variety of people, with different customs and ways of life. Most Africans are farmers who live in villages in the grasslands and coastal areas. Many are nomads, who wander from place to place, herding cattle, sheep, or other livestock. Some live and work in modern cities. A few primitive tribes hunt and gather wild plant food. They live much as their ancestors lived for thousands of years.

Negroes are the largest group of African peoples. They live mainly in regions south of the Sahara Desert. The people of the various Negro tribes can be quite different in appearance. Many tribes take their names from the languages they speak. The *Bushmen*, a tribe of hunters of the Kalahari Desert, and the *Hottentots*, nomadic herding peoples of the southwest, are sometimes referred to as Negroid (Negro-like). Their yellowish-brown skin makes them different from most other Negroes. The *Nilotes* include several tribes, such as the Dinkas, who live in the Nile River Basin. They are rather dark-skinned and are unusually tall and slender. The *Pygmies*, also called Negrillos, rarely grow taller than 4½ feet. They are hunters who live in the tropical rain forests.

North Africans are chiefly Caucasian (white) peoples. Most of them are Arabs and Berbers who dwell north of the Sahara. A few nomadic tribes, such as the *Bedouins*, roam this vast desert, living in tents and tending herds of camels, goats, and sheep. Other Caucasians of Africa include about five million people of Dutch, British, and French descent. Most of them live in the southern plateau and along the Mediterranean coast, where the climate is much like that of Europe. About a million Asians, mainly Hindus who came from India, live in eastern and southeastern Africa.

LANGUAGES. Africans speak more than 800 languages. Arabic is the chief tongue of northern Africa. Great numbers of eastern Africans speak Swahili. It is just one of 80 Bantu languages. Hausa is also widely spoken, especially in the west. The Bushmen and Hottentots speak a variety of Khoisan languages, which are quite unusual. They feature clicking sounds that are not found in any other language. English or French is the official language of many countries that are, or once were, European colonies. The Dutch of South Africa speak Afrikaans, a Germanic language developed by Dutch settlers in the 1600s.

RELIGION. The religions of Africa are as varied as the people. Many different groups have their own tribal religions. Most tribes believe in one god who created the universe and who controls human life. They

*The art of Africa is famous for its strong, simple shapes. Sometimes the shapes are covered with fancy designs. The artist who carved this wooden statue covered it with colored seed pearls.*

*Most Africans live in small villages. Here, you see a village hut in Uganda, a country of East Africa.*

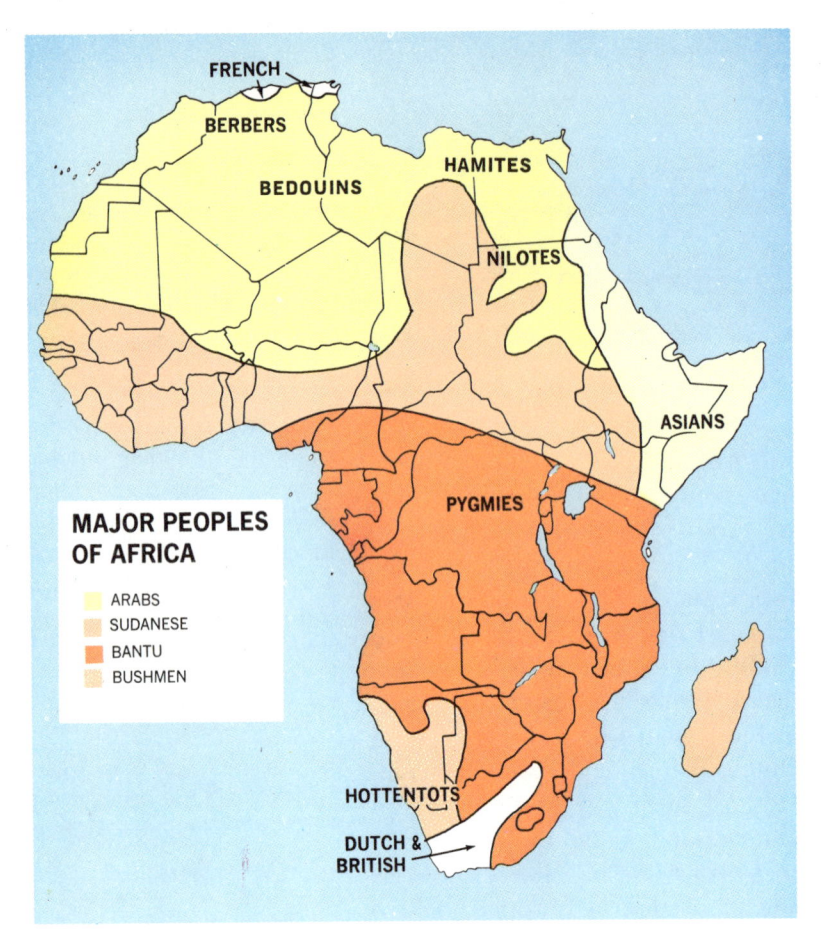

▲ Africa is made up of many countries whose boundaries were fixed by European colonial powers. The location of the countries' borders often has little to do with where the various peoples have lived for centuries.

▲ These fishermen in Chad are getting their nets ready to go fishing on Lake Chad.

may also worship their ancestors as minor gods, and believe in spirits that represent parts of nature, such as trees, water, or the sun. Religious rituals are an important part of tribal life. They mark events such as births, marriages, and deaths. Magic ceremonies are often performed to heal the sick and to make the land more fertile.

About 100 million Africans, mainly in the north, are Muslims. Many African peoples were converted to Christianity by European missionaries in the 1800s. Large numbers of Egyptians and Ethiopians are members of the Coptic Orthodox Church. About 300,000 people, including several Negro groups, are Jewish.

## History

Africa has a long and complex history. Ancient skulls found by archeologists show that the human race may have had its beginnings on the African continent millions of years ago. Rock paintings and tools of the Stone Age have also been discovered. But not much is known about the earliest peoples of Africa. The first highly developed civilization began in Egypt in the Nile Valley about 3,000 B.C. An important area of settlement after 1,000 B.C. was the Mediterranean coast of Africa. Phoenician and Greek invaders founded colonies there. As Egypt gradually became weaker, it was conquered about 725 B.C. by the Kushites, a Negro civilization on the Nile River south of Egypt. The Kushites built the oldest and greatest civilization of black Africa. It lasted a thousand years. Both Egypt and the Mediterranean lands had become part of the Roman Empire by the middle of the first century A.D.

Still another group of invaders, the Muslims of Arabia, began to conquer northern Africa about the year 700. Muslim influence spread in time to west-central Africa, where there were several large Negro kingdoms. Camel caravans were sent across the Sahara to trade with kingdoms of Ghana, Mali, and Songhai. Northern African goods such as cloth and wheat were exchanged for gold and ivory. Arab traders also brought their religion and culture to the coastal cities of eastern Africa.

The next great influence on African development after the Arabs came from Europe. The Portuguese set up trading posts on both the east and west coasts during the 1400s. At first they were interested only in African gold, ivory, and spices. But as colonies began to be established in the Americas, the Portuguese found that slave trade was even more profitable. The British and French also set up trading posts in the 1600s, and the Dutch started a colony at the Cape of Good Hope. The slave trade began to decline in the 1800s. But millions of black Africans had been captured and brought to the Americas by that time.

European explorers and missionaries penetrated the interior of Africa in the 1770s. Europeans became interested in colonizing Africa, when this continent's vast natural resources were discovered. Great Britain, France, Germany, Belgium, Spain, Portugal, and Italy competed for control of Africa, beginning in about 1850. These nations had divided up almost all of Africa among themselves by 1914. Only Ethiopia and Liberia were independent countries.

Colonial rule brought great changes to Africa. Transportation was improved, industries were developed, and new cities were built. Missionaries set up schools and hospitals in remote places. But not all the changes brought about by the Europeans were good. Often the white settlers did not understand the Africans' ways, and they tried to do away with the cherished customs of tribal peoples. Many Negroes were offered jobs in mines and factories, but they were not given the same rights and wages as white people. Europeans often took the best lands for themselves, leaving the less productive lands to the Africans.

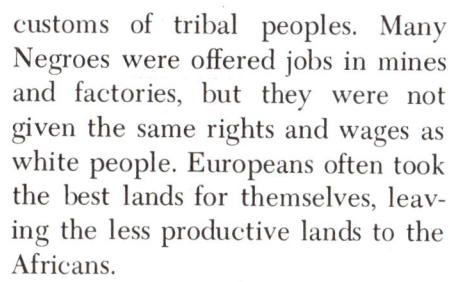

People in some parts of Africa began to demand the right of self-government in the late 1880s. The struggle for independence became stronger and more widespread after World War II. Most of the colonies gained their independence peacefully during the 1950s and 1960s. By 1976 Portugal and Spain had no more African claims, and France planned to grant independence to its possessions.

The new nations are struggling with many problems. Although they are making rapid progress in economic development, most of them are still very poor. Education is improving, but in every country most of the people cannot read or

▲ *Many different peoples live in Africa. The smiling woman at upper left is a Bantu, of whom 60 million live in Africa in 200 tribes scattered through many countries. At upper right is an Ethiopian Coptic priest. Ethiopians are an ancient, proud people. The children at lower left are from Nigeria, where 250 tribal groups live and speak many languages. The woman at lower right is a Berber, a very old people, often nomadic, who live in several North African countries.*

▶ *African governments are eager to industrialize their countries. Here, you see a gold mine in Vaal Rey, South Africa. Gold is an important African export.*

write. More people trained in science, medicine, and government are needed. Nearly every African government faces the difficulty of unifying groups of people who are widely different from one another. The Organization of African States, established in 1963, is trying to unite the new countries and to help other parts of Africa in their movements toward independence.

*For further information on:*

**Animals,** *see* ANIMAL DISTRIBUTION, NATIONAL PARK, RARE ANIMAL.

**Arts,** *see* ART HISTORY, FOLK ART, MUSICAL INSTRUMENTS.

**History,** *see* ANCIENT CIVILIZATIONS; BOER WAR; CARTHAGE; DIAS, BARTHOLOMEU; EGYPT, ANCIENT; GAMA, VASCO DA; LIVINGSTONE, DAVID; RHODES, CECIL; SCHWEITZER, ALBERT; SLAVERY; STANLEY, HENRY MORTON; WORLD WAR II.

**Language,** *see* ALPHABET, ARABIC, LANGUAGES.

**Man,** *see* CIVILIZATION, MAN, PYGMY.

**Physical Features,** *see* CONGO RIVER, CONTINENT, EQUATOR, JUNGLE, MEDITERRANEAN SEA, NILE RIVER, RED SEA, SAHARA DESERT.

*Also read the article on each country shown in the table.*

**AGASSIZ, LOUIS** (1807–1873) The ambitious son of a villager in Switzerland grew up to be one of the greatest naturalists of the 1800s. He was Jean Louis Agassiz. He gained his greatest fame for important work in *ichthyology*, the study of fish. He was a geologist who added to scientific understanding of glaciers and the ways continents form.

Even as a child in Switzerland, Agassiz was determined to be a great naturalist. He formed the habit of observing nature closely. This habit became the key to his life's work. He had to see nature at first hand, not just read about it in books. Once he risked his life to go into the center of a glacier to study it. Agassiz was a teacher as well as a scientist. He had a warm personality and was popular.

When he came to America at the age of 39, Agassiz was already world famous. He became a professor at Harvard University, and he founded Harvard's Museum of Comparative Zoology.

ALSO READ: GEOLOGY, ZOOLOGY.

▲ *Living things grow and age in different ways. This little girl has a lot of growing still to do. Her grandmother, like all people, stopped growing taller at about 21 years of age. Trees grow until they die.*

▼ *Louis Agassiz, Swiss-American naturalist.*

**AGING** On each birthday a person adds one year to his age. Growing older year by year is called *chronological* aging.

However, each person grows and ages at his own pace. Some babies take longer than others to learn to walk. Some children grow faster than others. Scientists believe that each person has a "biological clock" that sets his speed of aging. Most plants keep growing throughout their lives, but most animals do not. A human being is usually full-grown by age 21.

Scientists divide human life into three periods—youth, middle age, and old age. In youth, the speed with which the body obeys orders from the mind, called *coordination*, is quickest. The muscles of young people move easily and usually do not stay stiff or tired for long after hard work or play. Peoples' muscles tire more quickly in middle age.

In old age, the body has some parts that are weak and others that are strong. Parts of the body wear out at different speeds. Some worn-out parts of the body can be replaced. The heart has valves that work so hard pumping blood that they may become weak. Surgeons can now put into the heart man-made valves that work as well as natural ones.

Many older people may have bodies so stiff they can hardly move, but they may still have very active minds. The growth of the mind may be at a different rate from the aging of the rest of the body.

ALSO READ: ANIMAL, GROWTH, HUMAN BODY, PLANT.

**AGRICULTURE** Man's life was difficult before he "discovered" how to grow food. People lived in small groups, because it was difficult to provide a large number of people with food. The groups roamed the countryside, constantly looking for animals to kill or wild plants to pick. If they could not spear or trap an animal, and if they did not find plants, they went hungry. Agriculture, often called the "mother of civilization," changed all that.

The word *agriculture* comes from two Latin words meaning "to plant and to care for the fields." But agriculture is far more than planting and raising crops. Agricultural scientists today study soil, climate, how plants grow, how to stop plant enemies, and how to develop better plants. Other scientists study animals. They try to find new ways to raise better animals, and to prevent and cure diseases. Farms, ranches, plantations, orchards, gardens, dairies, sheds for beehives, and a great many laboratories and factories are now parts of agriculture. The areas where most plants and animals are cared for are called *rural areas*. "Rural" is an adjective meaning "open country."

Agriculture employs more than half the people on Earth. But in the United States, only 4 out of every 100 people are now involved in agriculture. Many machines are used on North American farms, ranches, and plantations. Scientific methods are used in crop production and livestock care. Although they are a small group of people, U.S. farmers produce more food each year than all the people in the United States can eat.

Other parts of the world cannot run farms with so few people as the U.S. does. Three of the main reasons for this are the lack of good cropland, the cost of buying and using machines, and the strict following of ancient ways of farming. About seven out of every ten people in Africa live in rural areas and work in agricultural jobs. Three out

▲ *A wall picture of ancient Egypt shows the time when all work in agriculture was done by hand, using animals and simple tools.*

▼ *Early planters believed the gods took care of crops and harvests. Even today, some primitive tribes dress up and dance in the hope they will get good crops.*

*Small American farms are fast disappearing. They are being combined into large farms. On these large farms, big and powerful machinery is used.*

*How would you like a job tending this flock of sheep? Breeding and raising animals is one of the main branches of agriculture.*

of every ten people in Europe are "farm folk." So are six out of every ten in Asia, and five out of every ten in South America. Some of the cattle and sheep stations (ranches) in Australia cover thousands of square miles, and four out of every ten Australians live and work in farm areas.

### The Start of Agriculture

People living in the sunny, fertile lands between the Mediterranean Sea and the Persian Gulf are believed to have started agriculture about 15,000 years ago. These people discovered that wild seeds planted in rows, kept clean of weeds, and watered regularly produced large harvests. They lived near their fields to guard them from both human and animal robbers. So they built year-round huts by their fields, with nearby pits for storing crops. After a time these places became villages. Then roads were made between the villages, and different peoples became acquainted.

The fruit trees and fields of grain attracted wild animals. After many failures, villagers captured and tamed some of the animals. The first type of animal to be tamed, or *domesticated,* was probably the sheep. Soon dogs were domesticated, then—hundreds of years apart —chickens, pigs, cattle, donkeys, and finally horses. Domestication of these animals took place mostly along the shores of the Mediterranean, and farther east, on the grassy plains of Russia, called *steppes,* between the Black Sea and the Caspian Sea. These changes caused agriculture to split into three major divisions.

### Kinds of Agriculture

STOCK FARMING. Some families chose to tame and care for herds of animals. These were the *stockmen.* In the years of the American Wild West, stockmen, especially cattlemen and shepherds, often lived on the frontier. Until recently, slow transportation forced dairymen and poultrymen to keep their animals close to the cities. Today, the Asian and African peoples called *nomads* (wanderers) are stockmen. They move from place to place, seeking food and water for their herds.

ONE-CROP FARMING. The ancient Greeks discovered many uses for the fruit and wood of the olive tree. Some Greeks became specialists in growing olives and processing olive oil. Many Egyptian farmers specialized in growing and harvesting cotton. They learned how to harvest the puffy bolls of the cotton plant, remove the seeds, and weave the fibers into cloth. The efforts of the ancient Greeks and the Egyptians were the beginnings of another major branch of agriculture—one-crop farming.

Examples of one-crop agriculture in the U.S. today are the Midwest wheat farms, the southern cotton plantations, and the citrus groves of Florida and California. Each of

If certain products were added up and divided among the 220 million people in the U.S., here's an idea of how much each person would get. The United States produces more of these products than any other country in the world. This table shows how many animals were marketed for each person in the U.S.

## AGRICULTURAL MARKETING IN THE UNITED STATES.

| | 3,742,000,000 | 133,000,000 | 78,000,000 | 60,000,000 | 10,000,000 |
|---|---|---|---|---|---|
| 15 | chickens for each person. | | | | |
| 1/2 | of a turkey for each person. | | | | |
| 1/3 | of a hog for each person. | | | | |
| 1/4 | of a cow for each person. | | | | |
| 1/22 | of a sheep for each person. | | | | |

### DISTRIBUTION OF CROPS ON A PERCENTAGE BASIS

Figures obtained from U.S.D.A. pertain to 1970. Slight variance on an annual basis.

- HAY 24%
- CORN 21%
- WHEAT 17%
- SOY 16%
- OATS 7%
- SORGHUM 5%
- BARLEY 4%
- COTTON 4%
- RICE 1%
- FLAX 1%

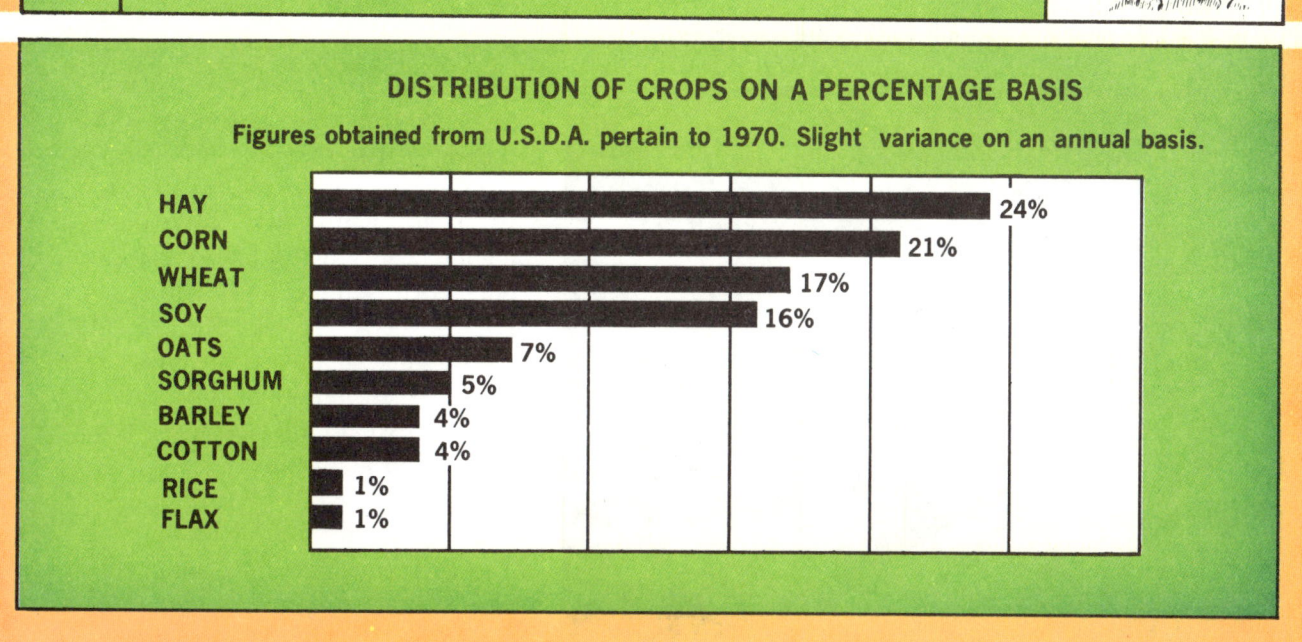

# AGRICULTURE

these places, as well as many other farming areas in the world, has climate and soil that are very good for the one crop of the region.

DIVERSIFIED FARMING. Several different crops can be grown on one farm. *Diversified farming* was, and still is, the most common type of farming. It got its start in America from European farmers such as those from Estremadura, in Spain. They brought their knowledge of this farming to the New World.

**European Farming in America**

Spanish soldiers conquered Mexico and Peru and first explored the southern and southwestern U.S. between 1521 and 1550. These Spaniards were called *conquistadors*, meaning "conquerors." Many of them grew up in Estremadura, one of the most beautiful areas of diversified farming in Europe. It is a region of many mountains, river valleys, and red-earth fields along the border between Spain and Portugal. It has been famous for more than 2,000 years for its crops of wheat, olives, fruit, and cork, and for its herds of sheep, goats, and pigs.

The conquistadors quickly realized that the mountains, plains, and climate of Southern California, Arizona, and New Mexico were very much like the countryside and weather of their Spanish homeland. The first Spanish settlers in the Southwest planted the crops they had known in Estremadura—oranges, olives, figs, grapes, and wheat. They brought cattle, horses, and pigs from Spain, too.

Spanish settlers moved into Florida, too, in the last half of the sixteenth century. The climate and soil of their new home reminded them of Andalusia, the region of Spain that is Estremadura's southern neighbor. So these settlers brought oranges from Andalusia and found that this fruit grew well in Florida. They learned about a New World plant food when they received the small, sweet nuts of the pine-nut tree from Indians. The Indians had used these *piniones* in soups, breads, and candies for a long time.

The French founded New Orleans and began other settlements along the Gulf of Mexico. They, like the Spanish, thought of their European homes when they began to farm. They brought pears and carrots from France to America.

Colonists in Massachusetts and Virginia found their land and climate much like that of their native England. So they brought familiar animals, such as sheep and cattle, and plants, such as peaches, to America. These settlers also got help from the Indians, who taught them how to plant and raise corn, squash, and tobacco.

All these New World settlers were fortunate that their new homes were much like their old ones. Plants do not grow successfully everywhere in the world. Plants do well in certain soils and climates. In different soils, or in different weather conditions, they may not grow at all.

**Names for Agricultural Land**

The three most common names for agricultural property come from the regions where European meth-

▲ *Women picking olives, which have ripened and fallen from the trees. In Europe, many olive growers have diversified farms. They grow several different crops.*

▼ *One-crop agriculture near Dacca, Bangladesh. The squares are rice paddies separated by dikes or walls of dirt.*

ods of caring for the land began. The words *ranch, plantation,* and *farm* are really lessons in the history of both language and agriculture.

*Ranch* comes from the Spanish word *rancho,* which first meant "where the cattle graze." It was used by the Spanish people who pioneered the Rio Grande Valley of New Mexico in 1598. The word spread to Texas, Arizona, and California, and then moved eastward. Most ranches today are west of the Mississippi River, but many of them have no cattle at all. They include mink ranches, horse ranches, fruit ranches, and even rose ranches.

*Plantation* comes from a Latin word used by English knights and lords. It meant a rural estate where servants tended the crops and cared for the livestock. Virginians began to develop large one-crop areas of tobacco or rice. Agricultural properties throughout the South were often called plantations, especially where planters owned slaves to do the hard work. Dairy herds, beef cattle, poultry, fruit, grains, beans, vegetables, and peanuts have now become important agricultural products in the South. Diversified farming has replaced much one-crop farming. Agriculturists in the South now prefer to be called farmers instead of planters.

*Farm* is an old English word that the Pilgrims brought to New England. The word meant "land that is rented" during the centuries when knights on horseback were the most important part of an army. The man who worked a farm was not a serf or peasant, but paid an annual rent to the lord or knight who owned the land. If an agriculturist owned his own land, but was not a knight or lord, he was called a *franklin.*

**Technology Comes to Agriculture**
Abraham Lincoln was President in 1863. At that time, seven out of every ten Americans worked and lived on farms, plantations, and ranches. Nearly everybody owned a horse, and almost every home had a horsebarn and a horse pasture. Horsepower was the chief method of getting the job done. Horses plowed and tilled the fields, hauled the wagons, carriages, coaches, and harvesting machines, and trampled the kernels of grain free from the stalks on the threshing floors. Horses and mules were the great servants of American agriculture from 1600 until 1920. Slaves on Southern plantations also played a very important part in shaping modern American farming.

Tractors, trucks, and hundreds of

▲*In early times, villages grew up when people joined together to care for the fields. Work was done with simple tools. (Top picture.)*

▲*The scythe was used for mowing for many centuries. A man could cut up to three acres in one day with this tool. (Middle picture.)*

▲*The harvester was invented in 1830. It picked up cut wheat automatically, while men tied the bundles of grain by hand. (Lower picture.)*

# AGRICULTURE

▲ *The modern combine cuts wheat and separates the grain from the chaff all at one time. One man does the work many men used to do.*

planting, spraying, weeding, and harvesting machines took the place of horses and mules in the 1920s. Scientists discovered ways to grow two or three times as much crop on the same amount of land. These inventions and discoveries made it possible for a family to farm three, four, or five times as much land as they could have with horses and mules. Fewer people were needed on farms. Machines and other materials needed for modern agriculture were expensive and complicated. Large properties and scientific training became necessary for successful farming. More and more farmers and ranchers sold their lands and moved to town. Hired workers were laid off or went to cities for better jobs. In 1900 about 35 of every 100 people in the U.S. worked on farms. By 1970, 28 of those 35 had found employment elsewhere.

A major division of the U.S. Government is the Department of Agriculture. Its director, the Secretary of Agriculture, is a member of the President's Cabinet. The 109,000 people who work for the Department are scientists, engineers, economists, and other specialists in modern agriculture. Each state in the U.S. has a department of agriculture. Many also have a state college of agriculture. The local advisors on agricultural affairs in each area, who have offices at each of the 3,000 county seats in the U.S., are called *county agents.*

Agriculture is faced with big problems despite the great changes created by machines and science. Among the most difficult ones are air and water pollution, high operating costs, new kinds of plant and animal diseases, and the growing number of people who must be fed.

Farmers who want to do well must make important decisions and answer questions before choosing which crops to plant. Is the lawn around your house or in a park nearby thick and green and fun to walk barefoot in all summer? Or does it turn brown and scratchy and ugly? What grass is best for your lawn? What flowers will grow in your garden? What kinds of fruit and vegetables will do well? These questions are similar to the ones that farmers must answer. Suppose that you are a farmer getting ready to choose the "crops" (plants) for your "farm" (your back yard or a nearby park). You must answer these questions if you want to have a successful farm.

You can get the answers to these questions from the department of agriculture of your state. The scientists who work there have studied these questions very carefully. They have lists of plants for your area. If you send them a small jar of soil from your "farm," they will tell you exactly what kinds of plants will or will not grow well.

Write to the agriculture department, and ask for information on plants that do well in your area. Also get an analysis (test) of your soil. Then, working with the results of the analysis and with the list of "crops," choose what to plant.

*For further information on:*
**Conservation,** see CONSERVATION, FERTILIZER, IRRIGATION, NATURAL RESOURCES, SOIL.
**Crops,** see CORN, FRUIT, RICE, TOBACCO, VEGETABLES, WHEAT.
**Farm Life,** see FARM MACHINERY, WEATHER.
**History,** see COWBOY; SLAVERY; WESTWARD MOVEMENT; individual countries.
**Livestock,** see CATTLE, GOATS, HORSE, POULTRY, SHEEP, VETERINARY MEDICINE.
**Processes,** see DAIRY FARMING, FISHING INDUSTRY, FOOD, MEAT, PLANT BREEDING.

**AIR** Air is all around you. You cannot see it, smell it, or taste it. But you can feel the wind blow. You can see the wind move waves on the water, clouds in the sky, and tree branches. Wind is moving air.

Without air you could not breathe. There could be no living plants or animals. Because sound travels through air, without air there would be silence. The movement of invisible air can support a large, heavy airplane. Air makes up a precious blanket of atmosphere wrapped around the Earth. Beyond this blanket lies airless space. Men must carry their own air supplies to be able to live and work when they travel in spaceships through this airless space.

Air is a mixture of gases and water vapor. The most important gases in the air are nitrogen and oxygen. About 78 percent of the air is made up of nitrogen, and about 21 percent of oxygen. The remaining one percent is mostly argon, plus very tiny amounts of some other gases. Almost all living things use the oxygen in air. Fire cannot burn without oxygen.

### Discovering Facts About Air

AIR CAN BE COMPRESSED. Get a small paper bag and blow into it until it swells up. Close the bag by twisting the end. Feel the bag. If the bag were just standing open, it would be filled with air. But by blowing into the bag, you have

▲ *For thousands of years, horses were the main working power of agriculture. They are still used on small farms by people who cannot afford expensive machinery.*

# AIR

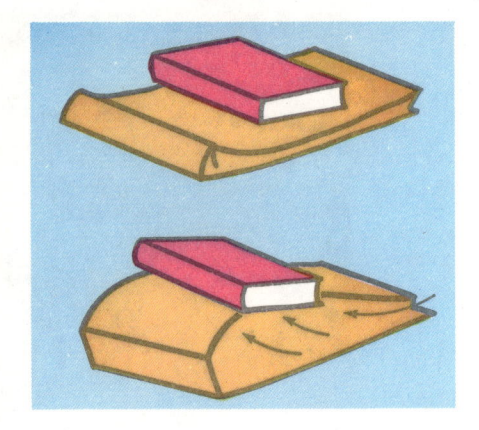

▼ *A window air conditioner takes warm air from the outside and sends cool, clean air into a house. The blower sucks in warm air. The filter cleans out dust and dirt. The evaporator has cold coils, which cool the air and remove moisture from it. The condenser fan blows air over the condenser to make the gas in the coils turn to a cooling liquid. The compressor is a motor that squeezes and pumps the gas through the coils. The blower does its second task by blowing cool air into the room.*

forced even more air into the same amount of space. The air from your lungs has been *compressed*, or squeezed together, in the bag, so the bag feels firm. If you could see into the bag, you would still not be able to see the air.

Now lay an empty bag on the edge of a table. Place a small book on top of it. Blow the bag full of air. The book will rise from the table. It is held up by the air in the bag. In the same way, air in tires holds a car off the ground. You are really riding on compressed air when you ride in a car.

AIR EXPANDS WHEN HEATED. Fasten a balloon containing a little air to the open top of each of two small-necked bottles. Place one bottle in a pan of hot water and the other in ice water. The air in the first bottle is heated by the hot water. The *molecules* (small particles) of air move faster and faster. The air *expands* and moves into the balloon. The balloon gets bigger.

Air in the other bottle cools and takes up less space than before, so the balloon shrinks and looks nearly empty.

When air expands, it becomes lighter. A small electric heater can heat an entire room. The heater warms the air next to it. The warmed air becomes lighter and moves upward. Cool air moves into its place. The new air gets warm and also rises. Then it cools and moves down. The air keeps moving in circles, and the whole room is soon heated.

AIR IS EVERYWHERE. Pack a glass full of soil from a garden. Add water to the glass. Watch the bubbles of air rise through the water. A lawn is often dotted with earthworms after a rain. The rain has forced air out of the ground, so the worms must come to the surface to breathe.

ALSO READ: AIRPLANE, AIR PRESSURE, ATMOSPHERE, GAS, WATER CYCLE, WEATHER.

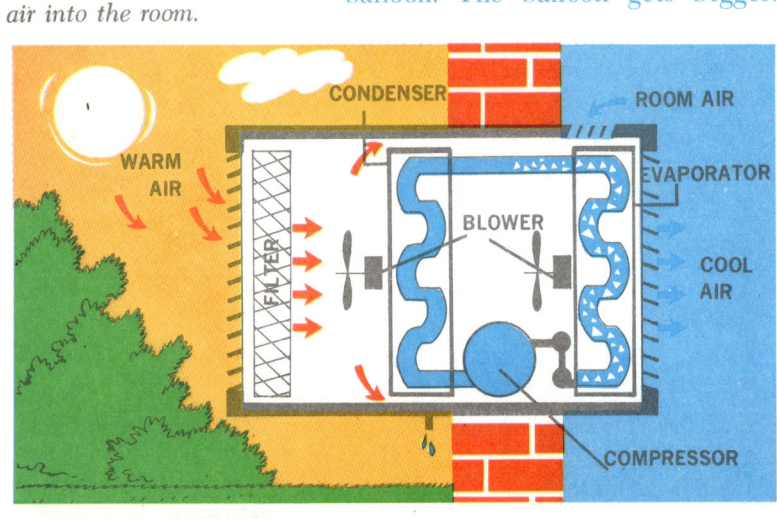

**AIR CONDITIONING** You can make an *air conditioner*, a machine that lowers the temperature of the air around it. You need an electric fan, a bowl of ice cubes, a thermometer, and an adult to help you. Put the fan on a table, and put the thermometer on the table about 15 inches in front of the fan. See what temperature the thermometer shows. Now turn on the fan, but be careful. Do not go near the fan while it is running. You can feel a cool breeze when you stand in front of the fan. Wait five minutes and see what temperature the thermometer then shows. Next, place the bowl of ice on the table, just in front of the fan. Does the breeze feel even cooler? After five minutes, what temperature does the thermometer show?

Air is seldom at the temperature comfortable for most people—about 70° F [21° C]. So men have learned to build machines that change air temperature. Machines that raise the air temperature are heaters. Machines that lower the air temperature are air conditioners. The work that these machines do is called *air conditioning*.

Air conditioners have other jobs besides changing the air temperature. The amount of water vapor in the air is called *humidity*. Humidity is also important to comfort. A person's perspiration usually evaporates into the air. This makes the person feel cool. (Put a drop of rubbing alcohol on your arm and blow on it. What happens?) But in summer, the humidity is often high. The air has no room for evaporated perspiration. So air conditioners remove water from the air. Perspiration evaporates and a person feels cool.

One more important job for air conditioners is to filter, or clean, the air. Air is filled with dust, pollen, and many other substances. Air conditioner filters are made of fine threads of glass called *glass wool*. The air conditioner's fan blows the air through the filter, which catches the dust and pollen.

Many home air conditioners are small, and fit in windows. The diagram is of a window air conditioner. New buildings often have *central* air conditioning, and one big machine cools the entire building. Pipes carry cool air from the machine to all the rooms. And sometimes the same pipes that carry cool air in summer carry hot air in winter.

ALSO READ: GAS, HEATING, HUMIDITY, REFRIGERATION.

**AIRCRAFT CARRIER** An aircraft carrier is a huge ship with a military airport on its top deck. But it is also many more things. It is a floating town, with movie theaters, restaurants, shops, and laundries. It has a church, a post office, and a hospital. In it are big shops that repair airplanes; places to store ammunition, bombs, and fuel; and almost everything else that would be found at a military airport.

A jet airplane needs a long runway on which to gain the speed needed to take off or to lose speed on landing. Airports on land usually have runways about 10,000 feet long—almost 2 miles. But there is

▲ *Cables across the deck slow down a landing plane much faster than a jet could stop by itself on a runway on land.*

[10,000 ft.=3.1 km]

◀ *The USS Enterprise, the world's largest aircraft carrier, launches airplanes into the air from a "runway" on the deck of the ship.*

# AIRCRAFT CARRIER

▶ *The USS* Langley *was America's first aircraft carrier. It went into service in 1922, carrying two-winged airplanes.*

[125 ft.=39 m]

▼ *An important carrier of World War II was the USS* Yorktown. *Its hangar deck had room for men to work on the weapons the airplane carried, while other men relaxed watching a movie.*

not much room on a carrier, so a plane is "thrown" into the air moving fast enough to fly. An airplane is launched much as a small model glider is put into the air with a rubber band. Hooks on an airplane are attached to a powerful steam catapult or "slingshot" that runs down a track on the deck.

On landing, another hook on the tail of an airplane catches cables strung across the flight deck. The ends of the cables are attached to cylinders that move in a big pipe filled with oil. The cables relax or "give" when an airplane first catches them, but they bring it to a stop in about 125 feet.

## History

Aircraft carriers got their start on November 14, 1910. On that day Eugene Ely flew an airplane off a wooden platform on the cruiser USS *Birmingham*. Aircraft carriers were not important in World War I, because they were not practical. But several countries worked to improve these floating airports.

Aircraft carriers became really important when Japan bombed Pearl Harbor, Hawaii, on December 7, 1941. The airplanes that carried the bombs came from Japanese aircraft carriers. This very successful attack almost wrecked the United States Navy stationed in the Pacific.

Less than three years later, in three great battles between June and October, 1944, planes from U.S. aircraft carriers practically destroyed all the Japanese carrier fleet. This sped the victory in World War II.

## Carriers Today

Today only three countries—the United States, Great Britain, and Australia—have large modern carriers with jet airplanes. The Soviet Union is building small carriers, but will possibly build bigger ones. However, the U.S. has more carriers than the rest of the world combined.

The most interesting aircraft carrier afloat today is the USS *Enterprise*. It is the only aircraft carrier powered by nuclear, or atomic, energy. It is also the biggest military ship ever built. The *Enterprise* is 1,123 feet long. The deck where the airplanes take off and land is 257

[1,123 ft.=348 m; 257 ft.=80 m]

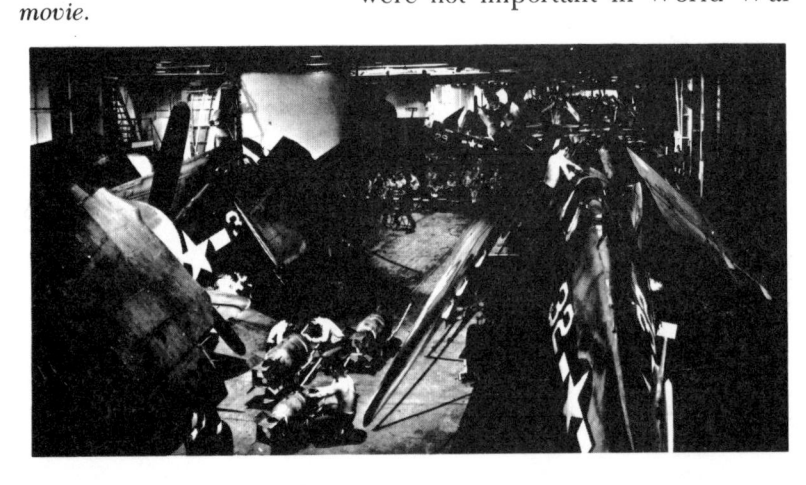

feet wide—almost the length of a football field. From keel to mast it is 250 feet high—equal to a 25-story skyscraper. In combat or on patrol duty, the *Enterprise* carries over 5,000 men and 85 jet airplanes. Most of the airplanes can fly faster than the speed of sound and can carry atomic bombs. The *Enterprise* is an attack carrier, designed to go anywhere in the world.

Another type of carrier is the antisubmarine warfare carrier. It is smaller and has slower airplanes, as well as helicopters, on board. The ship and the airplanes use complicated electronic devices to find and destroy enemy submarines that are trying to sink friendly ships or attack coastal cities.

Aircraft carriers, such as the USS *Hornet*, are also used to recover astronauts returning from space. Helicopters fly to the splashdown site and carry the men and capsules to the carrier.

Military experts argue about which is more useful—aircraft carriers or land-based airplanes. Both are expensive. The people who favor carriers claim that carriers can be anywhere in the world in a short time, ready to fight. They say it takes months to build airfields, supply them, and get them ready for use. Then, when the war is over, they must be left behind. But the floating airport comes home when war is over. It is ready to go somewhere else if necessary.

Most aircraft carriers built in the future will probably have atomic engines. They may be able to run for ten years on one load of fuel.

ALSO READ: AIRPORT, NAVY, SUBMARINE, WORLD WAR II.
[250 ft.=78 m]

**AIR CUSHION VEHICLE** An air cushion vehicle is a machine that rides on a layer of *compressed air* that holds it off the ground or water. It may stay only a few inches or several feet above the surface, depending on the vehicle's design. The advantage of being off the surface is that there is less friction between the machine and the surface. Friction is a force that opposes movement when one object or surface is rubbed against another. It is caused, for example, by a car's wheels turning against the ground, or by a boat's hull moving through water. The more friction there is between a vehicle and the ground or water, the slower the vehicle travels.

You probably cannot push even a small car. You would fight the weight of the car and the friction of its wheels on the axles. But if a strong wind underneath the car lifted it straight up, even one inch, you could probably move the car as long as the air held it off the ground. All you would have to do is

▲ *An aircraft carrier is a floating airport. The "runway," set at an angle, allows jet planes to take off and land without running into other planes or the tall radar and instrument house.*

▼ *An air cushion vehicle ferries passengers across San Francisco Bay. It rides on a cushion of air over land or water.*

# AIR FORCE

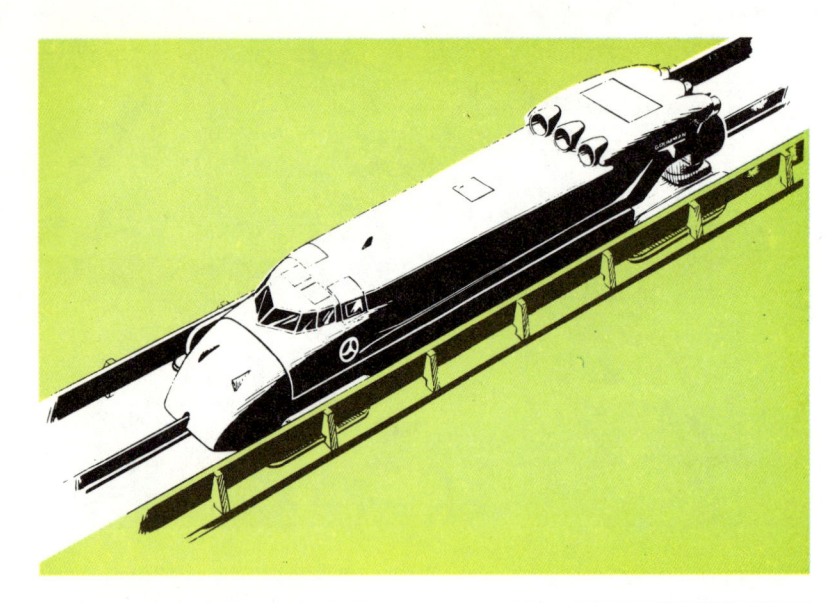

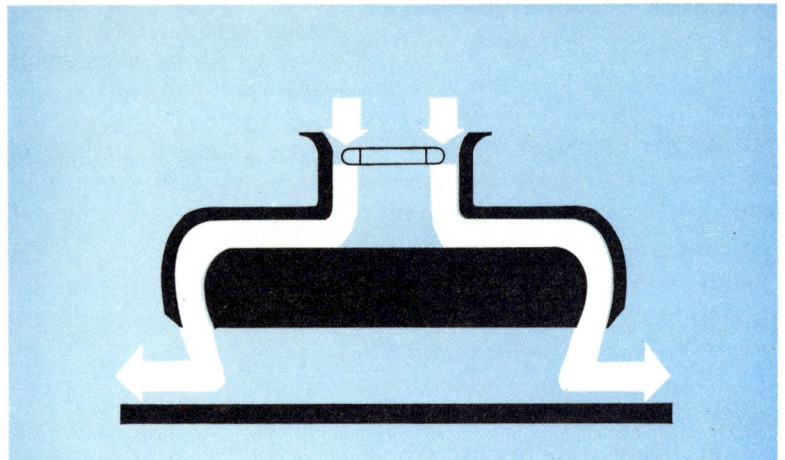

▲ *A track air cushion vehicle runs on a thin cushion of air above a track. The track guides the vehicle along. The vehicle was designed as a fast taxi between airports and cities. It can reach 150 miles an hour.*
[150 mph=242 km/hr]

▲ *Fans force the air through the channels at the side into an open "chamber." The pressure of the air in the chamber lifts the vehicle.*

push the car through air, and the friction between the car and the air would be very little. The wind would be an *air cushion*. An air cushion can also be formed by a strong wind blowing down from the car, to lift it off the ground. Air cushion vehicles use large fans to create the strong wind.

Air cushion vehicles (ACVs) come in several designs. One works only over water. Another must follow a big track. Other ACVs can travel over any flat surface.

Scientists and inventors thought of these machines as early as 1716. But they did not have the materials or the powerful engines to make them work. The first ACVs that really "flew" were built in the early 1950s. Big fans made the air cushions that lifted the vehicles off the ground. Propellers or jet engine exhausts then drove them forward.

Modern ACVs, like the one in the photo on the previous page, usually look like boats. Several fans may work to push the air down, and as many as four large propellers push the machine forward. Most ACVs travel about 20 miles an hour. But the one that follows a track may go 150 miles an hour.

Some ACVs have "skirts" made of a rubber-like material. These skirts are attached around the bottom of the machine. They hold the air cushion in place. An ACV with skirts can ride as high as ten feet above the surface. It can jump wide ditches and cross marshes. ACVs have also been tested that travel over ice and snow. Some ACVs have been driven over deserts, but sand sometimes gets into the engines. Air cushion vehicles called *hovercraft* are being used on a regular schedule to cross the English Channel between England and France. Many nations are using them to see how they compare with other kinds of transportation.

ALSO READ: AIR PRESSURE, TRANSPORTATION.

[20 mph=32 km/hr; 150 mph=242 km/hr; 10 ft.=3 m]

**AIR FORCE** One job of an air force is to defend its country by using airplanes and missiles against the country's enemies. Air forces have other jobs, too. One is rescuing people who are hurt or lost. All air forces do many of the same jobs, although each country organizes its air force differently. Only the United States Air Force (USAF) is described here.

## USAF Combat Commands

The *Military Airlift Command* (MAC) is one of the four main combat commands of the USAF. MAC furnishes air transportation for the Army, Navy, and Air Force. It carries anything needed in a hurry. MAC has all kinds of aircraft, from small helicopters to the huge C-5A jet transport, the largest airplane ever built. The C-5A is almost as long as a football field (246 feet) and can carry tanks and trucks, or as many as 900 soldiers.

MAC also runs a rescue service. It has helicopters and special airplanes to pick up wounded soldiers and pilots shot down over enemy territory. The rescue service has bases in many countries. It has saved many civilians who got lost or had accidents on mountains or in canyons, forests, deserts, or snowstorms. At the President's request, MAC flies medicines, doctors, food, and supplies to countries where there have been earthquakes, floods, and other disasters. MAC also helps pick up astronauts in the ocean when they return from space flights.

A special MAC squadron flies the President of the United States and his staff all over the world. The people in the squadron, from pilots to mechanics to clerks, are carefully picked. The squadron's aircraft range from small helicopters to big jet transports. The squadron [246 ft.=76 m] is often called the *Air Force One Squadron*, because any airplane the President flies in is *Air Force One*.

The *Strategic Air Command* (SAC) is another major part of the USAF. SAC is set up to attack military bases and factories in an enemy's country in case of war. SAC's main weapons are bombers and guided missiles. The B-52 is the biggest bomber. It can carry atom bombs. It can fly halfway around the world, at 650 miles an hour, without refueling. But it can be refueled while flying, by a *tanker airplane*. A tanker is like a flying gasoline pump. It hooks up with the bomber in flight and pumps fuel into its tanks.

SAC's intercontinental ballistic missiles (ICBMs) are kept in deep, concrete-lined holes in the ground, called *silos*. An ICBM carries an atom bomb in the nose. It can travel 7,000 miles at 15,000 miles an hour. Atomic missiles can be fired only by direct order from the President of the United States. They have never been fired.

The *Aerospace Defense Com-* [7,000 mi.=11,270 km; 15,000 mph=24,150 km/hr]

[650 mph=1,047 km/hr]

▼ *The B-52 Stratofortress is a long-range heavy bomber. It can even carry air-to-surface guided missiles. The B-52 was the most commonly used bomber during the 1950s and 1960s.*

# AIR FORCE

▲ *The F-104 Starfighter is a lightweight fighter-interceptor. It set a world speed and altitude record. The F-104 is one of the smallest and lightest jet fighters.*

▲ *An airman tries on a flight suit at an officer training school. Here, men who want to become officers undergo a course of study and exercise.*

▼ *An F-4 Phantom dives toward a target. The F-4 is swift, but it can also carry a heavy bomb load. It is multi-purpose and can be used as a fighter or bomber.*

mand (ADC) operates from a huge cave drilled out of a mountain, near Colorado Springs, Colorado. It has computers, radar, telephones, and radios to keep in touch with bases around the world. Its job is to protect the U.S. from enemy airplanes and missiles. ADC shares its cave with a group from Canada. Together, they make up the North American Air Defense Command (NORAD).

To shoot down enemy airplanes flying over Canada or the U.S., NORAD would use *fighter-interceptors* and *surface-to-air missiles* (SAMs). Fighter-interceptors are small, very fast airplanes that cannot go very far, but can fly almost straight up. The F-104G is a fighter-interceptor that carries atomic *air-to-air guided missiles* (AAMs). The Bomarc is a surface-to-air missile. It, too, has a small atom bomb in the nose. A Bomarc is fired from the ground like a rocket.

The *Tactical Air Command* (TAC) helps Army soldiers capture enemy territory. TAC has fighter-bombers to carry bombs, machine guns, cannons, and rockets to shoot at enemy tanks, trucks, trains, and storage places for ammunition.

The Air Force also works, usually secretly, to find out what enemy countries are doing. This is called *reconnaissance*. Reconnaissance satellites circle the Earth and take pictures of enemy territory. Reconnaissance planes can fly 2,000 miles an hour at 80,000 feet—twice as high as most airliners. Cameras in these planes photograph tiny details. Experts can recognize different kinds of cars in such pictures.

Other USAF commands train the men of the Air Force, handle supplies, and support the combat commands. The USAF presently has about 15,000 airplanes and almost 800,000 people. The people must be highly trained to take care of complicated airplanes, missiles, and radio and radar equipment.

[2,000 mph=3,220 km/hr; 80,000 ft.=24,800 m]

## History of the Air Force

The U.S. Air Force started August 1, 1907, as part of the Army Signal Corps, with one officer and two enlisted men. The division got its first plane in 1909, from the Wright brothers. It carried 2 people, flew 40 miles an hour, and cost 25,000 dollars. It was not easy to

[40 mph=64 km/hr]

learn to fly at that time because the two Wright brothers were the only instructors.

No American airplanes flew in combat during World War I. By the end of the First World War in 1918, the U.S. had 58,000 Air Service officers and men in France. Many of them had learned to fly in France and England, using British and French planes in combat.

From earliest days, Army pilots did not want to be controlled by Army ground forces. Most ground generals did not understand the airplane. They thought it should be used as a sort of long-range gun on the battlefield. The pilots believed airplanes should carry the war to an enemy's country and destroy his ability to make war. The pilots were considered rebels by many of the old-fashioned Army generals. General Billy Mitchell, assistant chief of the Air Service, was court-martialed (put on trial) for speaking up in public about his dreams of a real Air Force.

In 1926, a new group, the Army Air Corps, was formed. Then, 6 months before Pearl Harbor, the Army Air Forces were organized. Under the command of General Henry H. "Hap" Arnold, over 2 million men and women and almost 80,000 airplanes of the AAF helped win World War II. The U.S. furnished thousands of airplanes to its allies. They flew in both Europe and the Pacific. They were one big reason why the Allies won the war. In 1947, the U.S. Air Force was established as a separate military service, equal in status to the Army and the Navy.

ALSO READ; ARMY; MILITARY CAREER; MISSILE; NAVY; WORLD WAR II.

▲ *A U.S. airman on duty. His little friend is called Tilley.*

**AIRLINE** Airlines provide many kinds of rapid services. They carry mail so you can receive it in a short time. They quickly deliver air cargo in huge amounts. Airlines enable people to travel farther and faster than ever before.

There are several kinds of air-

▼ *F-100 Super Sabres roar across the sky. The F-100 was the first USAF plane to be able to fly at supersonic speeds in level flight.*

# AIRLINE

*A group of children enjoy a ride on an airliner. For many it was their first adventure in the air.*

*The most important person on an airplane is the pilot. He, together with the rest of the flight-deck crew, looks after the safety of everybody aboard the airplane.*

The first stewardess to serve on an airline was Ellen Church. She helped the passengers on a United Air Lines flight from San Francisco, California, to Cheyenne, Wyoming, on May 15, 1930.

lines. The *commuter airlines* fly small planes that carry up to 20 people between small cities, or from small cities to larger ones. *Local airlines* fly between medium-sized cities or from medium-sized to large cities. Their planes may be either propeller-driven or jet-propelled, and may carry from 20 to 100 passengers. *Trunk airlines* usually fly between large cities within a country. Most of their airplanes are jets that carry from 100 to 300 people. *International flag carriers* fly big jets between the major cities of the world. These four kinds of airlines are called *scheduled air carriers*. They must fly at the times they advertise to the public, whether their airplanes are filled or not.

*Cargo airlines* carry freight instead of people. They fly fresh vegetables, fruits, and flowers to restaurants, grocery stores, and shops. They carry automobile parts, furniture, and animals for zoos. They deliver almost anything that needs to be delivered quickly and that requires careful handling. Cargo airlines use all kinds of airplanes, including the biggest jets.

*Charter* or *supplemental airlines* do not have schedules. They rent their airplanes and crews to clubs and other organizations, usually for vacation trips or meetings. The trips are usually planned six months before the flight, and all the passengers must go and come back together. Because a charter airline knows ahead of time that the airplane will be filled with passengers, the fare for each passenger is low. It is usually about half the cost of the same trip on a scheduled airline. Supplemental airlines fly the same big jets and have the same kinds of crews that the international scheduled airlines use.

Great changes have been made since the first airline flight. On January 1, 1914, a flying boat carried two passengers from Tampa to St. Petersburg in Florida. The fare was 5 dollars for the 20-mile trip. The Boeing 747 of today is very long—(231 feet, 10 inches) and has four jet engines. It can carry 340 passengers for 6,000 miles at 600 miles an hour. It has a cocktail lounge and elevators to bring food up from the galley, or kitchen, to the passenger cabin.

[20 mi.=32 km; 231 ft. 10 in.=72 m; 6,000 mi.=9,660 km; 600 mph=966 km/hr]

## The People of an Airline

The cockpit of an airliner is called the *flight deck*. The crew, or people who fly the airplane, include the *captain*, the senior pilot who is in charge of the airplane, and another pilot called the *first officer*. The *flight engineer* is also a member of the flight crew. He is in charge of the mechanical operation of the airplane, which includes everything from the coffee makers to the engines. He watches all the meters and gauges in the cockpit and adjusts temperatures, power, fuel, and other things to be sure everything is working right. On long overwater flights, the crew also includes a *navigator*. The navigator's job is to know where the airplane is at all times. He tells the pilot what route to follow and how long the trip should take.

The *stewardesses* are called the *cabin crew*. There are usually 15 of them on a Boeing 747. Smaller airplanes may have two or three stewardesses. They serve food, but are also trained to take care of sick people and to get passengers out of the airplane quickly in case of an emergency. Many stewardesses speak several languages so they can talk to passengers from almost any country. Most stewardesses have been to college. They are very important to airlines because they help make the passengers' flight more pleasant.

The maintenance or engineering people take care of the airplanes on the ground. They are a very important part of the airline because they make sure that the airplanes are ready to fly safely. Passengers usually do not see them.

Air travel has become so popular that every year the number of passengers who fly on the world's scheduled airlines (not counting charter airlines and private planes) is larger than the total population of the United States.

ALSO READ: AIRPLANE, AVIATION, TRANSPORTATION.

**AIR MASS** see WEATHER.

**AIRPLANE** On a lonely beach at Kitty Hawk, North Carolina, on December 17, 1903, a man flew an airplane for the first time. The man was Orville Wright. The flight was not far, only 120 feet. The airplane never got more than 20 feet off the ground. Its top speed was only 30 miles an hour. But, unlike earlier aircraft, it was an airplane—it flew under its own power and could be controlled by the pilot.

Orville Wright's flight at Kitty Hawk was the first giant step in the development of air and space transportation that would land another American on the moon, only 66 years later.

Aviation is today one of the world's largest industries. Orville and Wilbur Wright can be called the "fathers of aviation" because they were the first to successfully design, build, and fly an engine-powered airplane. The first flight
[120 ft.=37 m; 20 ft.=6 m; 30 mph=48 km/hr]

was not just luck. The Wright brothers were not scientists or engineers, but they were good and careful mechanics. They had read everything they could find about earlier attempts to fly and why those attempts had failed. They studied very hard and made many experiments on the ground before they tried to fly. They built a simple wind tunnel, using an electric fan to test small models of different types of wings before they built an airplane. A wind tunnel is a chamber through which air is blown at different speeds, to test the flow of air around and the effects on model airplanes. The Wright brothers discovered the four basic forces that today's engineers and scientists must still work with to design and build huge jets.

**Why an Airplane Flies**
The forces the Wrights discovered are called *lift*, *weight*, *thrust*, and *drag*. These forces work in the same way on a small model airplane with a propeller driven by a rubber band, as they do on a giant transport plane driven by powerful jet engines.

Lift and weight are opposite forces. *Lift* makes an airplane go up, and *weight*—or *gravity*—makes it go down. The lift must be stronger than the weight, if an airplane is to fly. Thrust and drag are also opposite forces. *Thrust* makes the airplane go forward or faster,

▲*The Boeing 707 was the first American jet airliner. It can fly the Atlantic Ocean in six hours. It flies at almost 600 miles an hour and can carry about 200 people.*
[600 mph=966 km/hr]

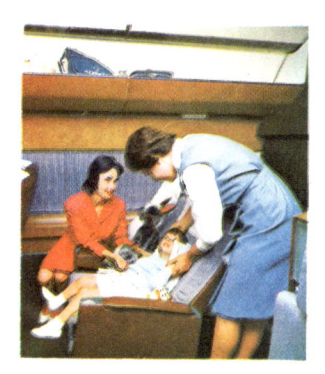

▲*An airline stewardess must be well-trained and cheerful. A stewardess is the link between the pilot and the passengers, especially in an emergency. She also tends to the needs of passengers during their trip.*

# AIRPLANE

▲ *The Wright brothers first flew in 1903. Their plane carried only one person and flew 30 miles an hour. It flew 120 feet.*
[30 mph=48 km/hr; 120 ft.=37 m]

▼ *Four different forces work to make an airplane fly.* Lift *is the opposite of* weight. Thrust *is the opposite of* drag.

and *drag* holds it back or slows it down. Thrust must be stronger than drag, for an airplane to take off.

To understand how these forces work on an airplane, you must look carefully at the airplane itself. The main parts of any airplane are the wings, the engine (or engines), the fuselage or cabin (the long part where the pilot and passengers or cargo ride), the landing gear (usually two large wheels or groups of wheels, and other parts to support an airplane on the ground), and the tail at the back.

LIFT. The movement of air around a wing creates lift. A wing of an airplane is curved on top and flat on the bottom. Air moving over the top must move faster than air moving under the bottom, because it has a longer distance to travel. The faster air travels, the less pressure it exerts. The air above the wing has a lower pressure than the air below. The higher pressure below forces the airplane up.

You can easily see how lift works. Tear a strip of paper about two inches wide and eight inches
[2 in.=5 cm; 8 in.=20 cm]

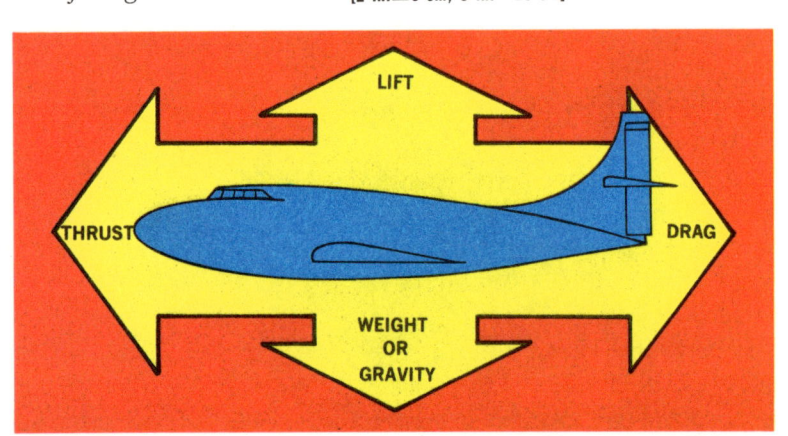

long, off a sheet of paper. Hold the strip at one end between your thumb and first finger so the long part hangs down over the back of your hand. Hold your hand near your mouth and blow across the top. The paper "wing" rises. If the paper were an airplane wing, the whole airplane would rise with it.

THRUST. The forward movement, or speed, of an airplane overcomes the drag of the air. A turning propeller pulls or pushes an airplane through air, much as a propeller pushes a motor boat through water. A jet engine works on the principle of *reaction*—the action of hot gases moving out the back of an engine cause a reaction of an airplane moving forward. If more thrust is supplied by either propellers or jets, more lift is created and an airplane can climb. Or, more speed is created if an airplane is flying level.

WEIGHT. The weight of an airplane is the weight of the machine, plus cargo, passengers, and fuel. This force, which must be overcome by lift, is called *gravity*.

DRAG. The drag, or resistance, is caused by the friction of air on every part of the airplane. An airplane is going as fast as it can when as much drag as possible is overcome by thrust. Designers reduce the amount of drag by making as many outside surfaces of the airplane as smooth and rounded as possible. The *landing gear* on most airplanes retracts, or pulls up, to reduce resistance during flight.

## Other Parts of an Airplane

The engines and the wing enable an airplane to fly. However, other things are needed to control its flight. The *tail* has *horizontal stabilizers* that look like tiny wings on the tail. It also has a *vertical stabilizer* that sticks straight up from the middle of the tail. These parts keep an airplane balanced in flight and are called *control surfaces*. The *elevators* are attached to the horizontal stabilizers. A pilot can move these up or down and apply more or less power to make an airplane climb or descend.

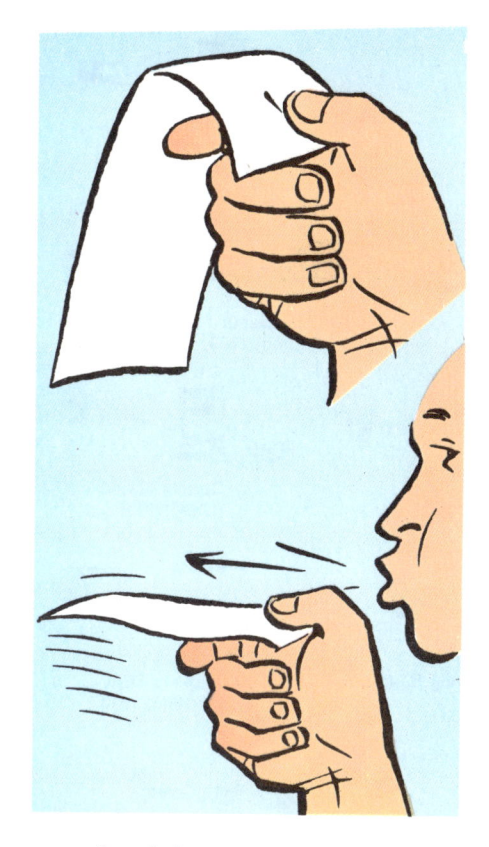

The rudder is attached to the vertical stabilizer but is not normally used to steer the airplane like a boat. The rudder is used to stabilize the airplane while two movable sections near the wing tips, called *ailerons,* are used to turn the airplane to the left or right. To turn to the right, the pilot raises the right aileron and lowers the left aileron. This tips the right wing down and raises the left wing. The airplane then banks to the right and makes a slow, smooth turn. Other wing sections, near the fuselage, are called *flaps*. Flaps can be turned down to make the curve of the wing top greater. The increased pressure difference increases lift. To keep an airplane cruising in the air at a particular speed, the thrust, or engine power, is kept constant and the control surfaces are kept in line

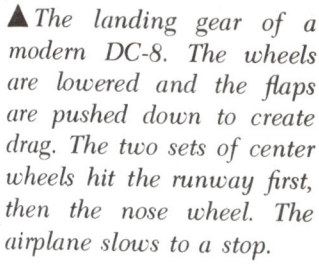

▲ The landing gear of a modern DC-8. The wheels are lowered and the flaps are pushed down to create drag. The two sets of center wheels hit the runway first, then the nose wheel. The airplane slows to a stop.

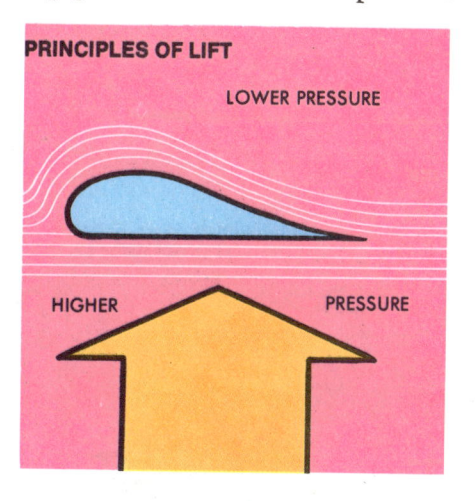

◀ The wing of an airplane is curved on top and flat on the bottom. The air (shown by the white lines) moving over the top, moves faster than the air moving beneath the wing. This difference makes the wing—and the airplane—go up in the air.

▲ The propeller pulls an airplane forward against the drag of the air. Pure jet airplanes do not have propellers.

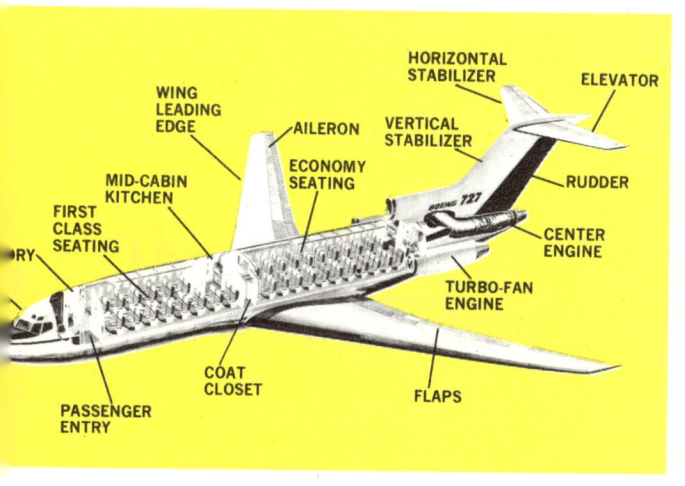

◀ The pilot has various devices to help him control the airplane, once it is in the air. Here is a plane with its wing flaps turned down.

# Famous Airplanes — 1903-1918

**Wright brothers' first plane** (USA) 1903

**Voisin-Farman** (France) 1907

**Curtiss "June Bug"** (USA) 1908

**"Henri Farman III"** (France) 1909

**Wright "A"** (USA) 1909

**Levavasseur "Antoinette"** (France) 1909

**Bleriot #11** (France) 1909 (first to cross English Channel)

**Curtiss** (USA) 1910

**Avro Biplane** (Britain) 1911

**Curtiss "Triad"** (USA) 1911

**Morane-Saulnier "L"** (France) 1913

**Sopwith "Tabloid"** (Britain) 1913

**Curtiss "America" flying boat** (USA) 1913

**Vickers FE-6** (Britain) 1913

**Sikorsky "Grand"** (Russia) 1913 (first multi-engine plane)

**Farnborough BE-2** (Britain) 1913

**Rumpler "Taube"** (Germany) 1913

**Martin "TT"** (USA) 1914

**Caudron G-III** (France) 1915

**DeHavilland DH-2** (Britain) 1915

**Nieuport 17** (France) 1916

**Albatros D-1** (Germany) 1916

**Avro 504-J** (Britain) 1916

**Bristol F-2B** (Britain) 1917

**Breguet 14** (France) 1917

**Fokker DR-1** (Germany) 1917

**SPAD 13 fighter** (France) 1917

**Gotha bomber** (Germany) 1917

**Sopwith "Camel"** (Britain) 1917

**Junkers D-1** (Germany) 1918

**Loening M-8** (USA) 1918

**Fokker D-VII "Jasta"** (Germany) 1918

**DeHavilland DH-4** (Britain-USA) 1918

**Curtiss F-5L** (USA) 1918

# Famous Airplanes —1919-first jets

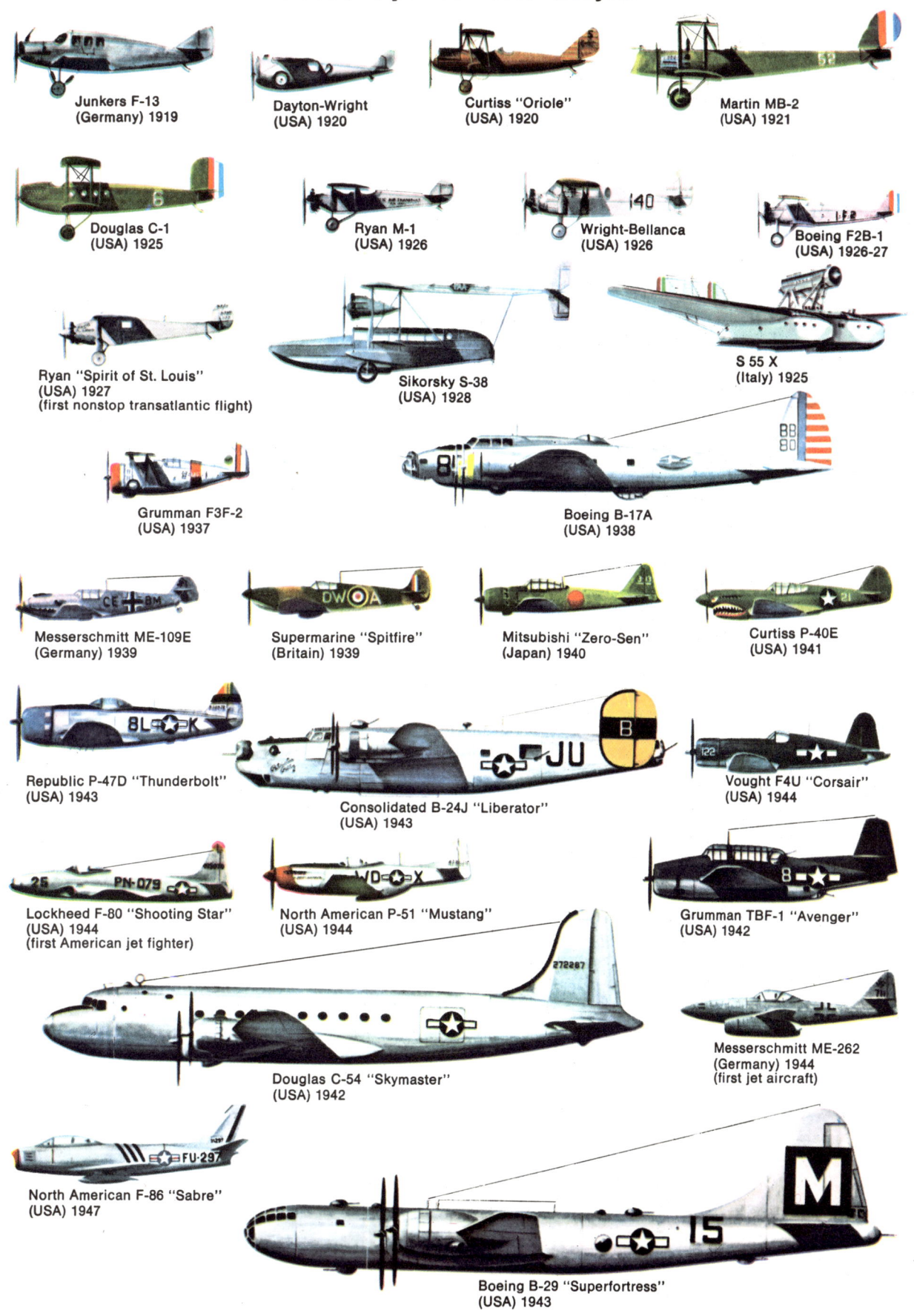

- Junkers F-13 (Germany) 1919
- Dayton-Wright (USA) 1920
- Curtiss "Oriole" (USA) 1920
- Martin MB-2 (USA) 1921
- Douglas C-1 (USA) 1925
- Ryan M-1 (USA) 1926
- Wright-Bellanca (USA) 1926
- Boeing F2B-1 (USA) 1926-27
- Ryan "Spirit of St. Louis" (USA) 1927 (first nonstop transatlantic flight)
- Sikorsky S-38 (USA) 1928
- S 55 X (Italy) 1925
- Grumman F3F-2 (USA) 1937
- Boeing B-17A (USA) 1938
- Messerschmitt ME-109E (Germany) 1939
- Supermarine "Spitfire" (Britain) 1939
- Mitsubishi "Zero-Sen" (Japan) 1940
- Curtiss P-40E (USA) 1941
- Republic P-47D "Thunderbolt" (USA) 1943
- Consolidated B-24J "Liberator" (USA) 1943
- Vought F4U "Corsair" (USA) 1944
- Lockheed F-80 "Shooting Star" (USA) 1944 (first American jet fighter)
- North American P-51 "Mustang" (USA) 1944
- Grumman TBF-1 "Avenger" (USA) 1942
- Douglas C-54 "Skymaster" (USA) 1942
- Messerschmitt ME-262 (Germany) 1944 (first jet aircraft)
- North American F-86 "Sabre" (USA) 1947
- Boeing B-29 "Superfortress" (USA) 1943

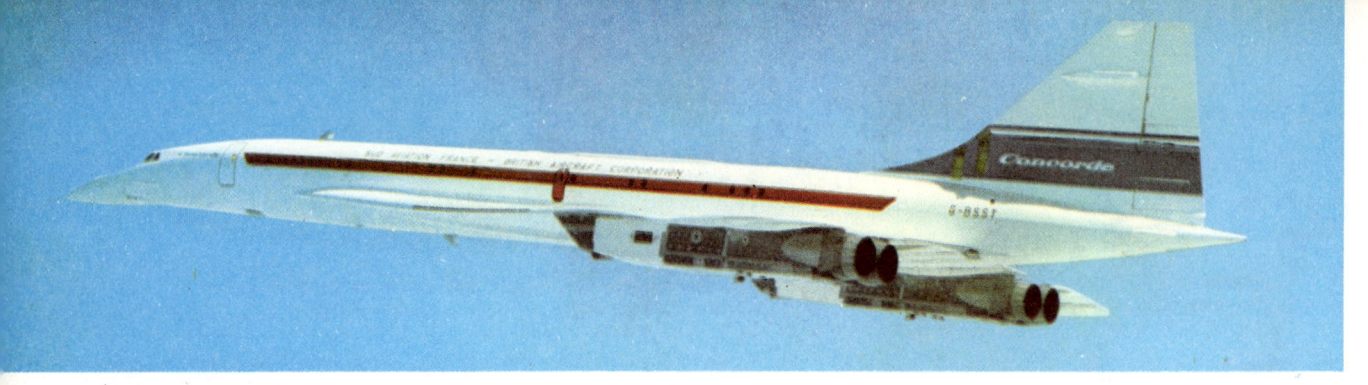

▲ *The Concorde is the newest kind of airliner. It is a supersonic transport (SST), which means that it flies faster than sound travels. It flies 1,400 miles an hour. It is built by France and England.*
[1,400 mph = 2,254 km/hr]

▲ *Small general aviation airplanes can go many places where there are no roads. This plane has carried scientists to McCall Glacier in Alaska.*

with the horizontal and vertical stabilizers.

Many important parts of an airplane can be seen only in the *cockpit* where a pilot sits. In the cockpit are all the controls and electronic devices that enable a pilot to fly the airplane safely. The *flight controls* consist of a wheel or control stick, and rudder pedals. The wheel, which looks much like an automobile steering wheel, controls the elevators and ailerons. To make a right turn, a pilot turns the wheel to the right and pushes the right rudder pedal. If he pushes the wheel forward, the airplane descends. The airplane climbs if he pulls the wheel back.

Even on a small airplane a pilot has a number of dials, gauges, switches, and lights on an instrument panel that looks much like an automobile dashboard. On large airplanes, instrument panels cover the front, sides, and ceiling of the cockpit. The instruments tell a pilot everything he must know about the condition of an airplane and its equipment. The instruments tell him how fast the plane is going, the direction it is flying, how much fuel is left, and many other things. Cockpit radio equipment permits him to talk to people on the ground to get landing instructions and weather information, and to be sure he will not run into another airplane in bad weather. Other radar sets and radios help him avoid bad storms and navigate his airplane. Large planes have *automatic pilots* that fly the planes for the crew.

### Types of Airplanes

Three kinds of power systems are used today to furnish thrust. (1) Gasoline engines turn propellers that pull or push an airplane through the air. These airplanes are called *conventional aircraft*. They usually fly at speeds of 120 to 225 miles an hour, but some can go faster. (2) Jet engines that turn propellers are called *turboprops*. Planes with such engines fly from 250 to 400 miles an hour. (3) Pure jet engines push an airplane through the air at very high speeds —600 miles an hour or faster.

Most airplanes today are monoplanes, which means they have only one wing. In the early days of aviation, airplanes had two wings (biplanes) or three wings (triplanes). Early airplanes had engines that were very heavy compared to the power they produced. More wings added more lift, but also more drag. However, the lift was more than the drag, so the airplanes flew but could not go very fast.

### The Airplane at Work

Different kinds of airplanes are used for many different jobs. The three main kinds of airplanes, according to use, are the general aviation airplanes, military airplanes, and airliners.

GENERAL AVIATION AIRPLANES. General aviation airplanes include every kind of airplane except military airplanes and commercial airliners. Over 125,000 general aviation airplanes were used in the United States in 1970.

Some people like to fly as a sport or hobby. The airplanes they use are usually small, one-engine planes that carry one to four people. Some

[120-225 mph = 193-362 km/hr;
250-400 mph = 403-644 km/hr;
600 mph = 966 km/hr]

*The Boeing 747 is a giant of an airplane. It started to fly in 1970. It can carry up to 490 passengers at one time.*

[2,000 mph = 3,220 km/hr]

[6,000 mi. = 9,660 km]
[600 mph = 966 km/hr]

[1,400 mph = 2,254 km/hr]

pilots of these small planes are very skilled and fly single-seat acrobatic airplanes for fun or to make money at air shows. An acrobatic airplane will not go very far or very fast, but it is strongly built. A pilot can fly an acrobatic plane upside down and do tricks in it that he could not do in a big airplane or in one not specially built.

The business or executive airplanes have come into use during the last 20 years. These airplanes range from six- or eight-passenger, conventional single-engine airplanes to multi-engine pure jets that carry 80 people. Many businessmen who want to work while they travel to faraway appointments use these airplanes.

Businesses use airplanes for many other jobs. Some airplanes, called *agricultural aviation* airplanes, spray fertilizers or insecticides on fields of cotton, wheat, or other crops. Such an airplane carries only a pilot and a lot of tanks and machines to spray chemicals on the fields.

Oil and mining companies use airplanes to carry people and spare parts to oil wells and mines in high mountains, swamps, and other hard-to-get-to places all over the world. Many parts of the world have few roads or railroads because of deserts, jungles, or year-long snow. Only airplanes can carry doctors, food, and other supplies to the people who live in these places. Sometimes, instead of wheels, the airplanes have skis to land on snow, or floats to land on water.

MILITARY AIRPLANES. The military use all kinds of airplanes, from very small ones to teach people to fly to huge eight-engine jet bombers, such as the B-52. Many military airplanes are much like civilian airplanes. However, the military have a special type of airplane called the *fighter*, which is not used in regular aviation. Fighters can fly over 2,000 miles an hour and carry guns and rockets. Some can also carry atom bombs. The United States Air Force Military Air Transport Service (MATS) operates aircraft that provide rescue, weather, photographic, and medical services for all U.S. armed forces throughout the world.

AIRLINERS. The airline industry uses many kinds of airplanes. Air taxis, which fly short trips and can use small airports, are much like business airplanes. Local service airlines fly short distances and use airplanes that carry from 40 to 80 people. Many of these airplanes are turboprops or conventional aircraft, because propeller-driven airplanes can use smaller airports than pure jets can.

Some huge *jet airliners* can carry 490 people for 6,000 miles at speeds over 600 miles an hour. They fly across the U.S. in less than five hours and cross the Atlantic Ocean in about six hours. Passengers may watch movies, eat meals, and live as if they were in a flying city. Supersonic transport (SST) passenger airplanes, which fly faster than the speed of sound, have traveled from continent to continent at a speed of 1,400 miles an hour. Some began regular service in 1976.

ALSO READ: AIR FORCE, AIRLINE, AIRPORT, AVIATION, JET PROPULSION, TRANSPORTATION, WRIGHT BROTHERS.

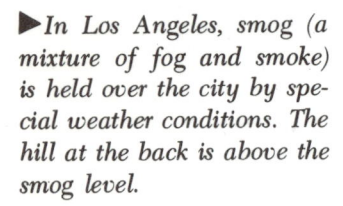

# AIR POLLUTION

*In Los Angeles, smog (a mixture of fog and smoke) is held over the city by special weather conditions. The hill at the back is above the smog level.*

*Smokestacks and burning rubbish often cause pollution. Here, dirty, black smoke shoots into the air from an oil refinery.*

**AIR POLLUTION** The photograph of Los Angeles, California, on this page shows a thick gray cloud covering much of the city. The cloud is *smog*—a mixture of smoke and fog—one kind of dirty, or *polluted*, air. Smog is unpleasant. It often causes shortness of breath, dizziness, watery eyes, and runny noses. Smog can also be dangerous, if it is extra thick and lasts a long time. One smog cloud choked London, England, for six days in 1952. When wind finally blew the smog away, 4,000 people had died.

Wind carries many substances through Earth's air. Among them are pollen from plants, sand from dry beaches, and dust from fields. These are natural substances. But man sometimes adds other substances to the air. Smoke pours from factory smokestacks. Chemical fumes rise from paper mills and metal-working plants. Garbage-dump incinerators spread black soot. Automobiles stream a blue, smelly haze that hangs over crowded cities. The air is polluted when it is filled with unnatural substances.

## What Pollution Can Do

Polluted air can destroy the balance of the exchange that goes on among plants, animals, and the oceans. Animals, including people, get necessary oxygen from the air they breathe. They exhale the gas carbon dioxide. Plants, even the tiny ones that live in Earth's oceans, all need carbon dioxide as much as people need oxygen. Carbon dioxide supplies the carbon that plants need to make food. Plants draw in carbon dioxide, then release oxygen. But *pollutants* such as soot, sulfur, lead, and automobile exhaust and factory fumes poison the air. Over a long period of time, these pollutants could poison all forms of life.

Air pollution causes other serious problems, too. Foul air damages crops. Air pollution wears away *(corrodes)* metals as though they had been put into acid. Look what pollution has done to the truck side shown on the next page. Layers of ash and soot from air settle on buildings and clothing, and cleaning costs rise. People cannot see clearly in heavy smog, so accidents happen more often. Fumes in the air even eat away buildings made of stone. Pollutants cause holes in glass and kill lawns and trees.

## Take a Deep Breath

Almost 1,000 tons of soot and ash land on every square mile of New York City each year. The 90 million

[1,000 tons=910 metric tons]

cars that Americans own add hundreds of thousands of pounds of poisonous carbon monoxide to the air every day. Each year more factories are built, more coal is burned to provide power and heat, more people drive cars.

The most serious fact about air pollution is that it endangers health. Eyes water and vision blurs. A person may not get the oxygen he needs when he breathes. He may choke on harmful gases instead. Old people, and people with heart or lung diseases, suffer most from polluted air.

People of all ages have become upset about the danger of air pollution today, and they are working to stop it. The United States Government formed the Environmental Protection Agency in 1970. This office studies pollution and works with people all over the U.S. to prevent further pollution of the air.

Another law passed in 1970 required automobile makers to produce engines by 1975 that give off only one-tenth the fumes of 1970 engines. This is a very important step, because automobile exhausts cause more than half the pollution in the U.S. Jet airplanes must now have devices that cut down the dirty black clouds of jet fuel exhaust that pour down around airports. The Los Angeles city government has laws to close down factories when there is danger of heavy smog.

Scientists watch the amount of pollutants in the air while they study new ways to control pollution. Many cities no longer allow people to burn leaves or trash. You and your family can help stop air pollution in the same way even if the place where you live has no law against trash burning.

Many newspapers print a *pollution index* each day. It usually shows whether the air was "good", "poor", or "unacceptable" during the day. (The terms used in your paper may be different.) Follow the changes in the pollution index for your town. Make a chart with six columns. Label the columns "Day," "Sunny," "Cloudy," "Rain," "Wind speed," and "Pollution Index." Fill in the chart each day for several weeks. Do you see a pattern develop? When is the pollution index "unacceptable"? When is it "good"?

ALSO READ: BREATHING, CONSERVATION, ECOLOGY, WATER POLLUTION.

▲*These holes in the side of a truck were caused by air pollution.*

**AIRPORT** An airport is a place where an airplane can take off and land safely. A simple airport may be just a piece of smooth ground. But ground gets muddy, so most airports, even far from cities, have runways. These are usually made of concrete or asphalt, like highways. But they are wider and thicker than highways. Runways are built following the most frequent wind directions. A small airport is usually owned by a person or a town. It is run by a *fixed-base operator* who provides the basic services needed at all airports. These include "parking lots" for the airplanes, taxiways (roads) to the main runway, fuel supplies, weather information and maps for the pilots, and mechanics to make repairs. Many fixed-base operators also give flying lessons.

Small airports can be as important as larger ones. Some small airports are the center of areas called *industrial air parks*. The airport itself is surrounded by factories and other businesses that need swift transportation. The Lock Haven, Pennsylvania, airport in the picture serves manufacturers, as well as privately owned aircraft.

▼*Not all airports are built for big planes. This airport in Lock Haven, Pennsylvania, is used by people who fly small airplanes.*

**The Large Airports**
Large airports in cities have two main types of customers—the airlines and the passengers. For the airlines, airports have maintenance services in huge buildings, called *hangars*. Airplanes can be parked in the hangars and worked on in any

# AIRPORT

▶ *A view of Dulles Airport near Washington, D.C., showing the terminal building, control tower, and runways. Can you think of anything more that an airport needs?*

▲ *An airport terminal building, where people get on and off airplanes. Look at the shape of this terminal in Los Angeles. It has six sides to it. Ten telescoping corridors reach out from the terminal to meet the planes.*

▼ *An airport runway at night. The lights help guide the pilot to the runway.*

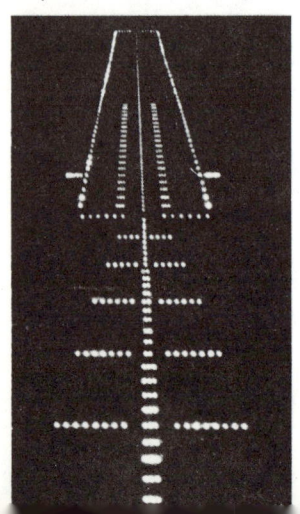

kind of weather, day or night, by expert mechanics. The mechanics make sure the airplanes are safe to fly. Communications services at airports include the control towers, where air traffic controllers watch the airports and tell pilots when to land or take off, and which of several runways to use. Landing and navigation aids, which are radio and radar stations, help pilots to find the airports and to land in bad weather. Airport weather services tell pilots what the weather is anywhere in the world, and what it will be like when they arrive at their destinations. Inflight food services furnish food for passengers in airplanes. Air cargo warehouses are big buildings where cargo is stored between flights.

An important job of the people who run airports is to keep airplanes safely going and coming in bad weather. Runways must be maintained so that rainwater quickly drains away. Troops of men and plows quickly remove snow. The light and radar aids on runways must always be ready to help pilots in darkness or fog. Airports often do such a good job that airplanes are flying after ground transportation has been almost halted by weather.

Each airline has ground services including people who check passengers' tickets, check in passengers' luggage, and announce arrivals and departures of planes. The skycaps who carry passengers' luggage, and the men who fill airplanes with fuel, are also part of the ground services. At large airports, passengers wait in lounges in the passenger terminal buildings before they get on the airplanes. They also go into these buildings when they get off at their destinations. The passenger terminal buildings have ticket counters, restrooms, telephones, barber shops, restaurants, drug stores, and various shops.

Some large airports are *international* airports, where flights go to and from other countries. These airports have United States officials who check all arriving passengers to see if they are legally allowed to enter the U.S. and to see if passengers are bringing into the country things they should not. Flights across oceans use very large airplanes that need much runway space, so international airports are usually very large. Dulles International Airport, near Washington, D.C., is an example. It is about four miles wide and five miles long. It
[4 mi. by 5 mi.=6 km by 8 km]

had three runways originally and a fourth was added. The longest ones are 11,500 feet long—over 2 miles—and 150 feet wide.

International airports are very busy, because they handle not only overseas flights but domestic flights as well. Some have flights of more than 50 airlines arriving and leaving each day. More than 21 million passengers go through Kennedy International Airport, near New York City, every year. Seven million of these passengers are going to or returning from other countries. The busiest airport in the world is O'Hare International in Chicago. An airplane takes off or lands there about every 45 seconds on a busy day.

Airports are noisy and busy, but without them, many cities and towns would be almost cut off from the rest of the world.

ALSO READ: AIRLINE, AIR TRAFFIC CONTROL, AVIATION.
[11,500 ft.=3,565 m; 150 ft.=47 m]

**AIR PRESSURE** Air is not very heavy. One cubic foot of air at sea level, and at 32° F, weighs only one ounce, which is about the weight of eight pennies. So much air is in
[1 cu.ft.=.03m³; 32° F=0° C; 1 oz.=28 g]

▲ *A great deal of air can be compressed into small tanks. These divers are checking the tanks. They will wear the tanks under water and breathe the air from them.*

the *atmosphere* above and around us that it presses on us from all directions with a pressure, or weight, of almost 15 pounds per square inch at sea level. The air pressure on our bodies amounts to thousands of pounds. We do not feel this great force because the fluid and air in our bodies are pushing out with an equal pressure.

The air above just one acre of ground weighs over 40,000 tons. The weight of air is only half as much four miles above the Earth. At 15,000 feet above the Earth, a pilot must wear an oxygen mask unless his plane has equipment to keep cabin pressure the same as ground level pressure. The mask is attached to a cylinder that feeds oxygen to the pilot. Most passenger airplanes have equipment to keep the pressure inside the cabins much like that of ground level. An instrumen called a *barometer* measures atmospheric pressure. Knowledge of air pressure is very useful in predicting the weather. High air pressure usually means fair weather. If air pressure is low, stormy weather is usually coming.

Air pressure can be put to work. When air is *compressed*, or squeezed together, in a small space, it rushes out through any opening with great force. A tool called a *pneumatic hammer*, or drill, uses the force of compressed air to drive the hammer deep into concrete, breaking it up.

▲ *An airport lobby, where people get their airline tickets and wait for their planes.*
[15 lbs./sq.in.=1.1 kg/cm²]

[1 acre=4,047 m²]
[40,000 tons=36,288 metric tons]

[4 mi.=6 km]
[15,000 ft.=4,650 m]

Test the pressure of the air yourself, using a bowl of water, a glass, and a napkin. Fill a deep bowl with water. Crush a paper napkin and force it tightly into the bottom of the glass. Turn the glass upside down and push it straight down into the water. Now pull the glass straight out. Feel the napkin. It should be dry. The air that was inside the glass when it was pushed into the water had enough pressure, or force, to keep water from filling the glass.

ALSO READ: AIR, AIRPLANE, ATMOSPHERE, WEATHER.

**AIRSHIP** You may have seen an occasional airship overhead—half-floating, half-gliding through the sky like a huge, over-sized, silver cigar. It is a huge "balloon" filled with lighter-than-air gas to make it rise. The airship has engines to move it through the sky and controls to steer it by.

There are two main types of airships—*rigid* and *non-rigid*. Rigid airships have a "skeleton" or framework of aluminum or some other lightweight but strong material. Layers of cloth are stretched over this frame. The cloth is painted with liquid *dope*. This shrinks the cloth, so it fits tight and hardens it to prevent serious damage if something hits the frame. Lightweight metal is sometimes used instead of cloth to cover the frame. A number of bags of light gas are inside the frame. If one bag breaks or leaks, the others keep the ship aloft. Rigid airships are usually called *dirigibles*, from a French word for "steerable." They are also called *zeppelins*, after Count Ferdinand von Zeppelin of Germany, who designed the first rigid airships that worked well.

Non-rigid airships are called *blimps*. Blimps do not have a complete inside frame. They depend on the pressure of the gas inside to keep them inflated to their normal shape. They may have a number of separate gas sections so that a gas leak in one section will not cause the blimp to come down suddenly.

**Development of the Airship**

Henri Giffard of France in 1852 flew a long sausage-shaped balloon filled with hydrogen, for 17 miles at 5 miles an hour. He used a 3½-horsepower steam engine to turn a big three-bladed propeller for power, and used a boat rudder to steer. Other men tried other ways of developing power. However, nothing worked very well until the lightweight gasoline engine was invented and used in early airships and airplanes.

Count von Zeppelin had four airships flying passengers between German cities by 1910. German zeppelins bombed London early in World War I. However, British airplanes soon proved their ability to shoot down the huge, slow airships.

[17 mi.=27 km; 5 mph=8 km/hr]

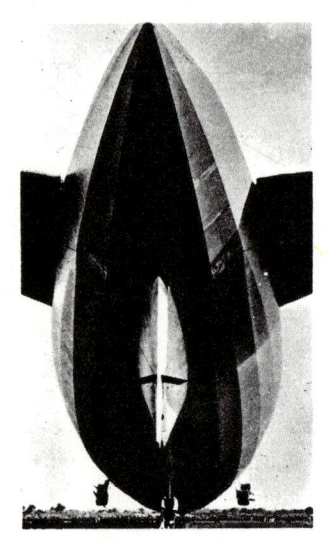

▲ *The* Graf Zeppelin *was a dirigible that carried many passengers. It had a rigid framework.*

# AIRSHIP

## The Age of the Airship

The high point in airship history came in 1929, when the German *Graf Zeppelin* flew around the world in 21 days. It had a crew of 40 and carried 20 passengers. The huge silver airship was 776 feet long, and flew 80 miles an hour. The *Graf Zeppelin* started its famous flight in Lakehurst, New Jersey. It landed only three times, first in Friedrichshafen, Germany, next in Tokyo, Japan. It then flew over the Pacific Ocean to Los Angeles, California. From there it returned to Lakehurst. The *Graf Zeppelin* flew safely for 9 years, and carried more than 18,000 passengers on very long trips.

The Germans built the *Hindenburg*, encouraged by the success of the *Graf Zeppelin*. The *Hindenburg* was the largest rigid airship ever built—803 feet long and twice as big around as the *Graf Zeppelin*. It carried 78 passengers and 19 crew members. It made ten successful round-trips between Germany and the United States in 1936. But, on May 6, 1937, the hydrogen inside it exploded and the *Hindenburg* crashed as it was landing at Lakehurst. Of the 97 people on board, 36 were killed and the rest were badly injured. The tragedy ended the age of the airship. No large airship has been built since the *Hindenburg* disaster.

Many accidents to European airships were caused by explosions of the hydrogen gas used to lift them. U.S. airships use helium, a gas almost as light as hydrogen, but which will not burn. The U.S. has most of the world's helium supply. Germany had none for its zeppelins and had to use hydrogen.

Between 1920 and 1935, the U.S. Navy built three huge dirigibles—the *Shenandoah*, the *Macon*, and the *Akron*. The *Macon* and the *Akron* each carried five small airplanes that could take off and land from the airship in flight. All three airships eventually crashed because they were not strong enough to fly in bad weather.

One type of airship that worked successfully was the U.S. Navy blimp. Ten of these were used in World War II, to carry antisubmarine bombs and to escort 80,000 U.S. ships across the ocean. The only airships in operation today are a few blimps manufactured in the United States and Germany. They move so slowly and calmly that they are useful for shooting television pictures from above, for a "bird's eye view" of important news events.

ALSO READ: AVIATION, BALLOON.

[776 ft.=241 m; 80 mph=129 km/hr; 803 ft.=249 m]

▲The *Hindenberg* exploded while landing at Lakehurst, New Jersey, in 1937. Since then, no other passenger dirigibles have been built.

◀Blimps are the only airships flying today. This is the blimp *Mayflower* built by Goodyear.

# AIR TRAFFIC CONTROL

**AIR TRAFFIC CONTROL** The traffic policeman of the air is air traffic control (ATC). This control system directs airplanes somewhat as a policeman directs cars. It keeps airplanes from running into each other by telling them when to turn, how high and fast to fly, and when to land. The job of controlling air traffic is complicated. Air highways in some areas are almost as crowded with airplanes as highways on the ground are crowded with automobiles. Different kinds of airplanes fly at different speeds, too. Some small airplanes fly at about 120 miles an hour. Big jet planes can fly at 600 miles an hour. Some military airplanes fly more than 1,200 miles an hour. Dozens of airplanes may be flying over an area at the same time. All have to share the sky in safety.

Radar is a device that allows an air traffic controller to "observe" an airplane as a blip of light on a screen. The blip moves as the airplane moves. Two-way radio lets him talk to the pilot of a plane. An air traffic controller uses these two main ways to keep track of all air traffic in his area.

The highways of the sky are called *airways*. The airways are run from *air route traffic control centers*. The control centers are in big buildings equipped with radar screens, powerful radios, comput-
[120 mph=193 km/hr; 600 mph=966 km/hr; 1,200 mph=1,932 km/hr]

ers, and many telephones. Each controller is in charge of all the airplanes flying in his *sector*, or area. When an airplane is about to leave his sector, he "hands it over" (by radio) to the controller of the next sector. He then tells the pilot to tune his radio to the new controller's frequency.

ATC provides *separation* between airplanes to keep traffic moving smoothly, quickly, and safely. This separation is like keeping all trucks and cars in separate lanes on a highway. Airplanes must be kept apart in three directions—up and down, side to side, and forward and behind.

When one airplane is flying above another, it must stay at least 1,000 feet higher. Controllers help keep these distances by assigning *altitudes*, or *flight levels*, to each airplane. Above 18,000 feet—where the big, fast passenger jets fly— airplanes are kept 2,000 feet apart. When they are side by side, airplanes must keep at a safe distance away from each other. Also, airplanes must usually be kept at least ten minutes' flying time from the airplanes in front and behind that are at the same altitude. In order to speed traffic, a controller may at times reduce the forward-and-behind distance to five minutes when he can see all the airplanes in his sector on his radar screens.
[1,000 ft.=310 m; 18,000 ft.=5,580 m; 2,000 ft.=620 m]

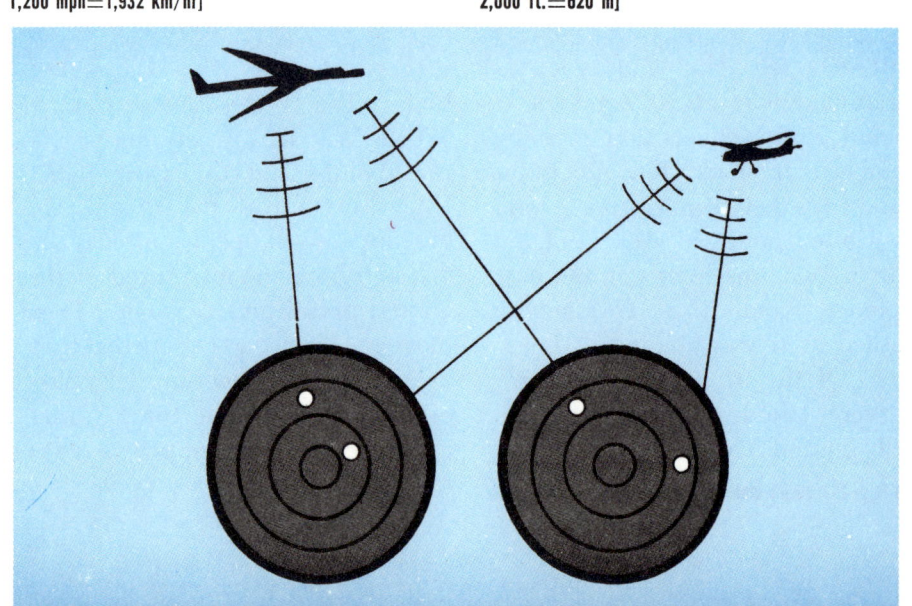

▼ *The Air Route Traffic Control Center in Leesburg, Virginia. These controllers are watching radarscopes in order to spot the planes in the area. The radarscope on the right is used for emergencies, especially when the main screen is crowded by too many planes. Some controllers wear headphones, in case a pilot needs to talk to them.*

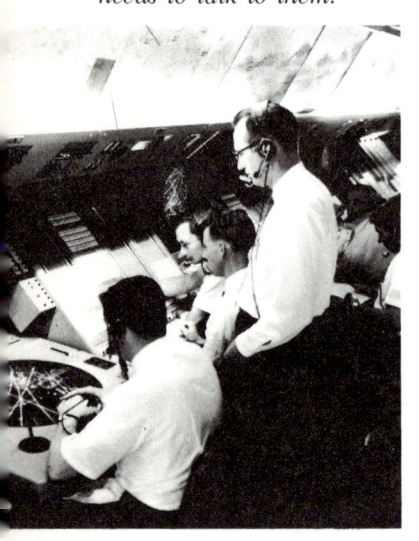

▶ *A radar signal bounced back by an airplane appears on the radar screen as a blip of light. The air traffic controller watching the screen then knows that an airplane is in the area.*

Powerful radar stations along the airways send up *signal patterns* in the shape of a cone, with the small end at ground level. There are enough radar stations along the continental United States airways, so that the cones overlap above 24,000 feet and all high-flying aircraft can be seen. At lower altitudes, planes may fly in spaces that the controllers cannot see on their radar screens. So pilots must make *position reports* over their radios. The pilots tell the controllers at what time they are over the stations, and their altitudes and speeds. A pilot is told to slow down, or hold, if his plane gets too close to an airplane in front of him. To *hold* means to circle the station until the traffic ahead is cleared.

Traffic jams happen at big airports, where different kinds of airplanes are coming in to land from all directions. Thirty miles from an airport all planes must call the *airport traffic control tower*. The control tower takes over from the air route traffic control center. The tower has special radar equipment that can detect all airplanes at all altitudes. The controller in the tower tells each pilot when to land and which runway to use.

The control tower is also in charge of the radar and radio landing aids at the airport. These are called *precision approach radar* (PAR) and *instrument landing systems* (ILS). A skillful pilot can safely land an airplane by using them, just by looking at the instruments in the airplane cockpit. In bad weather or at night, a pilot may not be able to see the runway until he is only 100 feet above it. But with PAR and ILS, he can still land safely.

Air traffic control in the United States is run by the Federal Aviation Administration (FAA), which is part of the U.S. Department of Transportation. The FAA works

[24,000 ft.=7,440 m; 100 ft.=31 m]

with governments of other nations so that air traffic control works the same way all over the world.

**ALABAMA** When Alabama was Indian country, the Alibamu tribe lived along one of its rivers. The name *Alibamu* meant "I clear land." These Indians made clearings in the forest. In the clearings, they raised corn, squash, and beans. White settlers gradually turned *Alibamu* into *Alabama*. The state later took this name.

Alabama is in the Deep South. It is bordered on the west by the state Mississippi, on the east by Georgia, on the north by Tennessee and on the south by Florida and the Gulf of Mexico.

### The Land

Nature has divided the state into two natural parts. One part, northeastern Alabama, is high and hilly. It belongs to the great Appalachian Highland. Trails used for hiking and riding twist through the hills. There are waterfalls and caves to visit and lakes for fishing and swimming. Beautiful flowers and shrubs brighten the woods. Farms here have always been small because the land is not very good.

The rest of Alabama is part of the Gulf Coastal Plain. The plain is

▲ *Imagine many airplanes circling above an airport waiting to land. Or, suppose a pilot cannot see the runway because the weather is too bad. The control tower has special equipment to advise pilots when and how to land and take off.*

# ALABAMA

**State flower**
Camellia
**State bird**
Yellowhammer
**State tree**
Southern pine
**Capital**
Montgomery (142,500 people)
**Area**
51,609 square miles (ranks 29th)
**Population**
3,577,000 people (ranks 21st)
**Statehood**
December 14, 1819 (22nd state admitted)
**Principal river**
Mobile River (formed by Tombigbee and Alabama rivers)
**Highest point**
Cheaha Mountain (2,407 feet)
**Largest city**
Birmingham (308,600 people)

[51,609 sq.mi.=133,667 km²; 2,407 ft.=746 m]

low. In some places, it is almost flat. In others, it is gently rolling. More than half of Alabama is in the coastal plain. Not all of this part is good for farming. Some land is swampy. Some has poor soil. Pine woods cover much of the poorer land. Bald cypress trees grow in the swamps, with gray streamers of Spanish moss hanging from their branches.

Alabama's coastal plain has much good soil. The very best lies in the Black Belt. This strip curves through central Alabama. It is one of the most fertile areas in the world. The soil that gave the belt its name is dark because thickly growing plants decayed in it for hundreds of years. Summers are long and hot in Alabama. Winters are mild. There is usually plenty of rain. Farmers like the climate.

## History

Among the Indians of Alabama were the Creeks, Chickasaws, Choctaws, and Cherokees. The Indians saw Spaniards, Frenchmen, and Englishmen follow one another, in that order. After the American Revolution, the land was given up by the British and became part of the United States. The government made the Indians give up their hunting grounds. Most of them were moved to reservations. Alabama became a state in 1819.

As the Indians moved out, white people and Negroes came in. The whites were farmers. The Negroes were slaves. Together, whites and blacks built up the state.

White men who could not afford to buy good land went into the hills. They did their own work in stony fields. These people made a very poor living. Some white men, though, were rich. They bought land where the soil was good. Their big farms were called *plantations*. The owners, planters, raised cotton. They raised so much that Alabama became known as the "Cotton State." Many planters grew rich. But the men, women, and children who worked in the cotton fields earned nothing. They were slaves.

Alabama left the Union in 1861 and joined the Confederate States of America. Alabama's capital, Montgomery, was also the capital of the Confederacy until the Confederate government moved to Richmond, Virginia. The Civil War ended in defeat for the Confederate States. All slaves were freed. Workers had to be paid. Although they were offered very little, the Negroes went back to the cotton fields because they had no other way to earn a living.

It was bad for Alabama to rely on just cotton. The Negro field hands never made a good living raising it. Neither did white farmers whose farms were small. And in some years, cotton did not sell very well. Such years were hard for everyone, even the plantation owners. By planting only one crop, they allowed cotton to wear out the soil.

An insect, the boll weevil, helped save Alabama and the rest of the South. It destroyed so much cotton every year that farmers began raising a number of other crops. Ala-

▼ *In Alabama, the owners of cotton plantations often had very large houses. This one in Mobile was built in 1830. It is now a museum.*

bama no longer depends on cotton. In the town square of Enterprise, Alabama, stands a monument honoring the boll weevil!

During the 1880s, businessmen began building factories in Alabama. The wages they paid were not high. But factories gave some Alabamians a better living than they could earn on farms. As manufacturing grew, wages were raised.

The poorest people of the state were the Negroes. But they, too, made progress. Black leaders appeared in Alabama. One was Booker T. Washington. Born a Virginia slave, he built Tuskegee Institute, for the education of Negroes. At the institute is the workshop of the Missouri-born Negro scientist, George Washington Carver.

People from Alabama have contributed much to the world. William Gorgas, a U.S. Army doctor, helped stop yellow fever, a disease that almost prevented the building of the Panama Canal. Helen Keller, who as a baby was made deaf and blind by a serious illness, learned to communicate with others. The example of her courage has helped many handicapped people. Georgia-born Martin Luther King, Jr., went from being a minister in Montgomery to winner of the Nobel Peace Prize for his work in civil rights. And scientists at an Alabama university discovered a new chemical element, francium.

### Alabamians at Work

The nickname "Cotton State" no longer fits Alabama. Farmers earn more from broiler chickens, cattle, eggs, and milk products than from cotton and all other field crops put together. Among the field crops, however, cotton still leads. Peanuts and soybeans are about tied in second place. Corn is third.

Agriculture has today lost its first place to manufacturing. Metal production is the leading type of manufacturing. The Birmingham area is

▲ *Beautiful gardens abound in Alabama. This one is part of Bellingrath Gardens in Mobile.*

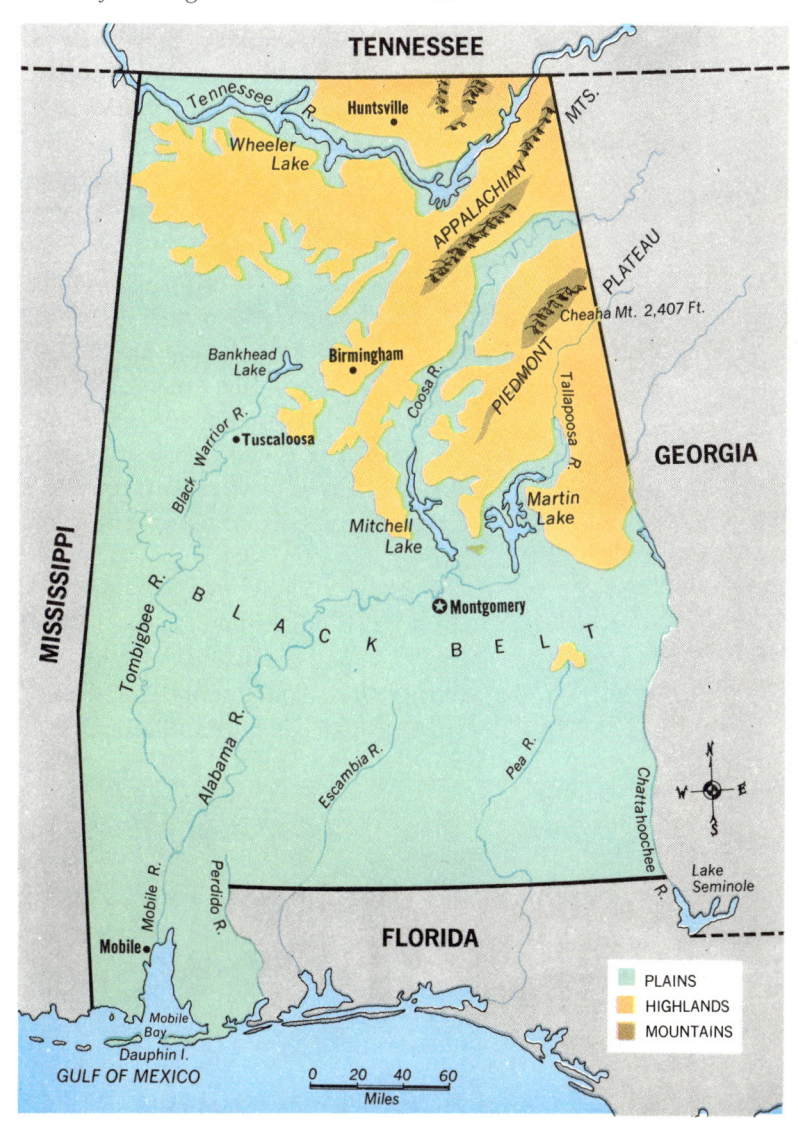

*Alabama's Capitol Building in Montgomery.*

the biggest iron-and-steel center in the South. On top of Red Mountain, overlooking Birmingham, is a tall statue of Vulcan, the Roman god of fire and metalworking. Other products are textiles, chemicals, paper goods, and food.

Manufacturing is aided by Alabama's raw materials. Coal is burned to make iron and steel and to produce electricity, too. Stone is used for building and for making cement. Gasoline, oil, and other products come from petroleum. Timber is made into lumber and paper.

Fishing is important to Alabama. Alabamians haul in several million dollars' worth of seafood every year. Crabs and oysters are taken from Mobile Bay. Boats go out into the Gulf of Mexico for shrimp, sardines, and other fish. Mobile Bay is also a major seaport. Goods from all over the South are shipped around the world from Mobile.

The Space Age brought a new kind of work to Alabama. In 1960 the National Aeronautics and Space Administration (NASA) opened a flight center at Huntsville. Scientists and engineers came there to work on rockets for space flight. They developed the mighty Saturn V that sent Americans to the moon.

ALSO READ: CARVER, GEORGE WASHINGTON; CIVIL RIGHTS; CIVIL WAR; KELLER, HELEN; KING, MARTIN LUTHER, JR.; WASHINGTON, BOOKER T.

*Remember the Alamo! In 1836, Texans fought for their freedom from Mexico at the old mission fort called the Alamo.*

**ALAMO** "Remember the Alamo!" was the Texans' battle cry during their fight for independence from Mexico. Often called the "Cradle of Texas Liberty," the fort of the Alamo in San Antonio was built as the Mission San Antonio de Valero in 1718 by Spanish missionaries. The mission-fortress was later nicknamed "Alamo," the Spanish word for "cottonwood," because of the cottonwoods around it.

San Antonio was part of Mexico in 1835. But Americans living there decided to rebel. A small group of Texas volunteers, led by William Travis, took over the Alamo in late December. Davy Crockett and Jim Bowie, the famous frontiersmen, were among them.

The Mexican General Santa Anna surrounded the Alamo with over 4,000 troops on February 23, 1836. To a man, the 150 men in the fort, plus 32 volunteers, refused to surrender. Fighting against these overwhelming odds, they held out for 13 days until the last man was killed. The only survivors were two women and two children.

This heroic resistance aroused all Texans. Sam Houston led Texas forces to victory against General Santa Anna six weeks later, and Texas won its independence. Many years later, the Alamo was restored. It is now visited by thousands of people each year.

ALSO READ: BOWIE, JIM; CROCKETT, DAVY; HOUSTON, SAM; TEXAS.

**ALARIC (about A.D. 370–410)** A group of German people called the *Goths* lived in the fourth century. The Goths were divided into two branches, the eastern *Ostrogoths* and the western *Visigoths*. Alaric was king of the Visigoths.

Alaric was born on the island of Peuce in the Danube River, now in Rumania. The Roman emperor gave him an army in 394. The next year the Visigoths elected Alaric king. He wanted more power. He and his forces tried first to conquer Greece, but they were driven out.

The Visigoths entered Italy twice to attack Rome, in 408 and 409.

*Alaric, warrior king.*

Rome paid a large ransom and was saved each time. In 410, Alaric made a third try. The Romans refused to give him the land and power he demanded. So he captured Rome, which had not been conquered by enemy forces for almost 800 years. The Visigoths occupied Rome for six days.

Alaric, however, still wanted land where his people could settle in peace. He led them south, planning to go on to Africa. But a storm destroyed their ships. They had to stop in southern Italy, where Alaric, their leader, died.

ALSO READ: ROMAN EMPIRE.

**ALASKA** The name of the largest state in the United States comes from a word used long ago in the Aleutian Islands. These islands lie off the southwestern part of Alaska. Aleuts called the mainland *alakshak*, meaning a land bigger than the islands. And Alaska is a "great land"—over twice the size of the second largest state, Texas.

**The Land**

Alaska can best be described in terms of three main parts.

TUNDRA. The cold, almost treeless plains called *tundra* lie along the western and northern coasts. In winter, the tundra is covered with ice and snow. Flowering plants and mosses appear when summer sunshine melts the ice. But ice underneath the surface does not melt, so the water does not drain off. The land is swampy all summer. The tundra slopes down to the Arctic Ocean north of Brooks Range mountains. Here the tundra is much colder in winter than it is on the west coast.

INTERIOR. The interior part of Alaska lies between two mountain ranges. On the north is Brooks Range. The Alaska Range is on the south. The interior stretches from the western tundra to the border of Canada. It is mostly the Yukon River basin.

Interior Alaska is colder in winter and warmer in summer than land nearer the ocean. Ocean temperature does not change so much as land temperature from summer to winter. Water is warmer than land in winter. It is cooler than land in summer. So winter winds from the ocean warm the land near the coast. And summer ocean winds cool the nearby land. Interior Alaska is not "protected" by the ocean, so its temperature changes much more from summer to winter.

SOUTH. Most of southern Alaska lies near the water. It follows the long southern coast. Southern Alaska may be divided into three sections.

The *southwest* consists of the Alaska Peninsula and many islands. Mount Katmai, a volcano, is near the northern end of the peninsula. This volcano has one of the largest craters in the world. The Valley of Ten Thousand Smokes was formed when Katmai erupted in 1912. Steam rises from thousands of holes that dot the valley floor.

At the eastern end of southern Alaska is the *panhandle*. This narrow strip has the Pacific Ocean on one side and the Coast Mountains on the other. Canada lies beyond

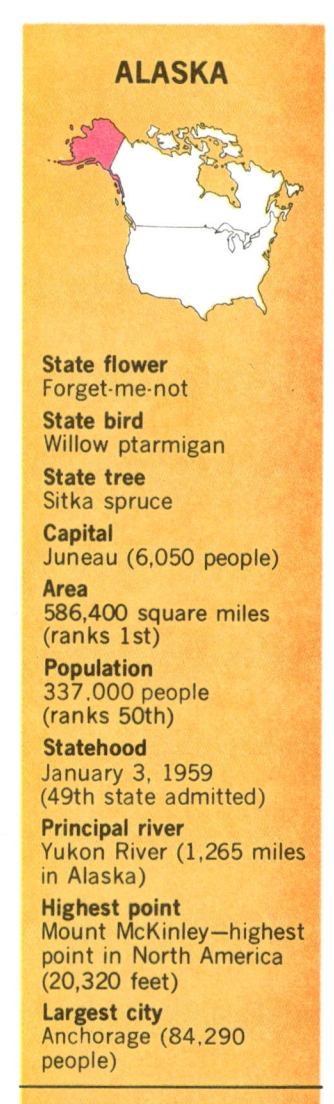

**ALASKA**

**State flower**
Forget-me-not
**State bird**
Willow ptarmigan
**State tree**
Sitka spruce
**Capital**
Juneau (6,050 people)
**Area**
586,400 square miles (ranks 1st)
**Population**
337,000 people (ranks 50th)
**Statehood**
January 3, 1959 (49th state admitted)
**Principal river**
Yukon River (1,265 miles in Alaska)
**Highest point**
Mount McKinley—highest point in North America (20,320 feet)
**Largest city**
Anchorage (84,290 people)

[586,400 sq.mi.=1,518,776 km²; 1,265 mi.=2,037 km; 20,320 ft.=6,299 m]

▲ *Some parts of Alaska have mild weather. Here, snowy mountains surround a beautiful green valley.*

the mountains. Green forests and blue water make the panhandle beautiful. It is a land of mild winters, cool summers, and much rain.

Between the southwest and the panhandle is south-central Alaska. Winters are mild here, too. The Alaska Range keeps out icy winds from the north. And winds blowing over the warm Alaska Current in the ocean raise winter temperatures.

Summers are cool and short in south-central Alaska, but summer daylight is long. (Summer periods of daylight lengthen as you go north.) The extra hours of sunshine make northern crops grow fast. Huge cabbages, turnips, and potatoes grow in the Matanuska Valley. Over half of the crops raised in Alaska come from this one valley.

# ALASKA

## The People

The population is small for such a large state. About one-sixth of the people are non-white. Most of the non-white population are Eskimos and Indians. More than one-third of all Alaskans live in cities and towns.

## History

Alaska was the "front porch" of the Americas 30,000 years ago. At that time, there was probably a land or ice bridge connecting Asia and North America. The Bering Strait flows over it today. The first people to reach the New World crossed from Asia to Alaska, probably looking for food. They were the ancestors of modern American Indians and Eskimos.

Most of the people moved southward. But some stayed in Alaska. The Tlingit Indians, the Aleuts, and the Eskimos of the north were there when the first white men came.

The Russians moved eastward through Asia in the 1600s and 1700s. From eastern Siberia they sailed across the short stretch of water to Alaska. They named the region *Russian America*.

The Russians came in search of furs. They fought the Eskimo and Indian hunters and killed a great many of them. Russia's czar (king) was in Moscow, half a world away. He found that he could not control his fur traders. Something else also worried him—Britain might capture Russian America. The land was too far away for the czar to defend.

He sold Russian America to the United States in 1867. The price was 7,200,000 dollars—less than 2 cents an acre! Alaska was truly a bargain. But many Americans did not think so at the time. They said that Secretary of State William H. Seward had wasted government money buying an "icebox." Many people called Alaska "Seward's Folly." They wondered how the huge

[2 cents an acre=$4.94/km²]

northern land could be governed.

The question was a fair one. For the next 45 years Washington, D.C., neglected Alaska. The U.S. government could not control the rough men who sailed there to get furs, fish, copper, and gold. At last Congress decided to give Alaskans a government of their own. Alaska was made a United States *territory* in 1912. As a territory, its governor was chosen by the President. Alaskans elected their lawmakers. Things went better from then on. But many Alaskans were not satisfied. They wanted the territory to be a state. Their wish was granted in 1959.

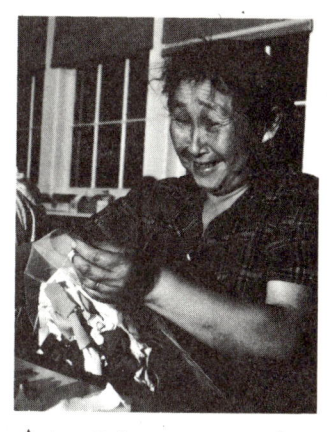

## Alaskans at Work

This state differs from the other 49 in several ways. Because it is so far north, little farming is done. Nearly 97 percent of Alaska's land is owned by the United States Government. Many people who live in Alaska are members of the armed forces, and their families.

Manufacturing is the leading industry in Alaska. Food items, especially canned and frozen fish and crabs, head the list. Lumber

▲ *An Eskimo woman busy making a hat for a hat making contest in Nunapitchuk, Alaska.*

▼ *Kodiak bears are brown bears of Alaska, especially of Kodiak Island. These large bears eat salmon from the cold rivers.*

and other wood products are second on the list of manufactured goods.

Underground resources bring in about half as much money as manufacturing. Petroleum comes first. Coal and gold follow it. Most of the petroleum comes from wells in southern Alaska. But geologists have found a rich field north of Brooks Range. Oilmen are now working on the Arctic tundra.

Another industry is tourism. Every summer thousands of people visit Alaska. Many come by plane. Others arrive by boat. They want to see the beautiful coast of the panhandle. A few motorists drive the 1,500-mile-long Alcan Highway that winds through Canada into Alaska. Tourists spend millions of dollars yearly for vacations in the "great land."

ALSO READ: ALEUT INDIANS; ARCTIC; ESKIMOS; INDIANS, AMERICAN.

[1,500 mi.=2,415 km]

▲ *Two farm women of Albania.*

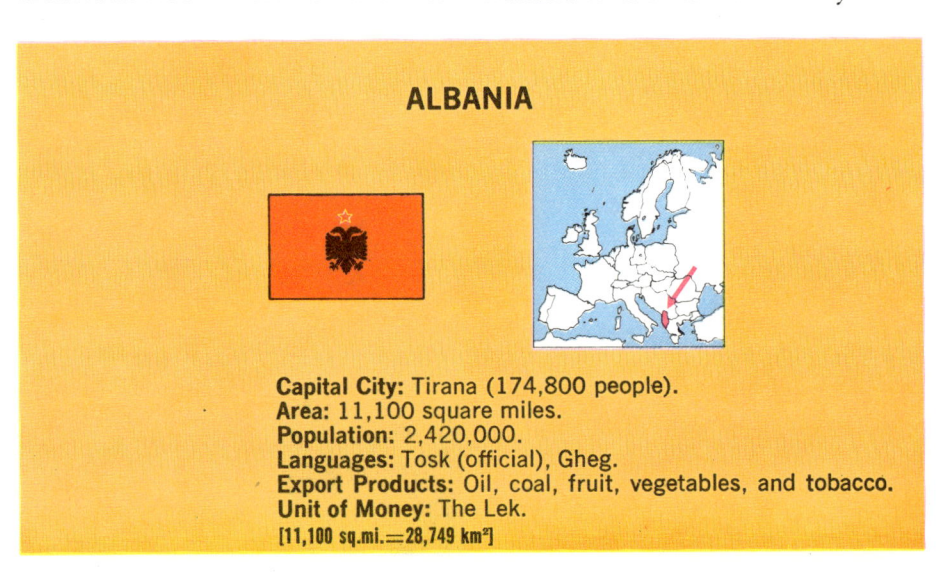

**ALBANIA** The very mountainous country north of Greece is Albania, the smallest Communist nation. Green valleys with many farming villages lie between rugged mountains. The larger towns can be reached by car. But pack animals are the only means of transportation to many mountain villages. In the mountains, the climate is moderate. But in summer it is hot on the beautiful sand beaches along the Adriatic Sea. (See the map with the article on EUROPE.)

Many women wear traditional baggy trousers and veils. Men often wear white felt caps, homespun breeches, and embroidered jackets. Albanians are known for their beautiful embroidery.

Foreign conquerors ruled Albania for many centuries. They came from the Italian peninsula, the Balkans, and the Middle East. Albania's national hero, Scanderbeg, fought fierce battles against the Turks in the fifteenth century. But the Turks conquered Albania in 1468 after Scanderbeg died. They made the country part of their territory, the Ottoman Empire. The Turks ruled Albania for more than 400 years. Today two-thirds of the Albanian people follow Islam, a religion brought by the Turks. The rest are Orthodox Christians and Roman Catholics.

In 1912 the Albanians finally overthrew the Turks and became independent. But Italian soldiers occupied Albania for four years during World War II. German troops later replaced the Italians. The Communist Party took over in 1946. It created a new government, calling Albania a "people's republic."

Albania is a poor country. Most Albanians are farmers. They raise

**ALBANIA**

**Capital City:** Tirana (174,800 people).
**Area:** 11,100 square miles.
**Population:** 2,420,000.
**Languages:** Tosk (official), Gheg.
**Export Products:** Oil, coal, fruit, vegetables, and tobacco.
**Unit of Money:** The Lek.
[11,100 sq.mi.=28,749 km²]

tobacco, livestock, grain, fruits, and vegetables. Few own their land. Most farms are owned by the government. A few Albanians are miners or fishermen. The country trades mostly with other Communist countries, especially China.

ALSO READ: COMMUNISM, EUROPE, OTTOMAN EMPIRE.

**ALBATROSS** see SEABIRDS.

**ALBERTA** Alberta is a western, or prairie, province of Canada. In both area (about the size of Texas) and population, it is the fourth largest of the ten Canadian provinces. Its principal cities are Edmonton (the capital), Calgary, Lethbridge, Red Deer, and Medicine Hat (named for the cap worn by an Indian medicine man). The province is named after a daughter of Queen Victoria.

The eastern side of Alberta has gently rolling prairie. The land builds up through foothills to the towering Rocky Mountains that form the province's border with British Columbia. The southern part consists of treeless plains, and is one of the few sections of Canada with so little rainfall that it requires irrigation to keep its farmlands blooming. The central part is known as the *parklands*, because of its many small lakes, rivers, and forests. A feature of the province's winter climate is a warm wind called a *chinook*, which may change the temperature from 40° F below zero [–40° C] to 40° F [4° C] above in 2 hours.

### History
Some of the oldest traces of life in Canada are found in Alberta. The Drumheller Valley is famous as a dinosaur burial ground. Millions of years ago the region must have been a tropical jungle. Later, Alberta was covered by a polar ice cap. As the ice retreated, hardy Indian settlers arrived from Alaska. Their descendants, the Sarcee and Blackfoot tribes of the Athapascan and Algonkian families, still live in Alberta. The first Europeans to arrive in the Canadian West were adventurers and fur traders from the Hudson's Bay Company of England.

Alberta became part of the new Dominion of Canada in 1870. The Royal Canadian Mounted Police established outposts and forts, and the railway soon arrived from the East. Cattle ranching began. The land was ideal for growing a new type of wheat called *Marquis*. In 1905, Alberta became a province.

### Industries
Coal, oil, and natural gas are found in Alberta in abundance. One-third of all Albertans earn their living from oil production and mining. No one yet knows the extent of Alberta's oil resources, but a deposit near Lake Athabasca in the north is thought to contain the world's largest single reserve. Alberta petroleum is sent to much of Canada and the western United States.

Ranching and farming rank second in importance, and Alberta is Canada's major supplier of meat. Calgary is the cowboy capital of Canada, and every July plays host to the world's largest "stampede," or rodeo, with hundreds of contests of bronco-busting, steer-riding, and chuckwagon races.

Many of the beautiful areas of Alberta have been set aside as national parks. One of the most popular is Banff National Park. Wood

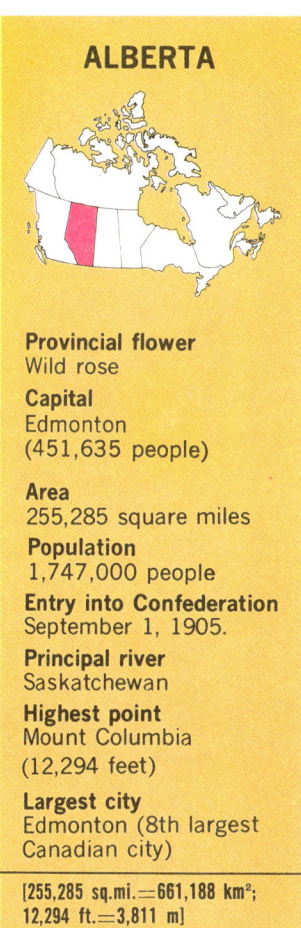

---

**ALBERTA**

**Provincial flower**
Wild rose

**Capital**
Edmonton
(451,635 people)

**Area**
255,285 square miles

**Population**
1,747,000 people

**Entry into Confederation**
September 1, 1905.

**Principal river**
Saskatchewan

**Highest point**
Mount Columbia
(12,294 feet)

**Largest city**
Edmonton (8th largest Canadian city)

[255,285 sq.mi.=661,188 km²; 12,294 ft.=3,811 m]

▼ *People who love nature would be happy here. This is part of Banff National Park in Alberta.*

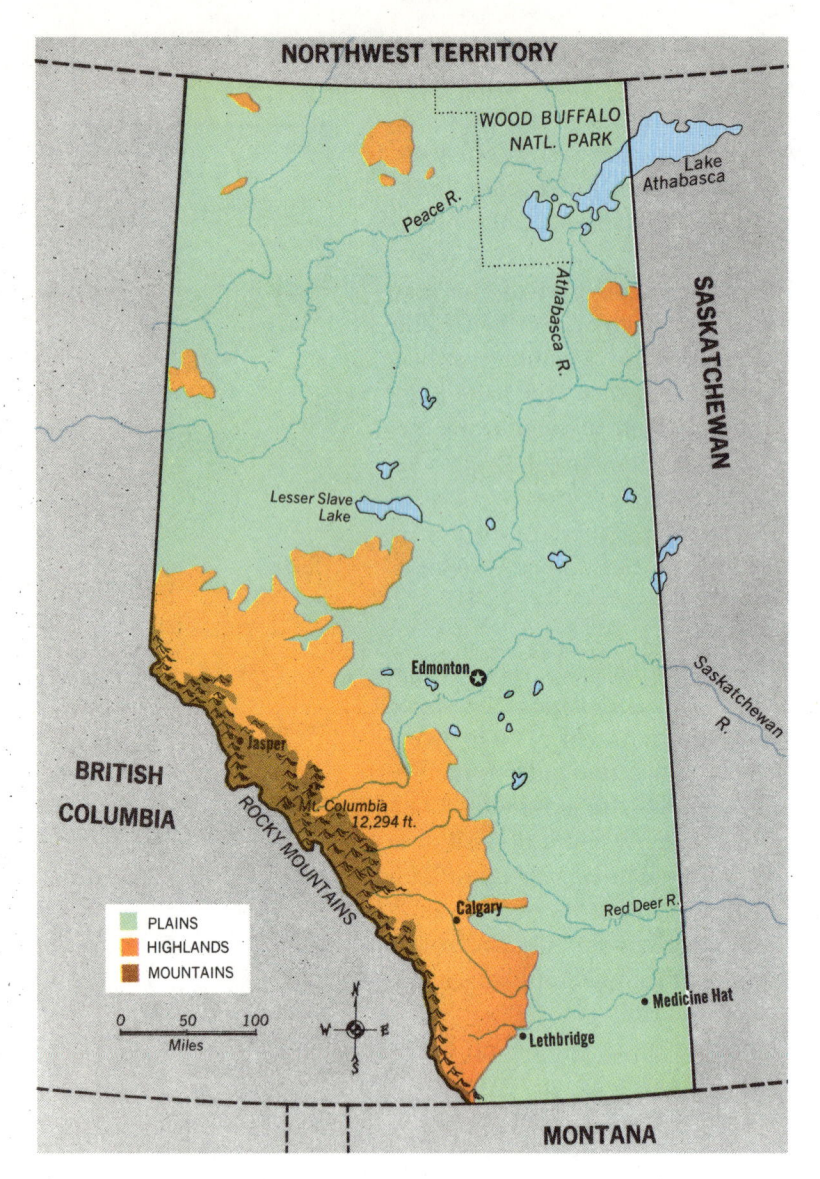

[17,300 sq.mi.=44,807 km²]

▼ An albino rabbit has white fur and pink eyes and ears.

Buffalo Park in the north, at 17,300 square miles, is the largest national park in the world. It is the home of the biggest herds of bison in North America, and is the nesting ground of the rare whooping cranes, which migrate to Alberta from southern Texas each year.

ALSO READ: CANADA, NATIONAL PARK.

**ALBINO** Animals, including human beings, are sometimes born with no coloring matter in their skin, hair, or eyes. They are albinos. White hair, pink eyes, and pinkish skin mark the albino.

Coloring matter in normal people and animals is called *pigment*. Pigments carry many colors: the yellow of a canary's wings, the stripes of zebras, the green of a cat's eyes. *Melanin,* a dark pigment, is the main coloring material of skin. A blonde person has less melanin than a Negro person. An albino's skin and eyes have no melanin. They look pink because blood vessels show through. Human albinos must wear dark glasses in the sun, because their eyes have no pigment for protection from strong light. An albino's hair is snow white. Look at the rabbit in the photograph. What color are his eyes?

Not all white animals are pure albinos. *Partial* albinos are more common. Most white horses, for example, have some coloring, perhaps blue eyes or a dark patch of skin. Certain black-and-yellow butterflies sometimes have white offspring, but they will have black markings on their wings. Rare white tigers have darkish stripes.

Albinos inherit their colorless condition from their ancestors, through *genes*, tiny parts of body cells. Genes control what a living thing inherits from its parents. An albino parent may produce normal young, and the young may later produce albinos. It may not happen again for many, many generations.

Plants can also produce albinos. They lack chlorophyll, a green material that makes food for the plant. Without food, albino plants quickly die.

ALSO READ: GENETICS, PHOTOSYNTHESIS, SKIN.

**ALCHEMY** The modern science of chemistry is only about 200 years old. For thousands of years, the study of metals and elements was a strange mixture of science and magic known as *alchemy*. It was practiced in ancient times by the Egyptians, Greeks, and Romans. Greek alchemists first introduced the belief that all matter is a mixture of four basic elements—air, earth, fire, and water. They thought that every form of matter could be

# ALCHEMY

made by mixing these four elements in the right amounts. From the Greeks and Romans, the study of alchemy reached the Arabs, probably about the eighth century. Later, in the Middle Ages, it reached Europe.

The men who practiced alchemy had three main goals. First, they wanted to change inexpensive common metals, such as lead, into gold, which they considered to be the "perfect" metal. Second, they wanted to find a medicine that would cure all diseases. And third, they wanted to make a substance that would make old people young and allow them to live forever. Alchemists believed that there was a magical substance, called the *philosopher's stone*, that could do these three things. Many strange recipes were invented in an effort to make this "stone." Some alchemists cooked "witches' brews," using ingredients such as hairs, bats' wings, and spiders. Of course, these brews never succeeded in curing sick people. Nor did the alchemists ever find a way to make gold from other metals. But some of their experiments led to the discovery of new elements, such as phosphorus, used today to make products such as matches, fertilizers, and detergents. Alchemists also invented some useful medicines.

At the end of the 1700s, the practice of alchemy began to fade. People no longer believed that the philosophers' stone existed. They began to see that many of the claims made by the alchemists were not based on scientific facts. But

◀ *Can people be made to live forever? Can tin be turned into gold? The alchemists of the Middle Ages thought they could do these things. Their work led to the modern science of chemistry.*

even though many of the alchemists' ideas were wrong, some of their discoveries helped pave the way for the development of modern chemistry.

ALSO READ: CHEMISTRY, ELEMENT, METAL, SCIENCE.

**ALCOHOL** see DISTILLATION.

**ALCOHOLIC BEVERAGE** Man probably made the first alcoholic beverage by accident, thousands of years ago. He might have kept some grape juice standing too long, before drinking it. When he finally drank the juice, it probably tasted sour and made him feel dizzy.

What this man discovered was a chemical process called *fermentation*. Fermentation occurs when micro-organisms, such as bacteria, yeast, and mold, are added to certain plant and animal substances. The two major products of fermentation are carbon dioxide, a gas, and alcohol, a colorless liquid. When prehistoric man let his grape juice stand too long, yeast spores fell into it from the air and grew in the juice. The juice fermented into an alcoholic beverage which has come to be called *wine*.

The manufacture of alcoholic beverages is one of the biggest industries today. Among the beverages made are beer, wine, whisky, gin, rum, and bourbon. Beer is made from cereal grains, and wine is made from fruits. Whisky (also called *Scotch*) is made from barley, gin is made from fermented grain flavored with juniper berries, and bourbon is made from corn. Fermented molasses produces rum.

Some people can drink alcoholic beverages without serious or long-lasting damage to their health. There are other people, however, who should never drink alcohol because they are victims of *alcoholism*, one of the major diseases in the United States. There are almost five million alcoholics in the U.S. An alcoholic is a person who cannot stop himself from drinking alcohol. He becomes addicted to alcohol.

Alcohol acts as a *depressant* on the body. A depressant dulls the centers of the brain that control speech, emotions, judgment, and coordination of movement. The depressant effects of alcohol become dangerous when a person drives an automobile after drinking alcoholic beverages. Alcohol may interfere with a driver's judgment, blur his vision, and destroy his muscle coordination. The National Safety Council has found that one out of five drivers who are in car accidents that kill people, has been drinking before driving.

Alcoholics Anonymous (A.A.) is an organization that has helped thousands of alcoholics conquer their addiction. The A.A. holds meetings where alcoholics help each other solve their problems.

ALSO READ: ADDICTION, DISTILLATION, FERMENTATION, YEAST.

▲ *Beer is a popular alcoholic beverage. Beer ferments in wooden vats as part of the brewing process.*

**ALCOTT, LOUISA MAY (1832-1888)** *Little Women*, the story of a New England family during the Civil War, was written by Louisa May Alcott. She wrote the story about her own family. She was Jo, and her real-life sisters—May, Elizabeth, and Anna—were the other March sisters—Meg, Beth, and Amy.

Louisa May Alcott was born in Pennsylvania, but she lived most of her life in Massachusetts. "Orchard House" in Concord, Massachusetts, where she sometimes wrote, is open to the public. Ralph Waldo Emerson and Henry David Thoreau, famous writers, were the Alcotts' friends. They sometimes taught Louisa and her sisters.

Louisa's father, Amos Bronson Alcott, was a writer and teacher, too. He had ideas about education that most people of that time did not accept. These ideas included a good education for girls. He was a very good teacher, but he did not earn much money. So Louisa opened a school when she was 16.

Louisa worked hard as a nurse during the Civil War. The letters she wrote about her experiences were published, and her name became known to the public. Money she earned from *Little Women* gave her a chance to spend time working in the women's suffrage movement (for voting) and in the temperance movement (against drinking alcoholic beverages).

Some of Louisa May Alcott's other well-loved books are *Little Men, Jo's Boys, Eight Cousins,* and *Under the Lilacs.*

ALSO READ: EMERSON, RALPH WALDO; THOREAU, HENRY DAVID.

**ALDRIN, EDWIN (born 1930)** Edwin "Buzz" Aldrin was the second man to walk on the moon. He was the pilot of *Eagle,* the Apollo 11 lunar module that carried Neil Armstrong and him to the bleak surface of the moon, in July, 1969.

Born in Glen Ridge, New Jersey, Aldrin is the only son of a United States Army officer. Aldrin graduated third in his class at West Point, the U.S. Military Academy. He joined the Air Force and became a jet pilot in the Korean War.

Buzz Aldrin studied space travel at the Massachusetts Institute of Technology, where he earned a doctor of science degree in astronautics. He became an expert in rendezvous and docking—the meeting and joining together of two craft moving through space. Aldrin's knowledge of rendezvous and docking techniques contributed to the success of the Apollo program.

Aldrin began astronaut training in 1964. His first space trip was on the Gemini 12, during which he "walked" in space outside his spacecraft for 5½ hours. Aldrin became Commander of the Air Force Test Pilot School in 1971.

ALSO READ: APOLLO, ASTRONAUT, MOON, SPACE TRAVEL.

**ALEUT INDIANS** The Aleutian Islands, off the Alaskan Coast, are the home of the Aleut Indians. The Aleuts call the islands the "birthplace of the winds" because strong, hurricane-like winds often blow there. Some Aleuts also live on the Pribilof Islands, other islands nearby, and the Alaskan peninsula.

For centuries, the hardy Aleuts used the Pacific Ocean as their source of all things. The Aleuts' boats were *kayaks* and *umiaks,* made of animal skins sewn together by Aleut women and stretched over a frame made of bone. There are no trees on the islands from which to make a wooden boat. The Aleuts

▲*Louisa May Alcott wrote* Little Women. *It was the story of the four March sisters—Meg, Jo, Beth, and Amy.*

▼*Edwin "Buzz" Aldrin, the second man to walk on the moon.*

used poison-tipped harpoons to kill whales and fish. They ate the whale meat and used whale blubber to make fuel for their stone lamps. These lamps gave heat and light to their homes, and were even used to cook food. The Aleuts' homes were holes dug in the ground and covered with sod, driftwood, and whale bones.

The Aleuts are closely related to the Eskimos of Alaska. But the Aleutian language and customs are different from the Eskimos'. The Aleuts' ancestors wore long garments made of bird skin, with feathers turned to the inside for warmth. They also wore light raincoats with pointed hoods, made from strips of seal intestines and decorated with bird feathers. The Aleut women once sewed beautiful, colorful clothing, using tiny sewing needles made of bird bones. The women also wove baskets of interesting designs out of beach grass and wild rye.

About 30,000 Aleut Indians were living on the Aleutian Islands and the Alaskan mainland when the Russian traders arrived in 1741 and started using the Indians to catch sea otters. Only about 1,200 pure-blooded Aleuts are living today.

Great numbers of the Aleuts were killed in massacres, or died from diseases brought by the white man, such as smallpox and tuberculosis. Marriages between white men and Indians also reduced the number of full-blooded Aleuts. Some Russians married Aleuts, so many of the Indians today have Russian names and are members of the Russian Orthodox Church.

ALSO READ: ALASKA; INDIANS, AMERICAN; ESKIMO.

## ALEXANDER THE GREAT (356–323 B.C.)

Alexander the Great was a mighty king and conqueror. He was one of the greatest military geniuses the world has ever known.

He was born in Pella, Macedonia. Alexander grew to be a handsome, brilliant man. Aristotle, the famous philosopher, came from Greece to teach him geography, politics, literature, medicine, and science. Alexander's father, King Philip II of Macedon, taught him to plan and win battles.

The young prince became king when he was 20. He then began the series of marches that continued until he ruled almost all of the then-known world. On his great war horse, Bucephalus, he first took

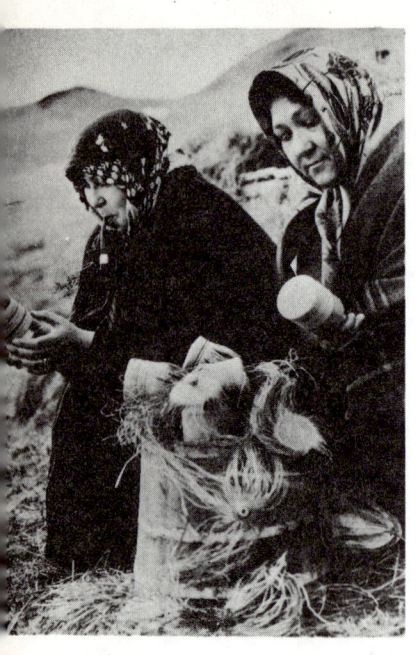

▲ *Aleut women on Attu Island in the Pacific Ocean weave some of the finest baskets in the world.*

▼ *Alexander the Great was a great conqueror of long ago. This section of a mosaic shows him in battle on his horse, Bucephalus.*

over Greece. He went on to conquer all of civilized Europe, Egypt, and then India. On his way he crushed the Persian Empire, and was made king of Egypt and Asia. He and his troops traveled over 11,000 miles. He spread Greek customs and ideas wherever he went.

In India his men refused to go farther. They were tired and frightened, and wanted to go home. Worn out, Alexander agreed to turn back. He died of fever in Babylon, at the early age of 33, but his burning desire for power and glory had been fulfilled.

ALSO READ: ANCIENT CIVILIZATIONS, MACEDONIA.

[11,000 mi.=17,710 km]

**ALFRED THE GREAT** (849?-899) Alfred was the king of Wessex, the southernmost of four kingdoms that became England. He is remembered as "the Great" because he led his people, the West Saxons, against the Danes—who had invaded Wessex—and defeated them.

Alfred became king in 871, after his father and three brothers had all ruled and died. Alfred, as a prince, had helped fight off the invading Danes. As king, he led an army against them. The mightiest Danish invasion came in 877, when King Guthrum landed in Wessex with his army. Alfred lost a battle to Guthrum, and went into hiding. While in hiding, Alfred made new plans for battle, and he defeated the Danes in 878.

Alfred built ships and towers along the coast to fight off the Danish invaders, should they break the peace. The Danish did start trouble again, in 886. Alfred once again defeated them, and also took over London. He drove the Danes from southern England in 897.

Alfred believed in the importance of education. He helped translate several books from Latin into Anglo-Saxon (Old English). He asked teachers from Wales and the European continent to come to his kingdom to teach. He also set up a school, and encouraged the development of arts and industries.

ALSO READ: ENGLISH HISTORY, VIKINGS.

**ALGAE** The slimy green scum that often floats on shallow lakes or ponds is a kind of algae, the simplest of plants. *Algae* is the plural form of the word *alga*. The plural form is usually used. There are many kinds of algae. These plants grow on land in damp places as well as water. Sometimes they grow attached to rocks or stones along the shore or way out at sea and are called *seaweeds*. They grow on other plants, on wood, turtles, water fleas, and even within plants and animals. Much of the green stuff in an aquarium is algae.

Some algae are so small that a thousand of them will fit on the head of a pin. Others are large, stretching for hundreds of feet. Certain small, fresh- and salt-water algae, called *diatoms*, are single cells with "glassy" outer walls made of silica. Diatoms are found in plankton and are the major food of many water animals.

## Algae Groups

All algae contain a pigment called *chlorophyll*, which gives plants their green color. But some algae contain other pigments that hide the green color. Although algae are plants, some of them can move about. They do this by sliding, twisting, gliding, or by floating with currents.

Most algae can be put in one of four groups according to their color —blue-green, green, brown, and red.

Blue-green algae, such as the pond scum in the photograph, are cells with no definite *nuclei* (cell centers). Cells of green algae have definite nuclei. Green algae grow in fresh and salt water, or in any place that is light, moist, and cool. Green

[100 ft.=31 m]

▲ *Alfred the Great.*

▲ *This pond scum is a type of blue-green algae.*

▼ *A drawing of the brown alga, bladder wrack. At the ends of the branches or "fronds" are bladders filled with air.*

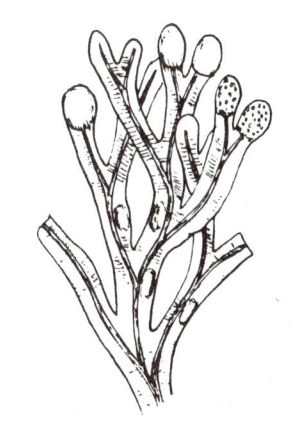

algae make up the largest of the four main kinds of algae. *Kelp*, a seaweed, is a brown alga. Kelp is sometimes attached to rocks near the shore. Some forms of brown algae are so small that they can be seen only with a microscope. Others are more than 200 feet long. Red algae can be found in oceans, especially in warm seas. Coral reefs are formed partly from red algae.

**Useful Algae**

Algae are food for fish and other animals. Even humans use algae as food. A single tablespoon of the alga called *chlorella* has as much protein as an ounce of steak. Chlorella also contains vitamins, fats, and starches. Scientists are working on ways to improve the flavor of chlorella so that people will want to use it as food.

The Japanese have made soup, noodles, tea, bread, and ice cream from kelp and other kinds of algae. The bread is pale green. So is the ice cream. But all these foods taste good. Algae are also used in food in the United States. Puddings thicken because of a product called *agar*, which comes from algae.

Why should people eat algae? For one thing, man may need new foods before very long. The number of people is growing faster than the food supply in many parts of the world. Science must find new foods. Some of these new foods may come from the plentiful supply of algae.

You can make algae cookies. Mix two cups of cake flour, one-half cup of sugar, one-quarter pound of butter, and two teaspoons of chlorella. An adult may help you find chlorella at a store. Roll the mixture flat and cut out shapes with the top of a glass or with cookie cutters. Put the uncooked cookies on a greased pan. Bake them at 375° F [191° C] for about 8 minutes or until the edges turn brown.

ALSO READ: CELL, FOOD WEB, PLANT, PLANT KINGDOM.

**ALGEBRA** (1) What number would you add to 5 to get 7? $5 + \Box = 7$.

(2) What number would you multiply by 3 to get 6? $\Box \times 3 = 6$.

(3) What number would you subtract from 5 to get 3? $5 - \Box = 3$.

In each of these examples, the correct number is 2. In (1), $5 + \boxed{2} = 7$; in (2), $\boxed{2} \times 3 = 6$; and in (3), $5 - \boxed{2} = 3$. Although you may not have known it, you were doing problems in algebra.

Several symbols, $+$, $\times$, $-$, $\Box$, and $=$, are used in these problems. Symbols are a quick, easy way of getting across an idea. Algebra is often called the study of mathematical symbols.

Two of these symbols are very important. One is the symbol $=$. This symbol means "is equal to." It means that everything on the left of the symbol "is equal to" everything on the right of it. When the symbol $=$ is used, the group of symbols and numbers is called an *equation*.

The other important symbol is $\Box$. You didn't know what number went in the box when you began the problem. The correct number was *not known* to you. The symbol $\Box$ in the examples is called an *unknown* for this reason. The problem was to find the *unknown number*. The symbol for an unknown is not usually a box. It is usually a letter, such as $x$, $t$, or $v$. Problem (1) written with a letter instead of a box would look like this: $5 + x = 7$. The mathematician knows that $x$ stands for an unknown number. To solve the problem, he has to find a number to use for $x$ that will make the equation true. So algebra can also be the study of rules that help you find an unknown number.

**How Algebra Is Used**

Here is an example of how algebra can be used to help you solve mathematical problems. Suppose you want to see a movie that be-

[200 ft.=62 m]

▲ *Two types of algae are clinging to this rock on the coast of New York. One is a type of green algae, called* sea lettuce. *The other is a brown alga, called* bladder wrack.

gins at three o'clock. You plan to ride your bicycle. The theater is 10 miles away, and you ride at a speed of 5 miles an hour.

The unknown number is *t*, the time you need to ride to the theater. The equation is: $10 = 5 \times t$, or, the distance (10 miles) is equal to your speed (5 miles an hour) multiplied by the unknown *t* (time required). At what time would you have to leave home?

This is a simple example, but algebra problems can be more difficult. Scientists often use algebraic equations in their work. The unknown might be how much fuel to put in a rocket, or how many seeds to plant in a cornfield.

**History of Algebra**

One of the oldest pieces of writing ever found is about algebra. The writing was carved on stone thousands of years ago by an Egyptian named Ahmes. The equation written on the stone is $\frac{x}{7} + x = 19$.

It took a long time for the study of algebra to progress. Greeks, Indians, Persians, and others knew a little about algebra. The Arabs learned more about algebra than any other people. An Arab mathematician wrote a book in 825, called *Hisab al-jabr w' almuqabalah,* meaning "the science of equations." We get our word "algebra" from the *al-jabr w'* in the title.

The Frenchman, Francois Vieta (1540–1603), is known as the "father of modern algebra." He collected all the known writings on algebra, and added many new ways to prove that algebraic equations are true. Since Vieta's time, algebra has grown and changed. Mathematicians today use many different kinds of algebra to solve many different kinds of problems. All have one thing in common—they are concerned with symbols and the rules for using them.

ALSO READ: ARITHMETIC, MATHEMATICS, NUMBER.

**ALGER, HORATIO, JR.** (1834–1899) "Poor but honest boy works hard to win fame and fortune." This "rags-to-riches" idea made Horatio Alger, Jr., one of America's most popular writers of novels in the nineteenth century.

Alger was born in Revere, Massachusetts. His family expected him to follow in his father's footsteps as a Unitarian minister. But he had plans of his own. After graduation from Harvard, Horatio traveled, and then worked as a private teacher and as a newspaperman. He returned to Massachusetts after several years, and gave in to his family's wishes. He became a Unitarian minister in 1864. Two years later, he moved to New York City and became the chaplain of the Newsboy's Lodging House, a home for orphans and runaway boys. The ideas for the stories that later made Alger famous came from the young people at the home. His first successful book was *Ragged Dick,* published in 1867. His later books—over a hundred in all—included *Sink or Swim, Do or Die,* and *Luck and Pluck.* These stories, showing that anyone could make good if he tried hard enough, fired the imagination of readers all over America.

ALSO READ: CHILDREN'S LITERATURE.

**ALGERIA** The African nation of Algeria covers a very large area. It is the second largest country in Africa—only Sudan has a larger area—and is one-fourth the size of the United States. It is bordered by seven other countries and the Mediterranean Sea. The Sahara Desert covers most of Algeria. Few people live in the vast region of rocky plains and great sand dunes, where rain may not fall for years. (See the map with the article on AFRICA.)

The people of the Sahara are nomads, wandering from oasis to oasis, caring for their goats and camels and living in animal-skin tents. But most Algerians are crowded into the

▲ *Horatio Alger, Jr., U.S. author.*

▲ *The Ragged Dick Series tell the stories of hardworking boys who lived a century ago. Alger's books about their adventures and success sold millions of copies.*

# ALGONKIAN

▲ *The entrance to the old part of the city of Algiers called the Casbah. The Casbah is named after an old fortress that stands in this part of the city.*

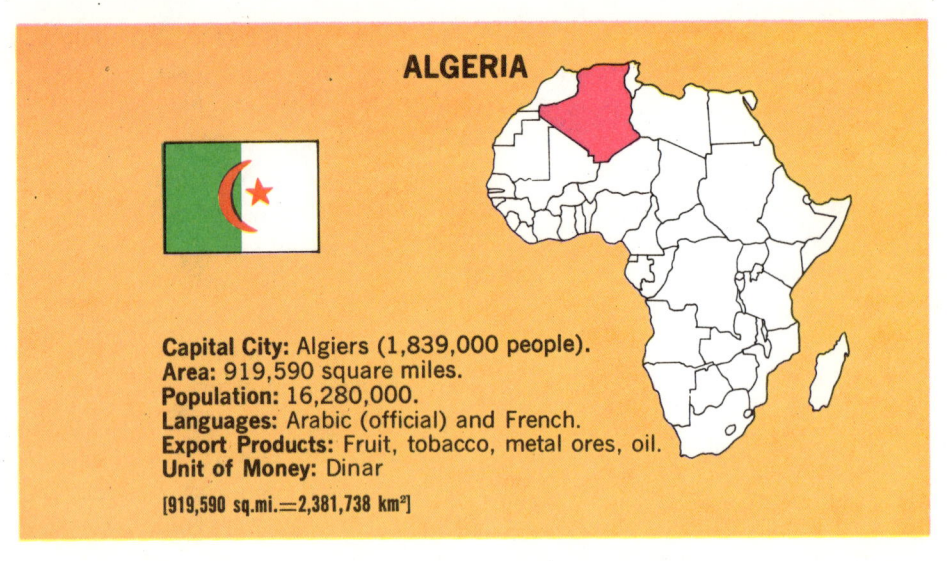

**ALGERIA**

**Capital City:** Algiers (1,839,000 people).
**Area:** 919,590 square miles.
**Population:** 16,280,000.
**Languages:** Arabic (official) and French.
**Export Products:** Fruit, tobacco, metal ores, oil.
**Unit of Money:** Dinar

[919,590 sq.mi.=2,381,738 km²]

narrow strip of land along the Mediterranean Sea. Algiers is the largest city and port, and the nation's capital. The first known settlers of the region were the ancient Berbers. However, Arabs conquered the land about a thousand years ago, and most Algerians are now Arabo-Berbers, who speak Arabic and follow the religion of Islam. A few pure-blooded Berbers still live in Algeria. They cling to old language and customs.

Many nations have controlled Algeria. It was called Numidia under ancient Roman rule. Arabs seized the country later on, then the Turks in the 1500s. The French captured Algeria in 1830, to stop pirates who hid there. The French stayed and slowly gained control of the whole country. The Algerians grew unhappy with French control, especially after World War II. They began to rebel in 1954. The Algerians and the French fought for eight years in one of the most bitter and bloody revolutions in history. More than 250,000 people died before Algeria won independence in 1962.

ALSO READ: AFRICA, BARBARY COAST, SAHARA DESERT.

**ALGONKIAN** Algonkian is a family of languages used by a large number of North American Indian tribes. The name is also spelled *Algonquian*. Algonkian-speaking Indians moved from Alaska to eastern Canada and the northern United States sometime before 3000 B.C. Each tribe adapted to its new surroundings. Tribes in Canada and New England hunted deer and moose, wore buckskins, and lived in bark-covered tepees or wigwams. New England tribes also learned to tap the sweet sap from sugar maple trees. Those in marshy regions near the Great Lakes gathered wild rice.

Algonkian-speaking people along the eastern seaboard met the white men who sailed ships from Europe

▼ *A warrior, dressed in eagle feather warbonnet, of the Blackfeet, an Algonkian-speaking tribe of Great Plains Indians.*

to settle the New World. The Indians taught the colonists how to plant corn, pumpkins, and squash; bake clams; make canoes; use seaweed for fertilizer, and even how to smoke tobacco. The Indians made it possible for the colonists to survive in the new land.

Algonkian-speaking tribes in the Northeast included the Delaware, Menominee, Illinois, Narraganset, Mahican, and Powhatan. Other Algonkian-speaking Indians lived in the Great Plains. They included the Arapaho, Blackfoot, and Cheyenne. The Naskapi, Cree, Ojibwa, Montagnais, and Algonkin tribes roamed eastern Canada. The Algonkin tribe, which gave its name to this language family, lived along the Ottawa River. They are now often called Ottawa Indians.

You may not realize it, but you already know some Algonkian words. The English colonists borrowed *raccoon*, *pecan*, and *squash* from Algonkian-speaking Indians, for example. Many American place names come from Algonkian words, too. Some of these names are Manhattan, Chicago, Illinois, Massachusetts, Mississippi, and Wisconsin.

ALSO READ: INDIANS, AMERICAN.

**ALIMENTARY CANAL** see DIGESTION.

**ALLEN, ETHAN** (1738–1789) Ethan Allen was a hero of the American Revolution. He was born on a Connecticut farm, and grew up on the rugged colonial frontier. He was an eager student, and he planned to enter Yale College. But Ethan's father died when the boy was 16. He had to go to work to support his family.

He served with the citizens' army (militia) during the French and Indian War (1754–1763). He moved to what is now Vermont when he was 31. He later helped to form the Green Mountain Boys, and he became their leader. These brave frontiersmen defended their farms from New Yorkers, who counted the region part of New York. When the Revolutionary War began in 1775, Allen and Colonel Benedict Arnold led the Green Mountain Boys in the daring capture of Fort Ticonderoga from the British. Allen joined a small group who tried to seize Montreal later that year. He was captured by the British. He spent nearly three years in jail in England, but he came home a hero. He later wrote the hair-raising autobiography, *Narrative of Colonel Ethan Allen's Captivity*.

Allen tried to convince Congress to make Vermont a state after the Revolution. But not until two years after his death in 1789 was Vermont admitted to the Union.

ALSO READ: AMERICAN REVOLUTION, VERMONT.

◀ *Ethan Allen, a hero of the American Revolution, demanding the surrender of Fort Ticonderoga.*

**ALLERGY** You probably have an allergy, if playing with a dog seems to make you sneeze, or if you feel itchy after eating chocolate. You are "sensitive" to something—your body does not like it.

The human body has a built-in safety device that sets off an alarm signal in the bloodstream if something harmful, such as a germ, enters the body. The blood begins to release disease-fighting substances called *antibodies* when it gets the signal. In some people, this alarm goes off in response to something that is usually not harmful at all—such as dog hairs or chocolate.

▲ *An allergy may make a person have red, runny eyes and a runny nose. Or, it may show as a red rash on the skin. Allergies that occur in late summer are often called* hay fever.

When this happens, antibodies increase the production of substances called *histamines,* which cause an allergic reaction, such as sneezing, itching, or vomiting.

A substance to which a person is allergic is called an *allergen.* It might be something a person swallows, breathes in, or touches. One of the most common allergies is *hay fever,* which is caused by pollen in the air.

Sometimes a person shows an allergic reaction, but doesn't know what has caused it. A doctor can usually find out what it is by doing a little detective work. He might ask, for example, if the patient has eaten a new food lately, or if he has a new pet. Or, he might test different allergens on the patient's skin. Once he knows what the allergen is, the doctor may tell the patient to avoid exposure to it, or he may give him a drug called an *antihistamine.* This drug counteracts the histamines in the body and thus stops the allergic reaction. Antihistamines were discovered by a Swiss chemist, Daniel Bovet, who received the Nobel Prize in 1957 for his work.

A doctor can also treat an allergy by giving the patient injections (shots). These shots contain tiny amounts of the allergen itself—so tiny that the body does not react. Then, over a period of time, increasing amounts of the allergen are injected. The body gets used to the allergen and no longer reacts when coming in contact with it.

Doctors can treat, and sometimes cure, allergies, although they still do not understand everything about them. Much remains to be learned about how allergies arise and why some people have them, while others do not.

ALSO READ: ANTIGEN AND ANTIBODY, BLOOD, DISEASE.

**ALLIGATORS AND CROCODILES** Alligators and crocodiles have lived in rivers and swamps in many of the warm parts of the world for about 135 million years. Biologists believe that these reptiles have changed very little in all that time, so they are sometimes called "living fossils." Alligators and crocodiles are found today in Asia, Africa, and North and South America.

▶ *The American crocodile lives in salt water. It is darker and greener than the alligator. When its pointed snout is closed, many teeth show on each side of its jaw. The American crocodile is rare.*

# ALLIGATORS AND CROCODILES

**Alike but Different**

One major difference between alligators and crocodiles is in their names. Ancient Romans building colonies in North Africa saw one of these animals basking in the sun and called it *crocodilus,* meaning "worm of the pebbles." The English word "crocodile" came from this name. Spaniards saw one of these reptiles in the New World and called it *el lagarto,* meaning "the lizard." From this, came the word "alligator."

How can you tell an alligator from a crocodile? For one thing, the crocodile's snout is long and pointed, while the alligator's is shorter and rounded. Also, when the crocodile's mouth is closed, you can see two huge teeth sticking out on each side of its lower jaw. The alligator has the same kind of teeth, but when its mouth is closed, they fit into a special groove, and you can't see them. Of course, it is not wise to get close enough to see the teeth of either reptile. Both can be dangerous, and the crocodile is usually fierce.

Crocodiles generally grow to be longer than alligators, although both start out life as tiny babies—a few inches long—hatched from eggs. Crocodiles 30 feet long have been seen, but alligators are rarely longer than 15 feet. Crocodiles are found in both fresh and salt water, while alligators prefer fresh water.
[30 ft.=9 m; 15 ft.=4.7 m]

Crocodiles have more green in their body color than alligators do.

In spite of their differences, alligators and crocodiles have much in common. They both belong to the same order of reptiles, *Crocodylia.* Members of this order are called *crocodilians.* Other crocodilians are the gavial of southern Asia, a close relative of the crocodile, and the long-snouted caiman, a Latin American cousin of the alligator.

Crocodilians have a tough, leathery skin covering an armor of bony plates. Temperature is very important to a crocodilian because it is a cold-blooded animal. It dies if its body becomes too hot or too cold. An alligator or crocodile crawls up from its mudbank in the morning, basks in the warm sun until its body temperature rises, and then goes hunting or looking for a mate. The animal returns to the mudbank

▲ *The American alligator is a reptile of freshwater rivers and swamps in the South. It is smaller than the crocodile, and it has a broader snout.*

▲ *The Nile, or African, crocodile is a man-eater. The Egyptians thought it was a god.*

to keep cool if the day is very warm. It comes out again in late afternoon. It may hunt at night.

On land, the crocodilian walks with its body high off the ground, dragging its tail. Its rear legs are longer than its front ones. In the water, the animal swishes its tail back and forth for propulsion and is a powerful swimmer.

A crocodilian is well suited for the time it spends in water. Its eyes and nostrils are on top of its head, so it can see and breathe when the rest of its body lies under water. It closes its nostrils to seal off its nose when it dives. The crocodilian can open its jaws underwater without inhaling water and drowning.

Crocodilians usually eat insects, fish, and small mammals. The jaw muscles of crocodilians are strong enough to drag a cow or a horse into the water, and some kinds of crocodilians are dangerous man-killers. Sharp teeth grip and hold the prey. New teeth grow in if some rip out. One animal was reported to have grown 45 sets of teeth by the time it grew to 13 feet in length. Crocodilian teeth are sharp, but they are not strong enough to chew prey. The animal swallows its prey whole or tears it up by twisting it into pieces. The muscles that close the jaws are extremely strong, allowing the crocodilian to snap his jaw shut quickly. The muscles that open the jaws are weaker. A man can hold a crocodilian's mouth closed with his hands.

### The Alligators

There are two species of alligators, the *Chinese alligator* found near Shanghai, and the larger *American alligator*. The American alligator lives in the southern United States, mostly in swamps in Louisiana, Georgia, South Carolina, and the Everglades of southern Florida.

Crocodilians make many noises, and alligators are the most "talkative." They make a wide variety of sounds, from grunts and hisses to roars that can be heard a mile away. Alligators were once common, but so many have been killed for their hides that the alligator population has shrunk. Ecologists have classified alligators as an endangered species. It is illegal to kill alligators in all four states where they are found.

Food for an alligator can be anything that it can outswim, ambush, or overpower. One zoologist cut open a dead alligator's stomach and found several pieces of wood, a fishing sinker, and a crumpled can. The alligator had swallowed these things to help grind the coarse food it could not chew.

Most female crocodilians bury their eggs in the sand or in a pile of leaves. The American alligator, however, builds a mound of plants three or four feet high. The female lays from 30 to 90 hard-shelled eggs. They hatch in nine weeks. The mother usually remains near the nest to protect the eggs. After the eggs hatch, she helps her young find their way out of the nest to begin life in the water. Most of the young alligators stay with their mother until the next spring.

Members of the alligator family in Central and South America are the caimans, also called *jacares*. The *black caiman* is the largest, reaching a length of 12 feet. The smallest is the *dwarf caiman*, rarely more than four feet long.

### The Crocodiles

Some American crocodiles share southern Florida swamps with the American alligator. But this 14-foot reptile is quite rare in the U.S. Most American crocodiles are found in South America.

The *American crocodile*, like the American alligator, eats a diet of fish and small animals. It will attack a man only in self-defense.

[13 ft.=4 m]

[3-4 ft.=1-1.2 m; 12 ft.=3.7 m; 14 ft.=4.3 m]

The man-eater of the crocodile family is the *Nile crocodile*. It is the best-known reptile of Africa, and was regarded as sacred in ancient Egypt. The *estuarine crocodile* is found mostly in coastal swamps and in the mouths of large rivers, but often swims to sea. This habit probably explains why the species has found such a wide range of homes—from India down to northern Australia. Both Nile and estuarine crocodiles can be 20 feet long.

The smaller *marsh crocodile,* or *mugger,* is found in India and Ceylon. The *gavial* of northern India has a very slender snout that looks like the handle of a frying pan. The animal may grow up to 20 feet in length. It feeds mainly on fish that it catches by snaps of its long jaws.

ALSO READ: DINOSAUR, LIZARD, REPTILE.

[20 ft.=6 m]

**ALLOY** You might think that a bright new penny is copper. But a penny is not all copper. It is an alloy of copper, tin, and zinc. A mixture of two or more metals, or a metal and a non-metallic element, is an alloy.

Fewer than 80 pure metals exist naturally, but thousands of alloys can be made from them. The first alloy was *bronze*, which was made as long ago as 3000 B.C. Bronze was probably first discovered by accident, when copper and tin melted together and hardened. Alloys are still usually made by heating the metals until they melt and turn into liquids. The liquids are then mixed and allowed to cool. The solid that forms after cooling is the alloy.

Alloys are used for many purposes. They are used most often to make objects less expensive or more useful than objects composed of pure metals. Pure gold is beautiful, but it is expensive and very soft. A ring of pure gold bends and scratches easily. A ring of gold alloy is much stronger. A reddish-yellow ring is probably made of an alloy of gold and copper. A white or silvery gold ring may be an alloy of gold and nickel, *white gold*.

Steel is one of the most useful alloys made today. It is a mixture of iron and other metals or non-metals, such as carbon and manganese. Other substances can be added to make the exact kinds of steel needed for special purposes. One example is the special steel alloy used to make steel sinks, which are used in many hospitals, restaurants, and houses. Steel sinks are very easy to clean, but pure steel would rust very quickly, so an alloy of steel, chromium, and nickel is used. Rust cannot form easily on a *stainless* steel sink. A smooth ride in a car is possible because of the springs between the passengers and the wheels. The springs would break if they were not very strong. An alloy of steel and vanadium makes them strong. Other parts of a car are also made of steel and other alloys.

Many different alloys of steel go into building large buildings and ships. As metal scientists, or *metallurgists*, learn more about metals,

▲*The lunar module lands astronauts on the moon. It is shown here being finished at the factory. It is made of many kinds of materials. Most of them are special alloys that protect men in space.*

▼*This funny face was made in bronze, probably the first alloy, in prehistoric times.*

## SOME COMMON OBJECTS AND THEIR ALLOY MAKE-UP

| Object | Metals in alloy (Metal shown first has largest amount in object) |
|---|---|
| Brass door knob | Copper and zinc |
| Aluminum pots and pans | Aluminum, copper, and manganese |
| Dime | Copper and nickel |
| 14-carat yellow gold ring | Gold and copper |
| Stainless steel knives and forks | Stainless steel, which is made up of steel (iron and carbon), chromium, and nickel. |

▲ *The title page of an almanac by Benjamin Franklin, called* Poor Richard's. *Some people read this almanac for the funny stories. Others wanted to find out things about the future.*

they are developing many other alloys that can do some jobs better than steel. One example is carboloy—an alloy of carbon, cobalt, and tungsten—that is used to make cutting tools.

Alloys are very important in building airplanes. A plane made of steel would certainly be very strong, but it would be too heavy to fly. Aluminum is a very light metal, but an airplane of pure aluminum would not be strong enough. An alloy of aluminum, copper, manganese, and magnesium is often used to build airplanes, because it is both strong and light. Alloys are also very important in building rockets and missiles. Flights to the moon would be impossible without the use of many new alloys, because spacecraft must be very light, but strong enough to work properly in the heat and cold.

ALSO READ: IRON AND STEEL, METAL.

**ALMANAC** If you want to know about the money unit of a country, or how many medals some athlete won in the Olympics, you can find out in an almanac. A reader can find many different kinds of information in such a book. Most almanacs have a calendar and facts about governments, history, and geography. They may also have weather information for cities and countries all over the world, and tables that tell the movements of the sun, planets, and stars.

People have written almanacs for thousands of years. The first ones, made in ancient Persia, contained astrologers' predictions. The word "almanac" probably comes from the Arabic *almanakh*, meaning "calendar." One of the most famous American almanacs was *Poor Richard's Almanac*, written by Benjamin Franklin. The book had poetry, proverbs, astronomy, and weather information in it. Today most almanacs, such as *The World Almanac, The U.S. Fact Book,* and *The Statesman's Year Book*, contain general information and tell the reader about events that happened during the past year. Some organizations, such as the United Nations, publish special almanacs that give facts about many countries. Farmers and sailors still use almanacs to tell when the sun will rise and set or tides will rise and fall.

You might enjoy making your own almanac, based on events at home or at school. You could predict when the first snow will fall, or when you will go on vacation. Other entries might show game scores of your favorite team; birthdays of family, friends, and pets; or notes on books, movies, and hobbies.

ALSO READ: ASTROLOGY; FRANKLIN, BENJAMIN; REFERENCE BOOKS.

**ALPHABET** All written languages are made up of marks called *symbols*. In most languages today, these symbols are *letters* that stand for the sounds of the language. An alphabet is a list of these letter symbols, arranged in a particular order. The word "alphabet" comes from *alpha* and *beta*, the first two symbols, or letters, of the Greek alphabet. Our English alphabet of 26 letters is sometimes known as the ABC's.

Man first tried to write down his language when he made pictures of objects by scratching or drawing or painting them on surfaces such as stone. Some of these pictures told a story or gave a message. For instance, simple pictures of a man, a boat, and the sun rising in the sky might have meant, "Father plans a trip down the river tomorrow morning."

People later began to use pictures to stand for words rather than for stories or ideas. Little by little, these pictures became simple shapes or marks that symbolized the separate *syllables* of words.

The earliest alphabets were probably developed sometime before 1000 B.C. by people such as the Phoenicians, who lived in the fertile regions east of the Mediterranean Sea. The Phoenician alphabet may have come from earlier Egyptian *hieroglyphics*, a system of picture writing. But the symbols of the Phoenician alphabet were not picture ideas. The symbols became letters that stood for the separate *consonant* sounds of language. Man thus had his first alphabet.

The Phoenicians were great sailors and traders who carried their alphabet on westward voyages to Europe and Africa. Other peoples wrote their own alphabets, using the Phoenicians' idea of setting symbols down in regular order, naming them, and having each one represent certain sounds. But the Phoenicians' alphabet had no vowels. Imagine reading an alphabet without vowels! Can you figure out this line from a well-known nursery rhyme written without vowels?

TH CW JMPD VR TH MN

The Greeks used the Phoenician letters, but made many changes. They were the first to develop an alphabet with *vowel* sounds. In the Greek alphabet, one could write the above nursery rhyme line,

THE COW JUMPED OVER THE MOON.

This Greek practice was later copied by the Romans, but they created their own symbols. A modern form of the Roman, or *Latin*, alphabet is now used most often in the Western world. Our own ABC's are Roman letters. Roman letters are also used for some of the newly written languages of Africa.

Early alphabets had only *capital* letters. Later, to save space, small, or *lower-case*, letters were made. The small, rounded letters were easier to write, too.

Several other alphabets are used in the world today besides the modernized Latin symbols. Greeks still use the Greek alphabet. But modern Greek uses sounds and rules for writing and speaking different from those in ancient times. Russians and other Slavic peoples use the *Cyrillic* alphabet, based on old Greek. The alphabets of modern *Hebrew* and modern *Arabic* developed from Aramaic, a language spoken and written in Palestine during the time of Christ. Modern Hebrew is spoken today in Israel. *Early Hebrew*, a much older language, was used to write the Old Testament of the Bible.

Chinese is the only major language of the modern world whose writing is not alphabetical. Its symbols, known as *characters*, stand for words instead of sounds. However, attempts are being made to create a uniform written language based on sounds. Japanese writing is based on old Chinese characters, but some

▼ *A page from a primer, a book used to teach the alphabet. Sentences and pictures are used to illustrate each letter in the alphabet. Did you learn the alphabet this way?*

▲ *Some letters from the Etruscan alphabet. Etruria was an ancient kingdom in Italy.*

symbols represent syllables instead of words.

Suppose that written alphabets hadn't been invented. You could never read a book or write a letter to a friend. And when your mother sent you to the store, you would have to remember everything very carefully, because you could not make a list!

Invent your own alphabet to stand for the sounds of the English language. You can start anywhere and make up your own order. What will you do with the sound "a"? Will your letter be long and pointed like an arrow, or rounded like an acorn? Or will you just make a funny little squiggle that doesn't look like anything at all, say, "That's 'a'!"? What about the "b" sound? Will yours look like a ball or a boat, or will it just be one special shape that always means "b"?

Say the word "car." Now say "kite." Does your alphabet need two different letters for these sounds ("c" and "k")? Can you use one letter for both? What will you do when "c" sounds like "s"? Would one letter be enough there? What about the "a" sounds in "father" and "face"? Some alphabets use one letter for each sound of the language. Other alphabets use one letter for more than one sound. Will your alphabet use one letter or two to show the "a" sounds of "father" and "face"? Can you think of other sounds for which you might want separate letters? How many letters will your alphabet use?

ALSO READ: ARABIC, BRAILLE, CHINESE, PICTURE WRITING, WRITTEN LANGUAGE.

**ALPS MOUNTAINS** The Alps form a mountain fence that curves along Italy's northern border. These beautiful mountains separate Italy from her neighbors—France, Switzerland, Austria, and Yugoslavia. Western Europe's highest peak, Mont Blanc ("White Mountain"), is on the French-Italian border. It is 15,782 feet high. (See the map with the article on EUROPE.)

Have you read the book *Heidi* by

[15,782 ft.=4,892 m]

Johanna Spyri? Heidi lived in Switzerland with her grandfather and his goats in a high pasture called an *alp*. This Swiss word gave the mountains their name. As in the story, most of the people in the Alps today live in villages in the meadows between peaks. A few herdsmen, with their cows and goats, live high in the mountains in summer. Some people farm in the alpine pastures. Other people cut trees for lumber. Skilled craftsmen make watches, clocks, toys, and wood carvings.

Snow collects on the slopes of the Alps. Thousands of people flock to the Alps in winter to ski and enjoy other sports. Tourists are also attracted year-round to the lovely scenery of the Alps. Waterfalls pour hundreds of feet down the sides of the mountains. Melted snow flows into deep, blue lakes and into such rivers as the Danube, Rhine, Rhone, and the Po.

ALSO READ: EUROPE, GLACIER, MOUNTAIN, SWITZERLAND.

**AMAZON** Greek myths told of a group of fierce women warriors called Amazons. The myths say that these warlike women lived near the Black Sea in Asia Minor, in what is now Turkey. Men could not live freely in the land of the Amazons. When the Amazons captured a man, they made him a slave. These women taught their girl children to hunt and fight. They sent away their boy babies. The Amazons were ruled by Queen Hippolyta.

Hercules, a hero of Greek mythology, went to the land of the Amazons to take Hippolyta's girdle, or belt. She gave it to him, but they argued. Hercules killed Hippolyta.

ALSO READ: HERCULES, MYTHOLOGY

**AMAZON RIVER** The Amazon River and its tributaries (smaller rivers) make up the largest river system in the world. The Amazon begins high in the Andes Mountains and empties into the Atlantic Ocean, almost 4,000 miles away. As the Amazon flows east across most of northern Brazil, it is fed by rivers from Peru, Venezuela, Colombia, Ecuàdor, and Bolivia. (See the map with the article on SOUTH AMERICA.) Only the Nile, in Africa, of all the rivers in the world, is longer than the Amazon. But the Amazon carries more water than any other river.
[4,000 mi.=6,440 km]

▲*There are many high mountains in the Alps. The tallest, shown here, is Mont Blanc. It has a glacier, a very slow moving mass of ice.*

▼*A band of women warriors, called* Amazons, *on a hunting party. Myths and legends tell that they lived long ago in a land where they did not allow men to live.*

▲ *The Amazon River is a vast highway through the jungles of South America. These Indians are moving fruit to market aboard a flatboat. The covering of leaves protects the fruit.*

▲ *A piece of amber.*

Francisco de Orellana, a Spaniard, first explored the Amazon in 1541. He later told how he and his men battled with female warriors. He gave the river its name because he thought they were the Amazons, a tribe of fighting women of Greek mythology.

Regular steamship service up the Amazon began in the nineteenth century, and settlements developed along the river. But much of the area remains unexplored even today. An explorer can travel thousands of miles and never cross a road or see a city. Most of the Amazon basin (land drained by the river) is a vast, dense jungle—the largest rain forest in the world. The basin is about three-fourths the size of the United States. About two million people (about three per cent of Brazil's population) live in the basin. A few Indians live a hard and primitive life deep in this hot and rainy jungle. They struggle to make their living by gathering the products of the forest, such as nuts, woods, and oils, and they hunt animals.

ALSO READ: AMAZON; INDIANS, AMERICAN; JUNGLE; RIVER; SOUTH AMERICA.

**AMBASSADOR** see FOREIGN SERVICE.

**AMBER** A piece of amber looks very much like a stone, but it is actually a fossil substance that formed from the sticky, gummy resin of pine trees millions of years ago. The resin was buried, and it hardened after many years in the ground.

Amber is usually golden or reddish-brown. It is almost transparent. In some pieces you can see the bodies of insects that were trapped in the sticky resin before it hardened. The ancient Greeks polished amber and used it for beads. It is often used to make jewelry today. The Greeks studied amber more than 2,500 years ago. They discovered that when amber was rubbed with fur, it attracted small pieces of straw and made crackling sparks of static. The word "electricity" comes from the Greek word for amber, *elektron*.

ALSO READ: ELECTRICITY, FOSSIL.

**AMBULANCE** An ambulance, with its lights flashing and its siren wailing, may someday save your life. An ambulance is a "moving hospital." It is a car designed to give first aid to people who are injured in accidents, or who suddenly become very sick. Ambulances carry injured and sick people to hospitals.

The first ambulances were made to follow armies. Wounded soldiers were either carried from the battlefield by their comrades or left lying where they fell. The wounded usually had to wait until the fighting stopped to get help. Napoleon's personal surgeon, Baron Dominique Jean Larrey, introduced the first ambulances in 1792. They were light carriages, each pulled by a single horse. They quickly took the wounded from the battlefield.

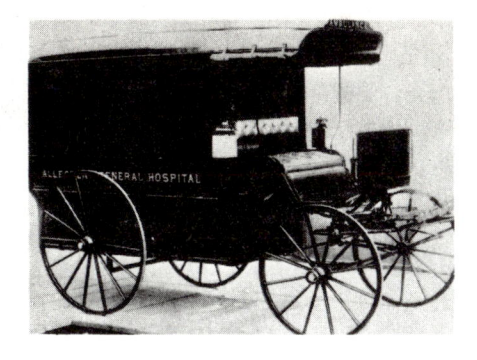

Horse-drawn and mule-drawn ambulances carried wounded soldiers during the American Civil War. A plan for an ambulance corps was proposed in Congress in 1862. But Congress did not give its approval until 1865, as the war was ending. So the corps played little part in the war.

Many hospitals in the United States began to develop ambulance services after the Civil War. Cincinnati General Hospital was one of the first. Bellevue Hospital in New York also started an ambulance service. Michael Reese Hospital in Chicago was probably the first U.S. hospital to use motor-driven ambulances, in 1899. Since about 1950, helicopters have often been used as ambulances.

Before a person can become an ambulance attendant, he must spend several weeks learning rescue and first aid. He must take a new training course every two years. Some states have additional requirements for people who want to serve in ambulances.

ALSO READ: HOSPITAL.

**AMENDMENT** see CONSTITUTION, UNITED STATES.

**AMERICA** The United States is often called "America," but this name really belongs to two great continents of the Western Hemisphere—North America and South America. Part of North America—the seven countries from Guatemala to Panama—is called Central America.

The two continents stretch 9,500 miles from north to south. They vary in width from just 30 miles in Panama to more than 4,000 miles across Alaska and Canada. The two continents were separate millions of years ago. Then volcanoes spilled lava that formed the narrow, connecting link known as Central America.

The Americas were explored thousands of years ago by groups of Asian people. Some of them were the ancestors of the Indians and Eskimos of today. For centuries, Europeans did not know that the Americas existed. Vikings visited eastern Canada about 1000 A.D., but their settlements died out. In 1492, Columbus reached the Caribbean islands but thought he was in Asia. A later explorer, Magellan, sailed around the southern tip of the Americas and across the Pacific. Europeans then realized that these lands were two new continents.

An Italian merchant named Amerigo Vespucci persuaded Spanish and Portuguese sea captains to take him along when they visited South America. He returned to Europe and wrote colorful letters claiming he had discovered a "New World." One of these letters reached a German geography professor who named the area of Brazil *America* (from Amerigo), in honor of Vespucci. The name became popular, and later became the name of both continents.

◀ *Ambulances were in service even before motor transport. This is a horse-drawn ambulance of 1889.*

▲ *An ambulance takes care of the patient until he gets to the hospital. Here, two attendants are about to take a patient into a hospital.*

[9,500 mi.=15,295 km; 30 mi.=48 km; 4,000 mi.=6,440 km]

*If you had the chance to name America, what would you call the two continents? Would you name them after an explorer, such as Eric the Red, Columbus, Magellan, Cabot, Cortez, Pizarro, or discoverers of other parts of America? Or would you name the continents after one of their Indian tribes?*

ALSO READ: CENTRAL AMERICA; EXPLORATION; INDIANS, AMERICAN; NORTH AMERICA; SOUTH AMERICA; VIKINGS.

**AMERICAN COLONIES** The discovery and exploration of North America caused great excitement among seafaring people of Europe. They looked upon America as a New World, as a "land of opportunity." Most of all, they saw it as a source of marvelous treasures. Many of the leading European nations were eager to get the valuable furs, important minerals, and other useful natural resources of North America, so they could grow rich and powerful. They dreamed especially of discovering huge fortunes in gold, silver, and precious gems.

The Spanish were first in the rush to claim some of the riches of North America. They established the first permanent North American fort at St. Augustine, Florida, in 1565. English colonies were not started until after 1600. The French made a claim to Canada and most of the Mississippi Valley. The Dutch got hold of the lands along the Hudson River, and the Swedes took over the region of the Delaware River.

England was the most successful of all the nations competing for America's vast wealth. The colonists from France and Spain were interested mainly in trading with the Indians and taking gold and furs back to Europe. But the English colonists were determined to set up permanent homes in the New World. In time, England gained control of a large area of land along the Atlantic coast—including the regions that had first been claimed by the Dutch and Swedes. England had established 13 permanent colonies by 1733. In the North were the *New England colonies*—Massachusetts, Connecticut, New Hampshire, and Rhode Island. The *middle colonies* were New York, Delaware, Pennsylvania, and New Jersey. The *southern colonies* were Virginia, Maryland, North Carolina, South Carolina, and Georgia. These colonies later became the 13 original United States of America.

**The Early Settlements**

A large group of men and boys landed at Virginia in the spring of 1607. They founded the Jamestown Colony, the first permanent English settlement in the New World. A second group of people, the Pilgrims, sailed on the *Mayflower* from Plymouth, England, to the coast of Massachusetts in 1620. There they set up the Plymouth Colony. Puritans came from England ten years later to found the Massachusetts Bay Colony, with settlements in Boston and Salem.

Many hardships and dangers awaited these Europeans who first made the long ocean voyage to the New World. America of the 1600s was a vast wilderness. The colonists had to get used to this strange New World. They had to give up many of their Old World habits of living. Even the kinds of food they were used to eating were no longer available to them.

The Indians often lent a helping hand to the colonists. Indians had already explored most of the land, and they knew the best ways to travel the waters and cross the mountains. They showed the colonists where to find minerals and other important resources. They also knew all about the kinds of foods that could be found. The Massachusetts colonists had never even heard of such vegetables as corn, squash, and sweet potatoes. The Indians showed them how to grow these crops and to prepare foods such as hominy, succotash, and popcorn.

But many Indian tribes were not so friendly to the newcomers. They were angry because the white men had forced them out of their homes and hunting grounds. They fought back with all their might. Men and boys in Virginia and Massachusetts had to learn to defend their homes and families from Indian attacks.

Not all the early settlers were prepared for the tough and dangerous life in Colonial America. The Jamestown colonists suffered from the burning heat of summer and the damp cold of winter. They worked hard. Many died of starvation and disease. But luckily, most of the early colonists were brave and hardy folk. They were ready to face all hardships in the struggle to build a new life in the land of opportunity. Many Europeans hoped to make new lives in the New World, so the settlement of America grew quickly after the founding of the earliest colonies. By 1700, the whole eastern coast was peppered with English towns.

### The People of the Colonies

Most colonial settlers were English, but many others were French, Irish, Scottish, Dutch, German, and Swedish. They all had one thing in common—they wanted to make new lives for themselves. Some were drawn to the New World by the promise of work, because in their home countries they were not able to make a good living. Others were excited by the chance to get some land to call their own. The English king had offered lands that were cheap, or even free. Still others fled their homes because they

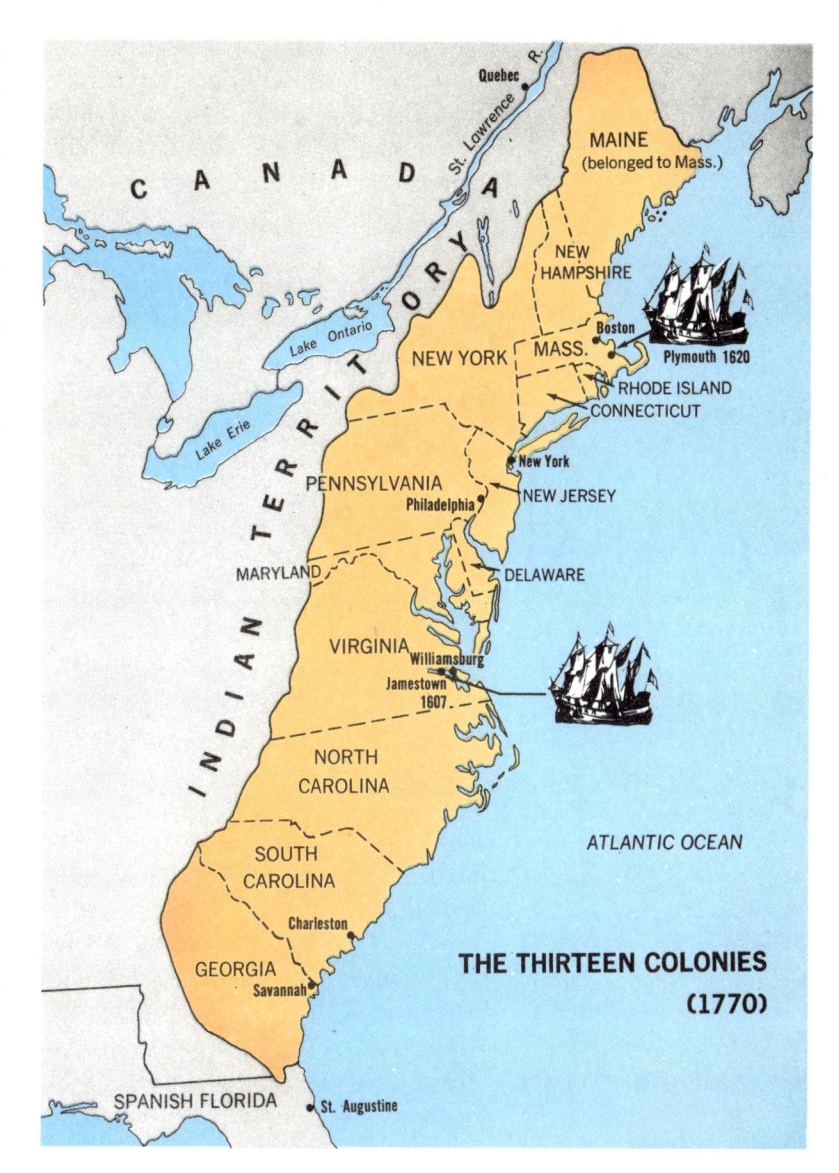

◀ *Corn husking. The colonists learned how to plant corn from the Indians. Corn became one of the colonists' favorite foods.*

were not allowed to worship as they wished there. They were told that England would allow freedom of religion in the colonies. The Pilgrims and the Puritans had been the first religious groups to come to America for this reason. Others were the Quakers, Roman Catholics, and French Protestants known as Huguenots.

Some Europeans who wanted to settle in the New World were poor people who did not have enough money to make the trip. So they offered themselves as *indentured servants* to wealthy colonists. An indentured servant agreed to work for his master for a certain number of years. In return, the master agreed to pay for the servant's trip and to provide him with room and board for the period of his service. But not all indentured servants came to America by choice. Some were criminals who had been forced to leave their countries. A few were black people from Africa who had been kidnapped by white Europeans. Many more Negroes were bought or captured in Africa and forced to become slaves. Most of them were brought to the southern colonies, where they were needed as farm laborers. Other slaves were brought to the North and put to work in the homes or shops.

**Everyday Life**

Each one of the three regions—New England, the middle colonies, and the southern colonies—had special conditions that made it different from the others. So people in each region developed different ways of living and working.

All the colonies depended on farming. The South was best suited for large-scale farming. The soil was rich and the climate was warm. Many southern colonists lived on huge plantations where tobacco and rice were grown for export to England. Every southern plantation was a tiny village. The plantation owner, or planter, was mayor, judge, sheriff, preacher, doctor, lawyer, and storekeeper for the community. He and his family often lived in a great mansion. His black slaves lived in small shacks away from the main house. Most of them spent their days at hard labor in the fields. Some were put to work as servants in the planter's home.

Each plantation had its own carpenter, cooper (barrel-maker), blacksmith, cobbler (shoemaker), tanner, and other craftsmen who provided the basic needs of everyday life. From the plentiful plantation trees came the wood for the carpenter and the cooper. The blacksmith used the wood for charcoal, which is needed to make ironware. Cotton and flax were grown and made into thread for weaving cloth. Cattle supplied milk and meat, as well as skins for the tanner and leather for the cobbler. Sheep's wool was woven or knitted to make clothing and bedding. Some planters were so rich they did not have to wear homemade clothing. They ordered fine silk gowns, satin breeches, and other fancy clothes from England.

The land in New England was rocky, the soil was poor, and the farms were small. Most towns were two rows of wooden or stone houses facing a *common* (a piece of land shared by the community) on which livestock grazed. Unlike the plantation family, the New England family did not raise crops for export to England. Each family grew only enough food for itself. The New Englander hardly ever bought ready-made English goods. People made all their own tools, clothing, and furniture. The North was blessed with rich forests, so there was plenty of lumber. New England woodworkers made especially fine furniture.

The main profit of the northern

▲ *Cutting and burning great logs was a must for the first American colonists. Much of America was covered by dense forests. The colonists needed the land to build cabins and plant crops.*

▼ *Roger Williams began the Rhode Island Colony so that people could freely worship God.*

colonies came not from the land, but from the sea. Fishing, shipbuilding, shipping, and whaling were all important industries. Trading ships traveled up and down the Atlantic coast, bringing goods to the other colonies. They also crossed the Atlantic and traded with Europe, Africa, and the West Indies. Whaling ships sailed out of Nantucket, New Bedford, and other New England ports. Voyages sometimes lasted two or three years. One lasted eleven years!

The middle colonies were known as the "bread" colonies. Their most important export was wheat. They also kept livestock and produced beef, pork, and lamb. Most of the farms were run by single families. But in the Hudson River Valley were large estates where wealthy landowners lived as comfortably as the planters of the South. The rich merchants of the cities also lived in splendid style.

▲ *Fancy carriages like this one belonged to the colonists who became rich.*

## Transportation

The early colonists traveled by foot over the Indian paths and wilderness trails, or they rode horseback. For many years, there were no roads outside cities. People found it easier to travel by water than by land. Vessels sailed regularly up and down the coast from port to port. Inland, large rivers, such as the Hudson, were heavily traveled.

Overland travel became easier as city streets were paved with cobblestones and wilderness trails were widened into dirt roads. In 1732, a stagecoach journeyed between New York and Philadelphia in record time—one week. Wealthy colonists imported splendid coaches from England. These coaches must have been a grand sight, painted with shiny gold and red paint, and drawn by four prancing horses.

But colonists who walked in the cities did not always have such a grand time. City streets were often used as garbage dumps. Hogs and other animals ran free in New York's streets, looking for food among the garbage. Rich people were able to buy *sedans* to avoid all this. The sedan was an enclosed chair with two poles attached to each side. Servants or slaves carried the chair, with its rider, on their shoulders.

## School and Church

Colonial children helped their parents with everyday chores. But schooling was also an important part of daily life for many children. The three R's—"Reading, 'Riting, and 'Rithmetic"—were the basic lessons taught by every schoolmaster, whether he was teaching in a public school or was hired as a private tutor. America's first public schools were in New England. The schools were free, but only boys could attend. Girls were rarely sent to public schools in colonial times. But both boys and girls could attend a "dame" school, run by a woman who taught in her home. The children learned their three R's seated around the kitchen fire. They made their own pens by carving sharp points from goose quills. They boiled bark to make a dark syrup that they used as ink.

On southern plantations, the planter's children were tutored by a schoolmaster who lived with the

▲ *The kitchen was the center of family life in most colonial homes. Every kitchen had a fireplace. With its crane and spit, the fireplace was used for cooking as well as heating. This is the kitchen at Wythe House in Colonial Williamsburg.*

▲ *American colonists did many things for themselves. Here, a man dressed in colonial clothes shows the art of flaxbreaking. The flax-break separates linen fiber from its woody core to prepare the fiber for spinning into thread.*

| COLONY | DATE FOUNDED | FOUNDER | REASON FOR SETTLEMENT | STATEHOOD |
|---|---|---|---|---|
| VIRGINIA | 1607 | Capt. John Smith | Profit and trade | June 25, 1788 |
| MASSACHUSETTS | 1620 | William Bradford | Freedom to be Puritans | Feb. 6, 1788 |
| NEW YORK | 1626 | Peter Minuit | Profit and trade | July 26, 1788 |
| NEW HAMPSHIRE | 1630 | John Mason | Left Massachusetts because rules were too strict | June 21, 1788 |
| MARYLAND | 1634 | George Calvert | Freedom to be Roman Catholics | Apr. 28, 1788 |
| CONNECTICUT | 1636 | Thomas Hooker | Left Massachusetts because rules were too strict | Jan. 9, 1788 |
| RHODE ISLAND | 1636 | Roger Williams | Thrown out of Massachusetts because he did not conform to Puritan thinking | May 29, 1790 |
| DELAWARE | 1638 | Peter Minuit | Profit and trade | Dec. 7, 1787 |
| NORTH CAROLINA | 1653 | Eight Lords Proprietors | Profit and trade | Nov. 21, 1789 |
| NEW JERSEY | 1664 | John Berkeley and George Carteret | Profit and trade | Dec. 18, 1787 |
| SOUTH CAROLINA | 1670 | Eight Lords Proprietors | Profit and trade | May 23, 1788 |
| PENNSYLVANIA | 1682 | William Penn | Freedom to be Quakers | Dec. 12, 1787 |
| GEORGIA | 1733 | James Oglethorpe | Colonization | Jan. 2, 1788 |

▲ *This splendid doll was made in colonial times. It is dressed in a plaid cotton dress and straw hat.*

family for several months of the year. Some boys—and a few girls—were sent to private schools in England. The first free school in the South was the grammar school at the College of William and Mary, in Williamsburg, Virginia.

Going to church was another important part of colonial life. The church was not only a place of worship—it was also the center of community life. People in the South enjoyed staying around the church after the services were over. Adults gathered in groups to chat, while boys and girls played tag or hopscotch or flew kites. But the mood in New England churches on Sunday was quite different. The Puritans believed that people should be quiet and serious on the Sabbath. Children were not allowed to shout and play. Every Sunday morning, after the drummer rolled the drums to announce the beginning of services, every man, woman, and child had to be in his or her seat at the meeting house. Sermons often lasted three hours in the morning and another three hours in the afternoon.

### Recreation

Life in colonial times offered many pleasures as well as duties. Fox hunting, horse racing, and week-long house parties made life gay. New England parties were happy occasions that often combined work and play. Neighbors gathered together to husk corn, make quilts, and even build houses. Growing up on a southern plantation was often a joyous adventure for white boys and girls.

Like today's Americans, the colonists especially enjoyed their holidays. Thanksgiving was first observed by the early settlers at Plymouth. But the colonists did not celebrate Christmas the way this holiday is celebrated today. The Puritans believed that it was wrong to be joyful about religion. Christmas did not become a real holiday until the middle of the nineteenth century. An important holiday in colonial times was the English king's birthday. But the colonists began to want independence. This desire grew stronger and stronger, until the colonists declared their break with English rule. A total of 169 years had passed between the time of the first permanent English colony, at Jamestown in 1607, and the Declaration of Independence from England in 1776. After the 13 colonies won their right to be an independent nation, a happy day on the American calendar was

Independence Day, the Fourth of July.

ALSO READ: AGRICULTURE, AMERICAN HISTORY, AMERICAN REVOLUTION, DECLARATION OF INDEPENDENCE, JAMESTOWN, MAYFLOWER, MAYFLOWER COMPACT, PILGRIM SETTLERS, PURITAN, RALEIGH, SIR WALTER; each state shown on the table.

**AMERICAN HISTORY** England did not start to colonize the east coast of North America until more than a century after Columbus and other explorers had begun their explorations of the Western Hemisphere. The first permanent English settlement in the New World was started in 1607 at Jamestown in Virginia. The Virginia Colony was governed by the British governor and the House of Burgesses. The people elected the *burgesses* (representatives) to this assembly beginning in 1619. The Virginia House of Burgesses was the first representative government in America.

A second English settlement was started when the Pilgrims landed at Plymouth, Massachusetts, in 1620. The Pilgrims left England because they were not allowed to worship God in their own way. They were part of a large group of Englishmen called *Puritans*, who wanted to "purify" the Church of England. Another group of Puritans founded the Massachusetts Bay Colony at Boston and Salem in 1630. The English had set up 13 colonies along the Atlantic Coast, from Maine to Georgia, by 1733.

Many North American Indians were friendly to the settlers and helped them learn the ways of the new land. But often bloody fights broke out between the colonists and the Indians. The Indians fought because the colonists were taking over their lands.

**The Roots of Revolution**
Wars fought by Spain, France, and England caused fighting in several parts of America during most of the 1700s. In America these were called the French and Indian Wars. Both the French and the British had Indians fighting for them. France lost the French and Indian Wars, and by 1763 Great Britain had gained nearly all French land in America, including Canada. The British needed money to pay their war debts. So Parliament decided to tax the colonies. The angry American colonists felt the taxes were unfair. But even though they protested, King George III and Parliament would not end the taxes. Colonists who took the side of the English king were called *Loyalists* or *Tories*. Other colonists wanted independence from England. They were called *Patriots*. Still others—probably a majority—had a "wait and see" attitude.

The Patriots felt that Britain was taking away rights that they deserved as free Englishmen. They could not get enough help from the British Parliament, or from the king and his ministers. The colonists therefore, defied the British government. This was particularly true in Massachusetts and in the city of Boston, beginning about 1761. Resistance had spread to other large cities by 1765. It continued to grow for ten years.

**The Fight for Independence**
One night in April, 1775, the Patriots learned that British troops planned to capture guns and ammunition stored by the colonists in Concord, Massachusetts. Leaders of the Patriots were in danger of arrest, so Paul Revere and other Minutemen rode for miles through the darkness to warn them. The American Revolution began the next day at the Battles of Lexington and Concord.

The fighting lasted for almost seven years, during which George Washington was the commander in chief of the Continental Army. He

▲*The settling of the West was one of the most lively periods of American history. The hard life did not stop the people of the frontier from dancing and having a lot of fun.*

# AMERICAN HISTORY

▲*New York City is one of the biggest cities in the world. Skyscrapers soar above a modern port where huge ships are anchored. It was a small town called New Amsterdam (shown in the drawing), until the English took it from the Dutch and renamed the city in 1664.*

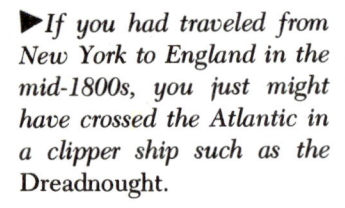

▶*If you had traveled from New York to England in the mid-1800s, you just might have crossed the Atlantic in a clipper ship such as the Dreadnought.*

kept the soldiers of the ill-equipped colonial army together until they won the war in 1781. In the peace treaty, signed in 1783, Great Britain recognized the independence of the United States of America, and turned over to the new country all British lands east of the Mississippi.

A national flag for the new United States was approved on June 14, 1777, during the Revolution. This first flag, the original Stars and Stripes, had one star for each state and 13 stripes to stand for the first 13 colonies.

The new nation needed laws to guide and protect its people. A first attempt at setting up a system of national law was made in the Articles of Confederation, which became law in 1781. But the system did not work, and a new Constitution of the United States was created in 1787. Adopted in 1789, it is still the basic law of the land today. Under the Constitution, a President is elected by the people every four years. The country called on George Washington again. He was elected the first President. He took oath of office in April, 1789.

### The Union Expands

Not all Americans were content to live in the settled areas of the eastern coast. Looking for land to farm, some began to move west toward the Ohio River even before the Revolution. The land between the Appalachian Mountains and the Mississippi River was quickly settled. It was soon divided up into states, which joined the Union. By 1800, 3 more states—Vermont, Kentucky, and Tennessee—had joined the original 13.

# AMERICAN HISTORY

The size of the country was more than doubled in 1803 by the Louisiana Purchase. The U.S., under the leadership of President Thomas Jefferson, paid France 15 million dollars for a huge tract of land that extended from the Mississippi River west to the Rocky Mountains, and from New Orleans all the way to Canada. Two young army officers, Meriwether Lewis and William Clark, explored this new land for the U.S. government. Lewis and Clark traveled beyond the Rockies to the Pacific Ocean. Their glowing reports of the western frontier made many Americans decide to move west.

The United States and England went to war again in 1812, fighting over the freedom of U.S. ships at sea. U.S. troops burned government buildings at York (now Toronto) in Canada. The next year, the British burned the U.S. Capitol, some other buildings, and the President's House in return. President James Madison had the house painted white to cover the scars and smoke stains. The home of the President of the United States has been called the "White House" since that time.

The U.S. continued to grow in size and political power after the War of 1812. Spain sold Florida to the U.S. in 1819. Settlements were founded beyond the Mississippi by pioneers who traveled to the West in wagon trains. Many Americans settled in Texas, which belonged to Mexico at that time. They fought with the Mexicans over laws and boundaries. In San Antonio, in 1836, an entire group of Texan Americans were killed by Mexican soldiers in the Battle of the Alamo. Angry Texans crying, "Remember the Alamo!" defeated the Mexicans a few weeks later. The Texans then went on to win their independence from Mexico. Texas was *annexed*, or added, to the Union as a state in 1845. The U.S. and Mexico fought over this annexation in the Mexican War from 1846 to 1848. The U.S. won. Mexico agreed to sell much of its western land, including California, to the U.S.

Gold was discovered in the new U.S. land of California. Many people, called "Forty-Niners," went west in the search for gold. Other travelers to the West went to make new lives for themselves and their families. The trip westward was long and dangerous. The Oregon Trail, which many of these pioneers took, was more than 2,000 miles long. Indian attacks troubled almost every wagon train.

## The Civil War

In the first half of the 1800s, debate between the North and the South on the question of slavery became more and more bitter. Slaves brought from Africa had been used on the large plantations in the South since colonial times. When cotton became a popular crop, more and more slaves were needed. The South's prosperity was based on the slavery system. Slavery was not profitable in the North, and most Northern states had laws against it. A large group of Northerners believed that slavery should not be allowed in new territories. They wanted to *abolish* (get rid of) slavery in the whole country. They were known as *abolitionists*. The

[2,000 mi.=3,220 km]

▼ Americans used to drive buggies along dirt roads. They would put up their horses at night in stables or pastures. Americans now drive along paved highways in shiny cars. ▲

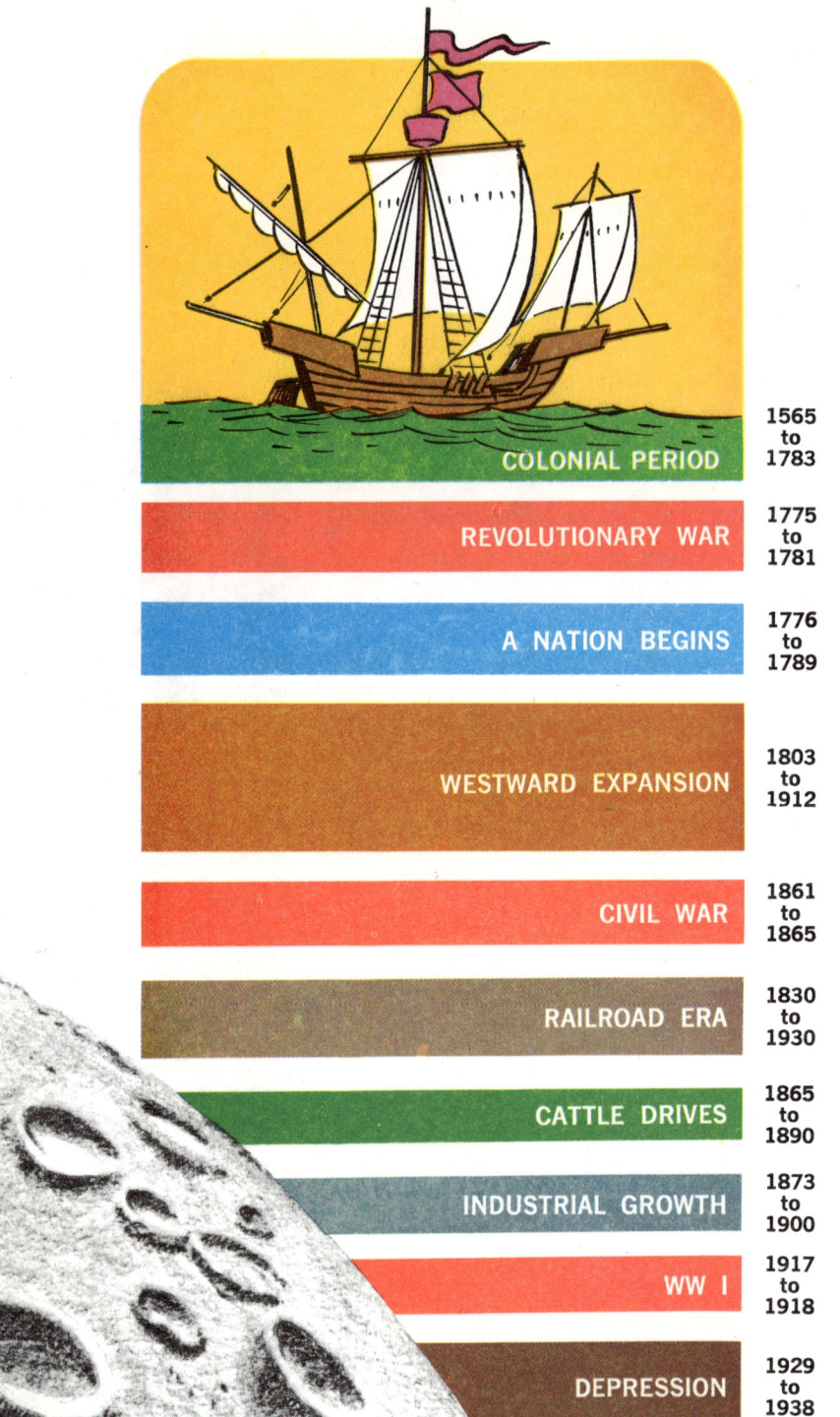

# American History timetable

|  |  |
|---|---|
| COLONIAL PERIOD | 1565 to 1783 |
| REVOLUTIONARY WAR | 1775 to 1781 |
| A NATION BEGINS | 1776 to 1789 |
| WESTWARD EXPANSION | 1803 to 1912 |
| CIVIL WAR | 1861 to 1865 |
| RAILROAD ERA | 1830 to 1930 |
| CATTLE DRIVES | 1865 to 1890 |
| INDUSTRIAL GROWTH | 1873 to 1900 |
| WW I | 1917 to 1918 |
| DEPRESSION | 1929 to 1938 |
| WW II | 1941 to 1945 |
| NUCLEAR AGE | 1945 to present |
| SPACE AGE | 1958 to present |

▲ Slave labor was the backbone of the Southern cotton industry. When Northern abolitionists demanded an end to such labor, slavery became one of the major issues leading to the Civil War.

▲ American soldiers in the Argonne Forest, France during World War I.

# AMERICAN HISTORY

▲ Santa Fe, New Mexico, was settled even before the *Mayflower* arrived in America. In 1609, Spanish Franciscan missionaries from Mexico built a chapel like this mission.

▲ In the right chamber on the lower floor of Independence Hall in Philadelphia, the Declaration of Independence was signed in 1776.

▲ When the American West was still young, hunters on the prairie did not know whether there would be peace or war when they met Indians.

▼ A Titan rocket blasts off from Cape Kennedy, America's spaceport.

▲ With the driving of a golden spike at Promontory Point, Utah, the first railroad across the United States was completed on May 10, 1869.

▶ The first Model T Ford was produced in 1908. In 1913, Henry Ford began to build them on an assembly line.

▶ In June, 1944, American troops freed Rome from German control near the end of World War II.

▲ *This drawing of the skull and crossbones expresses the colonists' hatred of the Stamp Act. "No taxation without representation," became one of the rallying cries of the Revolution.*

Southern states saw less and less reason for staying in the Union.

In 1860—the year Abraham Lincoln was elected President—several southern states *seceded from* (left) the Union and formed a new government. They called themselves the Confederate States of America. They chose Jefferson Davis as their president. The Civil War began on April 12, 1861, when Confederate soldiers fired on a U.S. fort, Fort Sumter, in the harbor of Charleston, South Carolina.

Abraham Lincoln remained President of the U.S. throughout the four-year war. General Ulysses S. Grant was the most famous of the commanders of the Union forces. Robert E. Lee was the commanding general of the Confederate army. In this war, brother often fought against brother, and friend against friend. After the North won this long and bloody war, two things were settled—slavery was abolished, and it was clear that no state could leave the Union. Just five days after the Civil War ended, President Lincoln was assassinated in Ford's Theater in Washington, D.C. by John Wilkes Booth, an actor who was a strong supporter of the South.

**The Railroad Helps Settle the West**

The U.S. went through a period of prosperity for the next 20 years, mostly due to the growth of transportation. Railroading became the biggest business of a big country. Railroads were built which ran all the way to the Pacific coast. This opened up the West for further settlement. Cattle raising, land development, lumbering, and silver mining made the western lands prosperous.

But the new settlers, miners, and ranchers faced a serious threat from the Indians. The American Indians were fighting not only for their lives, but for their way of life. They were being driven from their ancient hunting grounds, from the homelands that had been theirs for generations. One tribe that fought the hardest was the Apache. The Apache War raged in New Mexico, Arizona, and Texas. It lasted almost 40 years, and was probably the bloodiest Indian war. Other serious Indian wars were the Sioux War in North and South Dakota, Minnesota, and Montana, and the Nez Perce War in the Pacific Northwest.

In the East, where manufacturing had become the most important business, another kind of fight was going on. The long struggle between factory owners and workers had started. Labor unions were working to get better working conditions, higher pay, and shorter hours for workers.

By 1890 there was scarcely any frontier (completely unsettled land) left. The U.S. now stretched from the Atlantic to the Pacific. Forty-five states had been formed by the time the twentieth century started. Three more came into the Union in the next 12 years. The admission of huge Alaska and distant Hawaii in 1959 brought the number to 50 states.

**A World Power**

Another war took place before the end of the 1800s. The Spanish-American War, fought with Spain in 1898 over Cuba's independence, began when a U.S. battleship, the *Maine*, was blown up in the harbor of Havana, Cuba. America won this brief conflict, and the world began to realize that the young country was becoming a world power. Under President Theodore Roosevelt, the U.S. dug the Panama Canal, which made it possible for ships to go from the Atlantic to the Pacific without going around stormy Cape Horn at the southern tip of South America.

World War I started in Europe in 1914. Germany fought against France and England. America did not want to enter this war at first. But events forced the country to fight. President Woodrow Wilson and Congress declared war on Germany in April, 1917. With fresh American troops helping out, Germany was defeated in 1918.

For more than ten years the world tried to recover from the debts and social changes brought about by the war. But finally there was a worldwide economic depression. The Depression began in the U.S. in 1929. Many people did not have jobs or money during this time, and they could not buy food or clothing. The government started many new building projects to make work so that people could earn at least some money. Highways, dams, bridges, and public buildings were constructed.

The U.S. was at peace with the rest of the world for 20 years after World War I. Then World War II broke out in Europe. Germany, under Adolf Hitler and his Nazi party, aided by Italy, attacked and captured many European and North African countries. The U.S. still did not want to enter another world war. But the Japanese, who were allies of the Germans and Italians, bombed the American naval base at Pearl Harbor, Hawaii, on December 7, 1941. Congress declared war on Japan, Germany, and Italy. Not until the Germans surrendered in May, 1945, was the war over in Europe. Japan did not surrender until August of that year, after the U.S. had dropped atom bombs on two Japanese cities. This was the only time atom bombs have been used in war.

One of the results of World War II was the organization of the United Nations. Nearly all the countries of the world belong to the UN. The representatives of the member nations work together to try to solve world problems. When war broke out between the North and South Koreans in 1950, the UN sent troops to defend the South Koreans from the North Korean

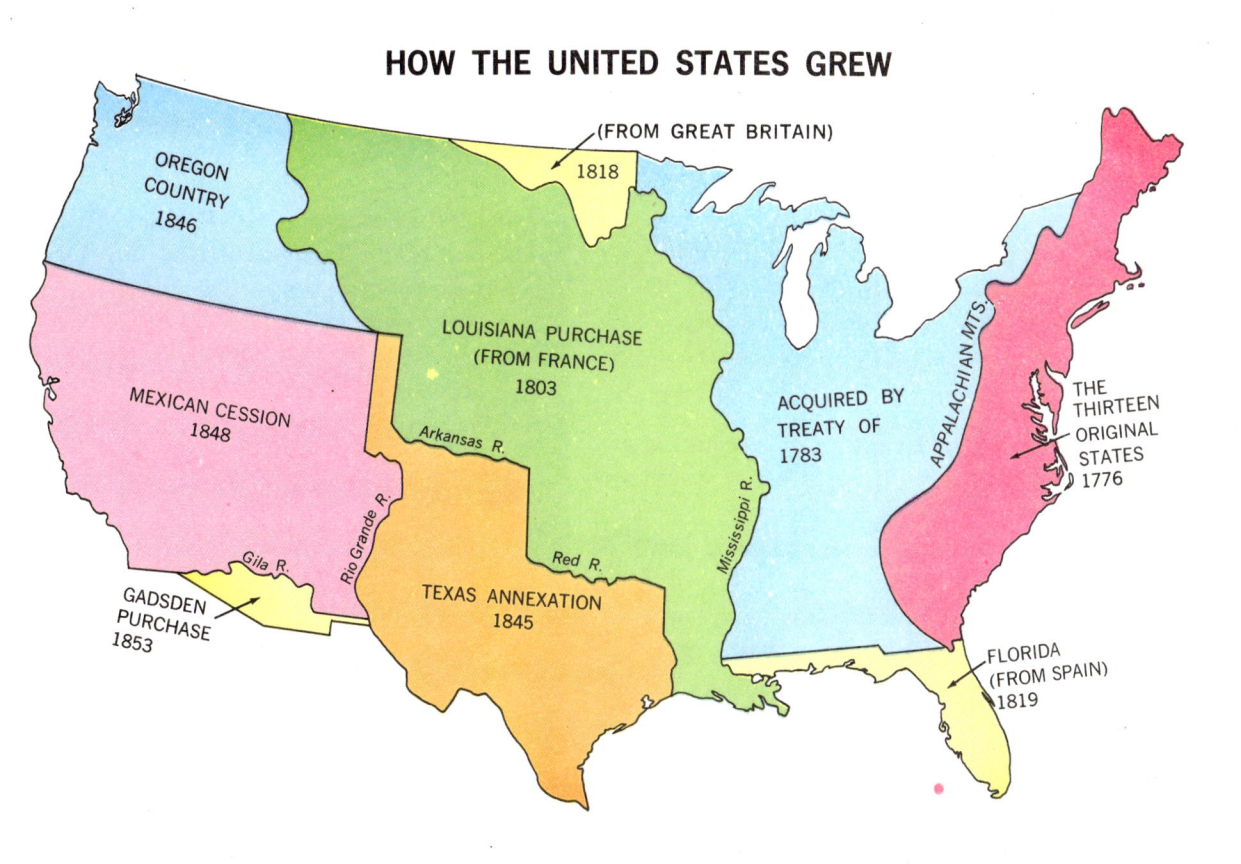

## HOW THE UNITED STATES GREW

Communists. The U.S. gave the largest share of men and equipment.

The United States had become more and more prosperous in spite of the Korean War. Americans were living better than any people on Earth. Both industry and the population were growing steadily.

In the 1950s and 1960s the U.S. sent personnel to help the South Vietnamese in their guerrilla war against the communist North Vietnamese. By 1965 U.S. troops were in combat in Vietnam. U.S. involvement led to discontent, and a peace accord was signed in 1973, ending America's longest war.

### Into the Future

The U.S. has problems of war, of dying cities, of poverty, and of air and water pollution. But at the same time the country is searching hard for solutions and is exploring new frontiers. The frontiers of space are just beginning to open. On July 20, 1969, two American astronauts became the first men to walk on the moon. They left on the moon a sign which read, "We came in peace for all mankind."

*For further information on:*
**Government,** *see* ARTICLES OF CONFEDERATION; CABINET, U.S.; CONSTITUTION, U.S.; FLAG; UNITED STATES GOVERNMENT.

**Life,** *see* AMERICAN COLONIES; CITY; EXPLORATION; INDIANS, AMERICAN; NEGRO HISTORY; PIONEER LIFE.

**Major Events,** *see* AMERICAN REVOLUTION, CIVIL RIGHTS MOVEMENT, CIVIL WAR, DEPRESSION, FRENCH AND INDIAN WAR, GOLD RUSH, INDIAN WARS, KOREAN CONFLICT, MEXICAN WAR, RECONSTRUCTION, SPANISH-AMERICAN WAR, WAR OF 1812, WORLD WAR I, WORLD WAR II, VIETNAM WAR.

*Also read articles on each state and each President.*

**AMERICAN INDIAN** see INDIANS, AMERICAN.

**AMERICAN REVOLUTION** "These United Colonies are, and of right ought to be Free and Independent States." So said the Second Continental Congress in the Declaration of Independence in 1776. Many events happened before the colonists were ready to take this stand. It took a long and hard struggle to make these words come true.

The British won the French and Indian War in 1763. They needed money to pay for the war and govern Canada and the eastern Mississippi Valley, which they had taken from the French. Parliament decided to raise funds by increasing taxes in the American colonies. The Stamp Act of 1765 required that tax stamps had to be bought for wills, deeds, and other legal documents. Every newspaper, magazine, almanac, or calendar sold in the colonies also had to be stamped. Americans were not allowed to have anyone represent them (speak and vote for them) when tax laws were made in England. "No taxation without representation," was the cry of the angry colonists. They wanted the right to make their own laws, not to be ruled by the English Parliament.

### Trouble in Boston

Another act of Parliament that the colonists hated was the Quartering Act. The colonies had to provide housing and supplies for British soldiers in America. The people of Boston and New York, where many troops were stationed, were especially upset by this law. A noisy crowd of men and boys gathered near Boston's Customs House on a cold March day in 1770. Some of the boys threw snowballs at a British sentry. The sentry called for other soldiers, and the crowd became angrier and angrier. Shots rang out. Three Americans lay dead and eight were wounded (two of the wounded died later). Crispus Attucks, a leader of the crowd and probably a runaway slave, was the first to die. This incident was called the *Boston Massacre.*

The Boston colonists were spurred to violence again three years later, in December of 1773. The British shipped tea to America. The tea tax was small, but the colonists were not allowed to vote on the tax. The Boston Tea Party was held when the ships arrived in Boston Harbor with their cargo. Colonists disguised as Indians dumped 342 chests of tea into the harbor. The British acted rapidly. They shut off trade by closing Boston Harbor. The British governor sailed to England, leaving General Thomas Gage in command. The Quartering Act, which had been stopped, was started again. And if a British official were charged with a crime against a colonist, he was sent to England for trial.

The people of Boston and of Massachusetts were angry. So were many other colonists. The First Continental Congress met in Philadelphia in September, 1774. Every colony except Georgia was represented. The Congress formed the Continental Association, adopted a declaration of rights, and decided not to import British goods. The delegates agreed to meet again the following May if Parliament did not rewrite the unjust laws.

## The Shot Heard 'Round the World

In April, 1775, General Gage marched his British troops from Boston, through Lexington, to Concord. Spies had told the British commander that guns and ammunition were stored in Concord. These spies also told Gage that two patriot leaders, Samuel Adams and John Hancock, were hiding in Lexington. Gage planned to capture the supplies and the rebels. But the Americans also had spies. When the red-coated British started their "secret" march, two Americans saddled their horses and sped through the darkness to warn the colonists at Lexington and Concord that the British were coming. Those heroic riders were Paul Revere and William Dawes. They were aided by Dr. Samuel Prescott, who took the warning to Concord after Revere was captured.

Gage's 700 or 800 redcoats met a band of Minutemen (farmers and shopkeepers who were "ready at a minute's notice") lined up on Lexington's village green. No one knows who fired the first shot. But, in the shooting that followed, eight Americans were killed and the rest scattered. The British marched on to Concord. British troops did not find Adams, Hancock, or the supplies, because Dr. Prescott had warned the colonists in Concord.

◀ *A group of patriotic Americans at the first Continental Congress in 1774. They came from far and wide to plan joint action against the British.*

▼ *The signing of the Declaration of Independence on July 4, 1776, was the highlight of the revolution and the birth of a new nation. To all the world, it served notice of a new order—the rights of the people had now replaced the rights of kings.*

# AMERICAN REVOLUTION

▶ *The Battle of Bunker Hill was one of the first battles of the war. During this fight, when ammunition was scarce, the American colonel, William Prescott told his men, "Don't shoot until you see the whites of their eyes."*

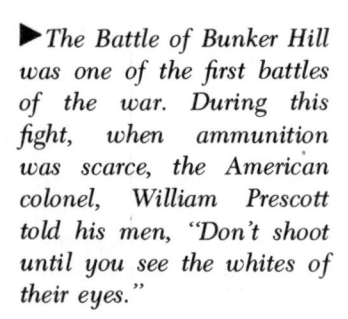

The British dumped several barrels of flour and set fire to some buildings at Concord before starting back to Boston. The redcoats found their return route blocked by angry Minutemen. Aroused by the news of the Americans killed at Lexington, hundreds of farmers and merchants swarmed toward Concord. The British fought off an attack on Concord's North Bridge. But their return march became a nightmarish retreat. Rifles and muskets were fired from behind every stone wall, building, or brushpile that could hide a Minuteman. Two hundred and seventy-three British soldiers had been killed or wounded by the time the redcoats finally reached the safety of their barracks.

One month later, Ethan Allen and Benedict Arnold led the Green Mountain Boys in the capture of Fort Ticonderoga, the most important British fortress north of the Hudson River. News of their daring attack encouraged the delegates to the Second Continental Congress in Philadelphia. The Congress now had to deal with a real war, so they called for a real army. The Congress chose a wealthy planter from Virginia to command this Continental Army. He was well suited for the job. He had been a lieutenant colonel in Britain's wars with France, and he later led several companies of Virginia volunteer soldiers. His name was George Washington.

The first major battle of the war—the Battle of Bunker Hill—was fought on June 17, 1775. It actually took place on nearby Breed's Hill. The British captured the hill, but more than twice as many British soldiers were killed or wounded as Americans. Many American colonists—called Loyalists—were still against breaking away from England, even though battles had been fought and men killed. This deep-seated struggle between American Patriots and Loyalists went on throughout the Revolution.

## The Declaration Leads to Full-Scale War

The Continental Congress continued to hope until the summer of 1776 that Great Britain would be fair to the colonies. Then a delegate from Virginia finally offered a resolution for independence. Thomas Jefferson wrote the first draft of the document that declared the colonies were free. John Adams and Benjamin Franklin made small changes. Other minor changes were made by the Congress. The Declaration of Independence was adopted in Philadelphia, on July 4, 1776.

That summer, the British shifted the fighting from Boston to New York. Washington's army was pushed from Long Island and Manhattan by troops led by Sir William Howe. Washington was forced to retreat into New Jersey and then into Pennsylvania. Washington and his men crossed the ice-packed Delaware River on Christmas night, 1776, in open boats and captured the garrison at Trenton, New Jersey. The troops at Trenton were German soldiers, called *Hessians*, whom the English paid to fight for them. The Americans won a small victory a few days later at Princeton, New Jersey. The British then began a major attempt to capture Philadelphia, the colonial capital. Philadelphia was taken from American hands in the fall of 1777. This was a staggering blow. The Continental Congress moved the capital to York, Pennsylvania, about 80 miles west of Philadelphia.

[80 mi.=129 km]

## The Tide Turns

The British tried to cut the colonies in half by advancing south from Canada with another army commanded by General John Burgoyne. But they were forced to surrender at the Battle of Saratoga in New York. This American victory was the turning point of the war. The French became allies of the Americans after Saratoga. French soldiers, ships, and money aided the American cause. Spain also helped, and the Netherlands loaned money for the fight.

But the American cause was in danger during the dreadful winter of 1777–1778. The British held Philadelphia. The government was in

▲ *In this famous painting, George Washington is crossing the Delaware River on Christmas night, 1776, to attack Hessian soldiers in New Jersey.*

▼ *A group of war-weary Americans encamped at Valley Forge. Although supplies were short, many men braved the terrible winter of 1777–78. They stayed with George Washington to fight again.*

▶ *In a spectacular sea battle, a blast from the American ship* Bonhomme Richard *put the British ship* Serapis *out of action.*

exile at York. And General Washington was camped in the snow at Valley Forge. His men were starving and frozen. The young French nobleman, the Marquis de Lafayette, was barely 20 when he joined General Washington and spent that winter at Valley Forge. Lafayette did not believe that men could survive such misery and hardship. Washington stated in one report that 3,000 men could not fight because they had no shoes or warm clothing.

Baron von Steuben, a friend of Benjamin Franklin, brought hope and encouragement to the Americans in the spring of 1778. Von Steuben, a former Prussian (German) officer, trained the Continental soldiers until they became better fighters, both in groups and as individuals.

The American Navy had had only four ships when the Revolution began. Congress later had more built. Many small, privately owned ships were used as *privateers*, seizing British supply and merchant ships. They also transported arms from France. John Paul Jones was a hero of the war at sea. With his ship, the *Bonhomme Richard*, he captured the British warship *Serapis* in a spectacular battle in 1779.

George Rogers Clark of Virginia captured several British forts in the region of Illinois and Michigan in 1778 and 1779. Clark's victories over the British and their Indian allies helped the Americans gain more favorable terms when the peace treaty was signed. Britain was forced to give all lands east of the Mississippi River to the Americans.

The British turned their efforts to the southern colonies in 1780 and 1781. They captured Savannah, Georgia, and won at Charleston, South Carolina. But they lost at Kings Mountain and Cowpens. American heroes of the South included Francis Marion, the "Swamp Fox," whose guerrilla-like (hit-and-run) warfare confused the British troops, and led to their defeat.

**Surrender at Yorktown**

Lord Cornwallis marched his British troops north and occupied Yorktown, in midsummer of 1781. He wanted to help the Royal Navy control Virginia, Maryland, and the Chesapeake Bay.

General Washington and the French leader, Count Rochambeau, cornered the British troops with the help of Lafayette and "Mad Anthony" Wayne. The French navy, led by Admiral de Grasse, blocked escape by sea. Lord Cornwallis surrendered at Yorktown on October 17, 1781. The colonials had won their revolution.

John Adams, Benjamin Franklin, and John Jay started peace talks for the Americans in April, 1782. When the Treaty of Paris was signed in September, 1783, Great Britain granted independence to the Americans and recognized the new United States of America.

*For further information on:*

**Background,** see AMERICAN COLONIES; BOSTON MASSACRE; BOSTON TEA PARTY; CONTINENTAL CONGRESS; DECLARATION OF INDEPENDENCE; FRENCH AND INDIAN WAR.

**Leaders for Independence,** see ADAMS, SAMUEL; FRANKLIN, BENJAMIN; HANCOCK, JOHN; HENRY, PATRICK; JEFFERSON, THOMAS; PAINE, THOMAS; REVERE, PAUL.

**Leaders in War,** see ALLEN, ETHAN; CLARK, GEORGE ROGERS; HALE, NATHAN; JONES, JOHN PAUL; LAFAYETTE, MARQUIS DE; MARION, FRANCIS; WASHINGTON, GEORGE.

**MAJOR EVENTS OF THE AMERICAN REVOLUTION**

- CAPTURE OF FORT TICONDEROGA (MAY, 1775)
- BATTLES OF LEXINGTON AND CONCORD (APRIL 19, 1775)
- BATTLE OF SARATOGA (OCT. 17, 1777)
- BATTLE OF BUNKER HILL (JUNE 17, 1775)
- VALLEY FORGE (WINTER 1777–1778)
- BATTLE OF TRENTON (DEC. 26, 1776)
- BATTLE OF BRANDYWINE (SEPT. 11, 1777)
- Philadelphia (CAPTURED BY BRITISH 1777)
- BATTLE OF YORKTOWN (OCT. 19, 1781)
- BATTLE OF GUILFORD COURTHOUSE (MARCH 15, 1781)
- BATTLE OF KING'S MOUNTAIN (OCT. 7, 1780)
- BATTLE OF COWPENS (JAN. 17, 1781)
- Charleston (CAPTURED BY BRITISH 1780)
- Savannah (CAPTURED BY BRITISH 1778)

★ BRITISH VICTORY
☆ AMERICAN VICTORY

◀ In 1781, the British general, Cornwallis, was defeated at Yorktown and surrendered his sword. America had won its fight for independence.

◀ "Give me liberty or give me death." Patrick Henry uttered these famous words before a convention of Virginians in 1775. They expressed the mood of an America ready to fight for freedom.

▲ *André Marie Ampère.*

**AMPERE, ANDRE MARIE (1775–1836)** André Ampère was a French mathematician and scientist who studied electricity and magnetism. He was born at Polemieux, near Lyons, France. His father was beheaded during the violence of the French Revolution when André was 18. A few years later, young Ampère's wife died of tuberculosis Ampère was greatly depressed by the loss of his wife and father. He tried to forget his sadness by working harder and longer every day on his scientific experiments.

In 1820, Hans Christian Oersted, a Danish scientist, discovered that an electric current can move the needle of a compass. Ampère heard about the discovery, and seven days later, he was able to explain it by the use of mathematics. He also showed that when a wire carrying an electric current is placed horizontally across a line running north and south, the needle of a compass held under the wire will be deflected to the east. Ampere's work also led to the invention of the galvanometer, which detects currents, and the telegraph.

The principles described by Ampère are used today in the operation of radio, television, electric motors, and other equipment. The unit of flow of an electric current was named the *ampere* to honor Ampère for his work.

ALSO READ: ELECTRICITY, MAGNET.

**AMPHETAMINE** see ADDICTION, MOOD MODIFIERS.

**AMPHIBIAN** Animals that spend part of their lives in water and part on land are called amphibians. Usually, they hatch from eggs laid in streams or ponds. As adults, they move to land to live. The word "amphibian" comes from a Greek word that means "leading a double life."

The animals in the class Amphibia are placed by scientists midway between fishes and reptiles in the animal kingdom. They probably developed millions of years ago from fish that stayed out of water for longer and longer periods. They were the pioneers for all backboned land animals. None of the early amphibians exists today. Most forms of amphibians died out altogether. Those that survived evolved into the frogs, toads, and salamanders we know today.

Although they breathe air, amphibians must return to the water to lay their eggs. The young amphibians, called *larvae* (tadpoles or pollywogs), hatch in the water and have gills and tails. As they grow, they go through a *metamorphosis*, or change. They usually lose their gills and tails, grow legs, and begin breathing with their lungs. Then, like their parents, they live on land.

Amphibians usually have legs and a moist skin, which may be soft and smooth or rough and gritty, but with no scales. The easiest way to tell the difference between an amphibian and a reptile is that amphibians do not have scales, and their toes are without claws.

There are two main kinds of amphibians—those with tails as adults and those without. All amphibians have tails when they are babies. Some kinds lose their tails as they grow, but salamanders keep theirs. They have long bodies and short stubby legs. They look much

▶ *The salamander is an amphibian that, as an adult, has a tail.*

as they did when young. Some kinds of very primitive amphibians with tails but no legs are called *caecilians*. Caecilians spend their lives burrowing in warm, moist earth. Not many people have seen caecilians. If they do, they often think the caecilians are earthworms.

The other amphibians—those that lose their tails when they become adults—are frogs and toads. A toad has stubbier legs than a frog, and its body is usually wider and flatter. A frog has smooth skin. A toad has rough skin, which often feels lumpy to the touch because of glands that make it look warty.

You can watch the way amphibians change from water-living to land-living. In early spring, explore a pond or quiet stream. When you spot the small, blackish, fish-like tadpoles, scoop one or two up into a glass jar. (See the picture of a tadpole with the article on FROGS AND TOADS.) Have ready at home an aquarium or large glass bowl. Put rocks and soil at one end and water from the pond at the other. Put the tadpole in the water. Feed it once each day with lettuce, watercress, or plants from the pond where you found it. If you need to add water, let tap water stand for a day before putting it in the aquarium.

In a few weeks, the tail of the tadpole will begin to shrink. Legs will start to form, and lungs will take over from the gills. Soon, the frog or toad will venture onto land. Unless you have a large aquarium that you can cover with a screen, release your hopping animal in the country or a park near the water where you found the tadpole.

Amphibians have eyes similar to those of mammals. But they probably do not see very well. They have nostrils, but it is doubtful that they have a good sense of smell. They do not have visible ears, yet they do have eardrums—round, flat areas of skin you can see below and behind their eyes.

Most amphibians make their homes near freshwater ponds and lakes, or in damp places on land. Many amphibians hibernate during the winter in cool climates. When an amphibian senses danger, it either stays still, blending in with its surroundings, or it runs away. If a hungry fish or some other animal bites the tail of a salamander, the salamander grows a new tail. Regrowth of a body part, such as a tail, is called *regeneration*. Many amphibians are helpful to man, because they eat large numbers of insects.

ALSO READ: AQUARIUM, FROGS AND TOADS, METAMORPHOSIS, REPTILE, SALAMANDER, TERRARIUM, VERTEBRATE.

▲ *The caecilian is a primitive amphibian without legs. It burrows underground. Caecilians are found in South America and southern Asia.*

◄ *An American toad. Like its relative, the frog, the toad is an amphibian.*

▼ *The tree frog has long, padded toes, which cling to surfaces. See how it blends in with the leaves.*

**AMSTERDAM** In the city of Amsterdam, in the Netherlands or "Holland," there are more than 50 canals and over 400 bridges. No wonder travelers who visit Amsterdam call it the "Venice of the North." Amsterdam is a city built in, on, and around water. It seems to float on a forest of stilts. Even the Royal Palace rests on thousands of wooden piles placed there in 1650. The modern buildings in Amsterdam rest on strong concrete piles that go deep into the sandy soil. There are millions of piles.

Amsterdam is the capital of the Netherlands, but government affairs are conducted in another city, The Hague. Amsterdam is a major European port. It is also a center of the diamond-cutting industry. Many international banks have headquarters in the city. Amsterdam was the home of the famous seventeenth-century artist, Rembrandt van Rijn. Many of his paintings are owned by the city's Rijksmuseum.

Amsterdam became a city long before Columbus sailed for the New World. People still use buildings that date back to 1300. The Dutch won independence from Spain in the sixteenth century. The Netherlands became one of the great powers of Europe, and Amsterdam was the financial capital of the continent.

ALSO READ: NETHERLANDS, REMBRANDT VAN RIJN.

▲ *Canals flow across Amsterdam. Along their sides are old houses, built by rich merchants, called* burghers, *in the 1600s. The Dutch had a powerful and wealthy empire at that time.*

▼ *Roald Amundsen, polar explorer.*

**AMUNDSEN, ROALD (1872-1928)** The first man to reach the South Pole was Roald Amundsen, a Norwegian explorer. Amundsen was born in Borge, near Oslo, Norway. He attended the University of Christiania and then joined the Norwegian navy.

Amundsen made a three-year expedition in the Arctic beginning in 1903. He was the first to navigate the Northwest Passage, a northern water route from the Atlantic to the Pacific. But Amundsen's greatest voyage began in 1910, at the other end of the Earth.

Actually, he was headed for the North Pole, but he heard that Robert Peary had already reached it. So Amundsen headed to the South Pole in his ship, *Fram*. He learned that an Englishman, Robert F. Scott, was also heading there.

Amundsen reached Antarctica in January, 1911. He and his men had to wait out the bitter cold, windy winter on the edge of the ice before they could head for the South Pole. The following October (Antarctica's spring), they set out with 52 well-trained dogs to pull their sledges. They climbed glaciers and went around huge cracks in the ice. They fought fog and blizzards. Finally, on December 14, 1911, Amundsen placed the Norwegian flag at the South Pole. Scott and his men found the flag there a month later.

Amundsen died in the Arctic, 17 years later. He was searching for another explorer, Umberto Nobile, who had disappeared. Nobile was later rescued.

ALSO READ: ANTARCTICA; ARCTIC; NORTH POLE; NORTHWEST PASSAGE; SCOTT, ROBERT F.

**ANATOMY** see HUMAN BODY.

**ANATOMY MIX-UP** Anatomy Mix-up is a fun game to play at parties, or even on a rainy afternoon when you and your friends want something to do.

Everyone sits on the floor in a circle. One person is It. It goes to another person in the circle. It points to a part of his own body, such as his eye, and says, for example, "This is my knee." The other person must do the opposite—point to his knee and say, "This is my eye." If the other person cannot do this correctly by the time It counts to 5, he becomes It. The game goes on until all parts of the body have been used. Try some funny combinations to mix up your friends.

## ANCIENT CIVILIZATIONS

Many civilizations have grown up and disappeared in places all over the world. The term "ancient civilization" is often used to describe the way of life that developed around the Mediterranean Sea, starting with the Sumerian civilization more than 5,000 years ago and ending 1,500 years ago with the fall of the Western Roman Empire in 476 A.D.

Early civilizations in China, India, Africa, and North and South America are sometimes called ancient civilizations, too. But the contributions of these people to the way people of the Western World live today are not so easily traced. Thousands of years ago, men lived in small tribes. Almost everyone in a group worked at hunting, gathering wild plants, and fighting other tribes. Tribes roamed all over, searching for food. Gradually, men made some important discoveries. First men discovered that they could plant seeds and raise crops. Then they *domesticated* (tamed) animals, both to help in farming and to keep for food.

The first cities developed in areas that were especially good for farming. Soon so much food was being raised that not all men had to be farmers. Men worked as full-time priests, government officials, craftsmen, merchants, artists, and musicians. Life became very complex. Writing was developed to help people conduct the business of their cities.

ANCIENT CIVILIZATION CONT.
IN VOL. 2

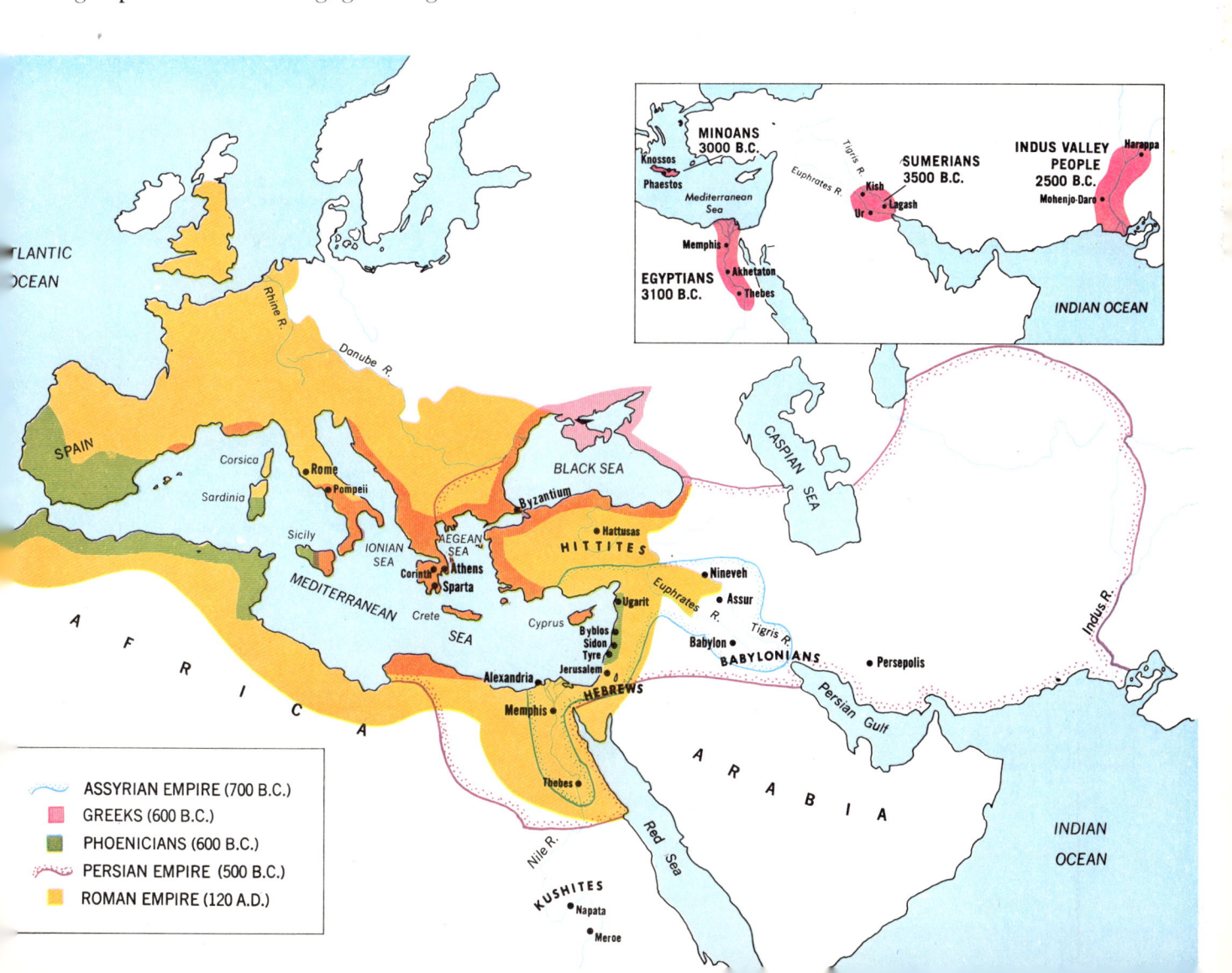

| CIVILIZATION AND LOCATION | DATES | WHAT DID THEY ACHIEVE? | FAMOUS CITIES | WHY DID THEY DECLINE? |
|---|---|---|---|---|
| Sumerians lived between the Tigris and Euphrates rivers in what is now Iraq. | 3500 B.C. — 2000 B.C. | First people to develop word-writing, before 3000 B.C. Called *cuneiform* (wedge-shaped) writing, written on lumps of clay. | Kish, Lagash, Ur | Were conquered. But their art and architecture were so good that the invaders learned and copied from it. Babylonia later developed out of the Sumerian civilization. |
| Egyptians lived along the Nile River. | 3100 B.C. — 525 B.C. | Built huge temples and large tombs called pyramids out of stone. Invented another form of word-writing called *hieroglyphics*. | Memphis, Thebes, Akhetaton, Alexandria | Rebellions and invasions weakened the empire. Finally, conquered by the Kushites. |
| Minoans lived on the island of Crete near Greece. | 3000 B.C. — 1100 B.C. | Made pottery and wall paintings full of bright, gay patterns. Built large outdoor theaters and loved to watch outdoor sports. | Knossos, Phaestos | Fell as Greece grew in power. Earthquakes may have speeded its end. |
| Indus Valley Peoples lived in what is now West Pakistan. | 2500 B.C. — 1500 B.C. | Famous for their well-planned cities with neat blocks of buildings facing paved streets. Sewers ran under many of the streets. Fine craftsmen worked in the cities. Some of them were toymakers. | Harappa, Mohenjo-Daro | Vast floods damaged the cities. Invaders from the west probably conquered the people of the Valley. |
| Hittites lived along the Halys Rivers in what is now Turkey. | 1900 B.C. — 1200 B.C. | Probably the first people to make things out of iron. | Hattusas | Allies of the Hittites rebelled. The Hittite city-states gradually lost power. |
| Babylonians lived between the Tigris and Euphrates rivers in what is now Iraq. | 1900 B.C. — 538 B.C. | Great lawmakers. The Code of Hammurabi is one of the oldest known sets of written law. Even trade was governed by law. There were many scientists and mathematicians. They were the first people to count seconds and minutes by 60s. | Babylon | Conquered by the Persians in 538 B.C. |
| Phoenicians lived along eastern coast of the Mediterranean. | 1100 B.C. — 842 B.C. | Invented an alphabet improved by the Greeks and used in the west today. Very skillful in making cloth and other goods. Traded in many parts of the world. Good sailors. | Byblos, Tyre, Sidon, Ugarit | Cities grew weaker as Assyria grew in power and took over most of the region. |
| Chou Dynasty China | 1027 B.C. — 256 B.C. | Iron tools replaced bronze. Literature and the visual arts reached great heights. Confucius and Lao-tse, great philosophers and teachers, lived at this time. | Peking, Chungking | Generals and politicians argued with each other. China broke up into small, warring states. |
| Hebrews were originally nomadic. Lived at various times in what is now Israel and Jordan. | 1000 B.C. — 587 B.C. | Created a great literature. Most important was the Old Testament of the Bible, the books of which were probably written between about 900 B.C. and 150 B.C. King Solomon, a well-known king of Israel, built a great temple in Jerusalem. | Jerusalem, Hebron | The Babylonians conquered the Hebrews and destroyed the great temple in Jerusalem. |
| Assyrians lived along the Tigris River in what is now Iraq. | 800 B.C. — 612 B.C. | Formed the first great army with iron weapons. This helped them to win many battles. | Assur, Nineveh | Conquered by the Babylonians. |
| Greeks lived in the southern part of what is now Greece. | 800 B.C. — 197 B.C. | Built fine buildings and sculptures. Wrote great poetry and drama. Had many wise scientists and philosophers. Democracy began in Greece. | Athens, Sparta, Thebes, Corinth | The Roman Empire was gaining strength taking away trade and turning farmers into soldiers. Rome finally conquered Greece. |
| Romans spread from the city of Rome west to England and east to Mesopotamia. At its height, included all lands around the Mediterranean Sea. | 735 B.C. — 476 A.D. | Excellent administrators, first to control a vast area from a central place and still let cities govern themselves. Used their army to build bridges and roads to improve the lives of conquered peoples. | Rome, Pompeii, Byzantium | Civil war and political assassinations tore the Roman Empire apart. The empire split in half in 395 A.D. The western Romans became easy prey for invaders. The eastern empire continued until 1453 A.D. |
| Kushites lived in Africa along the Nile River, south of Egypt. Expanded through much of Africa below Sahara desert. | 725 B.C. — 350 A.D. | The city of Meroe became a great, iron-making center. Made beautiful pottery, built pyramids, temples, and palaces. Developed a written language not yet deciphered. | Meroe, Napata | Conquered by their neighbors, the Ethiopians. |
| Persians lived in an area from the Indus River to the Aegean Sea at the height of the empire. | 700 B.C. — 331 B.C. | Built huge palaces of mud, brick, and stone. Beasts of legend appeared in their wall paintings and sculptures. Mail was delivered by "Pony Express." | Persepolis | The Persian Empire crumbled before the army of Alexander the Great in 331 B.C. |